The Stage and the Page

PUBLISHED UNDER THE AUSPICES OF THE

WILLIAM ANDREWS CLARK MEMORIAL LIBRARY

UNIVERSITY OF CALIFORNIA, LOS ANGELES

The Stage and the Page
London's "Whole Show" in the
Eighteenth-Century Theatre

Edited by
GEO. WINCHESTER STONE, JR.

Clark Library Professor, 1976–1977

1981
UNIVERSITY OF CALIFORNIA PRESS
BERKELEY • LOS ANGELES • LONDON

318824

University of California Press
Berkeley and Los Angeles, California

University of California Press, Ltd.
London, England

Library of Congress Cataloging in Publications Data

Main entry under title:

The Stage and the Page.

(Publications from the Clark Library professorship,
UCLA ; 6)
Seminar papers given at the Clark Library, University
of California, Los Angeles, 1976–77.
Bibliography: p. 231
Includes index.
1. Theater—England—London—History—Congresses.
2. English drama—18th century—History and
criticism—Congresses.   3. Music in theaters—
Congresses.   I. Stone, George Winchester, Jr., 1907–
II. Series: California. University. University at
Los Angeles. William Andrews Clark Memorial Library.
PN2593.S73   792'.09421'2   80-19027
ISBN 0-520-04201-8

Printed in the United States of America

1 2 3 4 5 6 7 8 9

CONTENTS

Preface

In the spring of 1968 the chancellor of UCLA instituted the Clark Library Professorship, providing for an annual appointment of a senior professor working in the area of the major holdings of the William Andrews Clark Memorial Library. In addition to his other duties the professor was charged with the responsibility of organizing and presiding over a series of seminars on a general theme, each seminar to be given by a scholar of distinction. The essays in this volume explore the proposition that drama receives its fullest aesthetic value when presented on stage and that our ancestors in the eighteenth century embraced in their aesthetic appreciation the "whole show" of the evening in *all* of its components. The seminars drew a large and continuing group of participants from among graduate students, faculty, staff, and visitors from the universities and libraries in the Los Angeles area and southern California. A unique feature of the publication of the papers is the cassette of theatrical music and songs that accompanied the seminar on the musical component of theatrical evening. It is conceived as a vocal and instrumental footnote documenting the comments by Professors J. Merrill Knapp and Stoddard Lincoln.

I take this opportunity to thank the following persons for the honor conferred upon me in my appointment as Clark Library Professor, 1976–1977: Chancellor Charles E. Young, Vice Chancellor William P. Gerberding, Director Robert Vosper, and the members of the Clark Library Committee. I am also most appreciative of the cheerful help given by the Librarian, William E. Conway and his entire staff. Their courtesy and interest make working in the Clark a continuing pleasure.

G. W. S., Jr.

The Clark Library
June 27, 1977

vii

ILLUSTRATIONS

Musical

To accompany the essays by Professors Knapp and Lincoln (chaps. 7 and 9), a cassette of music and songs is provided from Garrick's *The Enchanter* (music by J. C. Smith) and *May Day* (music by Dr. T. A. Arne) on Side 1, and for Garrick's burletta, *Orpheus* (music by F. H. Barthelemon (side 2). The cassette is provided from a recording of the original Clark Library lectures by the Audio Visual Department of UCLA.

Pictorial

Promptbooks being the basis of the performance of plays, Professor Shattuck's essay (chap. 10) includes the following four illustrations, which give insights into the manner of turning text into stage copy. They come from *The John Philip Kemble Prompt Books*, with permission of the Folger Shakespeare Library.

Coriolanus, from Act I, sc. iii, making it Act I, sc. iv, in the acting version (p. 182).

Coriolanus, from Act IV, sc. iv, from the *Kemble Prompt Book* (p. 184).

Pizarro, by R. B. Sheridan, Act II, sc. ii, in the Kemble acting version (p. 186).

Pizarro, by R. B. Sheridan, Act V, sc. ii, from same (p. 189).

INTRODUCTION

Over the years the course of drama and theatrical study has tended to separate critical concern into two channels — one seeing *dramatic text* as all important, the other seeing *stage presentation* as most basic to the aesthetic effect achieved by the dramatic form. The series of essays in this volume suggests the values of conjoining the two streams of critical enjoyment under the controlling thought that (especially in the eighteenth century) the stage *and* the page contributed to a varied "whole show" of an evening delightful to its audience in performance in *all* of its components, and to be read afterward with the performance readily recalled to mind. Awareness of the interdependence of stage and page suggests a wholeness of critical approach beneficial both to critical dramatic theory and theatrical experience.

Three of the essays — Robert D. Hume's "The Multifarious Forms of Eighteenth-Century Comedy," John Loftis's "Thomson's *Tancred and Sigismunda,* and the Demise of the Drama of Political Opposition," and Leo Hughes's "Afterpieces: Or, That's Entertainment," are concerned with literary genres and their relation to performance and popular taste.

Two of the essays deal with fundamentals of stage and theatre structure, and with essentials of scenic presentation — those by Donald C. Mullin, "Theatre Structure and Its Effect upon Production," and Ralph G. Allen, "Irrational Entertainment in the Age of Reason." Both structure and scene are vital to dramatic performance.

Four of the essays (and their accompanying musical cassettes) deal with the fundamental use of theatrical music to enrich an evening's entertainment — "The Prevalence of Theatrical Music in Garrick's Time," by G. W. Stone, Jr., "Theatrical Music in Garrick's *The Enchanter* and *May Day,*" by J. Merrill Knapp, Jr., "Garrick's Fail-Safe Musical Venture, *A Peep Behind the Curtain,* an English Burletta," by Phyllis T. Dircks, and "Barthelemon's Setting to Garrick's *Orpheus*" by Stoddard Lincoln. A cassette providing vocal and instrumental illustration of the music is available for purchase at the Clark Library.

Three of the essays, "Drama as Promptbook," by Charles H. Shattuck, "Reviving the Gesture Sign: Bringing the Dance Back Alive," by Shirley Wynne, and "Schemes of Show: A Search for Critical Norms," by Bernard Beckerman concern themselves with translating the stage onto the page, with the vagaries of acting copies, and with suggestions for a new critical approach to drama study.

The conviction of the authors as to the value of an eclectic approach is refreshing. Their developments of some special themes corroborate the general thesis of the series: isolation of textual study from dramatic performance is a disservice to critical relish of an ancient and very modern art. And performance was rich and varied. One should bear in mind that an evening's entertainment in a London theatre in the mid-eighteenth century entailed a fixed format of seven elements—each important: music (three pieces before the curtain rose); an engaging prologue; a mainpiece (tragedy, comedy, ballad opera); entr'acte singing and dancing; an epilogue (sportive or moral); an after-piece of one or two acts (farce, pantomime, or procession), and final music. And it was the "whole show" that counted!

Part I

LITERARY GENRES AND THEIR RELATIONSHIP TO PERFORMANCE AND POPULAR TASTE

COMEDY
Editor's Headnote

In "The Multifarious Forms of Eighteenth-Century Comedy" Professor Hume examines that most popular form of stage show in the century more closely and perceptively than it has been for many a year. Finding older terminology vague and outworn, and seeing plays always in relation to audience expectation and response, he finds five kinds of comedy prevailing: farcical (to beget amused contempt or benevolent indifference); satiric (to nourish a feeling of superiority or disdain); humane (to exude benevolence and good will); reform (to beget strong approval or relief); and exemplary (to beget outright admiration). He also suggests five distinct periods in the century during which the various kinds seemed not only to flourish but to dominate popular taste. This domination lay not so much in the page, as on the stage where the quality of the acting and the power of actor personality prevailed.

1. The Multifarious Forms of Eighteenth-Century Comedy

Robert D. Hume
Professor of English, Pennsylvania State University

Eighteenth-century comedy is a large and untidy subject—and one that still suffers from the prevalence of misleading and derogatory clichés. Much has been written about a few of the plays and playwrights, some of it quite good. In four important respects, however, scholars are still failing to come to grips with problems inherent in the subject. First, we still lack a satisfactory sense of the structure of the period. The eighteenth century is not, theatrically speaking, an undifferentiated morass. Hence we need to take subperiods into account. Second, our understanding of the various ways in which eighteenth-century writers conceive "comedy" as a genre is fuzzy. Third, the laughing-sentimental terminology we have inherited is an unsatisfactory way of characterizing the plays of the time. No such dichotomy can validly be drawn: In order to escape the limitations of false categories we need to establish a new terminology — one that fairly represents the aims and potentialities of the plays themselves. Finally, we need to ask just what right we have to treat stage vehicles as printed literature, and on what terms we can safely and profitably do so.

I

Many scholars have a curiously unstructured concept of the eighteenth century, and Nicoll's generic discussions by half-century have provided minimal help. People have spoken loosely of the neoclassical and preromantic periods, or the Age of Pope and the Age of Johnson — concepts widely employed yet misleading in their simplistic generality. And such designations are no use to the historian of the drama. Fortunately the checkered history of the theatre does provide a reasonably clear sense of both how and why the drama developed as it did. Five fairly distinct phases appear in eighteenth-century drama. They are so obvious that I am almost embarrassed to point them out — but evidently they were not so obvious to scholars who did not have *The London Stage* to draw on, and because no one has yet said the obvious, I will go ahead and do so.

The drama of the first period I have designated "Augustan."[1] Whether this muddy term was the best choice we need not pause to debate. Chronologically, we may say that the first phase comprises the years 1708-1728. The closing date is provided by the triumph of *The Beggar's Opera* and the rapid changes it triggered in the London theatre world. The opening date — provided by the new theatrical union decreed by the Lord Chamberlain — is a little more arbitrary. By 1708 or 1710, however, a basic change has occurred in the norms of English drama. The hard, satiric, mostly Tory comedy of the Carolean period has gradually given way to something else — a humane and reform-minded comedy whose ideology tends to be more bourgeois and Whig.

The change occurs gradually and untidily over a span of nearly thirty years. But by 1708 Congreve, Southerne, and Vanbrugh have fallen silent, and Farquhar (whose career is a minipattern of the change) is dead. The theatre was in an unhealthy state, and even after the permanent reestablishment of a second company in 1714 the managers remained stodgy, careful, and unventuresome. Staging new plays was always an expensive gamble, and in periods of stasis and noncompetition the new plays were few and mostly unexperimental. Thomas Davies tells us that Barton Booth "often declared in public company, that he and his partners lost money by new plays; and that, if he were not obliged to it, he would seldom give his consent to perform one of them."[2] A. H. Scouten observes that "Booth could afford to talk in such a way so long as Nance Oldfield, Wilks, and Cibber were still helping him attract spectators; nevertheless, this attitude meant slow death for the drama."[3] There are fewer interesting plays from this period than from any other time in the century—only the lull that follows the Licensing Act is anything like as stodgy. The successful new plays are mostly reprises of the tried and true by professional theatre people such as Cibber, Centlivre, and Charles Johnson.

The second phase is probably best christened the "New Wave" in eighteenth-century drama. It is triggered by the simultaneous triumphs of *The Beggar's Opera* and *The Provok'd Husband* in 1728, which brought about a startling change in the London theatre. The thirties' boom, so maddeningly truncated by the Licensing Act in 1737, reflects a sudden realization that an enormous, untapped theatregoing public had grown up in London— and that it could be exploited. An explosion of theatrical activity is the immediate result. Where two companies had been cautiously coexisting we abruptly find four and five groups competing vigorously and successfully, some of them quite ready to offer new and radical plays.[4] Henry Fielding's "off-off Broadway" venture at the Little Theatre in the Haymarket is famous, if not much studied. The big patent houses, inherently conservative, were forced to compete against innovation-minded rivals: The result is a tremendous upsurge in new plays. Few of them are very good. But we must remember that Robert Walpole was able to cut off this movement before it achieved maturity. If the Carolean theatre had been suppressed in 1669—an imaginable

suppostion — how would we now view the products of its apprentice playwrights? The 1730s writers experiment vigorously in new
play types, trying ballad opera, bourgeois tragedy, and topical
revues. John Loftis, writing about the New Wave drama from a
very different vantage point, sees it as finally displacing and
abandoning long-dominant "Restoration stereotypes."[5] The political and social concerns of these writers, and the multiplicity of
venues, ought to have produced a glorious period in English
drama. Instead, Walpole's intervention produced a profitably
conservative theatre and something like a wasteland in new plays.

The third phase (1737–1760) we may dub the "Lull," or the
"Low Georgian" period. Given a safe monopoly, Covent Garden
and Drury Lane take no chances. Shakespeare required no
author's benefits and entailed less risk than something new. The
greatest demand for fresh work was in afterpieces. Some considerable new plays were mounted — Thomson's *Tancred and Sigismunda* (1745), Hoadly's *The Suspicious Husband* (1747), Home's
Douglas (1756), some Foote farces, and Garrick's early work — but
though the theatres were operating profitably, one senses little
vitality in the trickle of new plays. Reflecting on the state of the
theatre in the 1750s, George Winchester Stone, Jr., remarks on its
"quietness and regularity."[6]

Exactly why the theatre came to life so relatively abruptly circa
1760 we need not inquire here. Signs occur that both dramatists
and audience were irked by the lack of new plays and by the
complacent enjoyment of the monopoly by the patent theatres.[7]
At all events the drama revived somewhat, and the next two
decades were to see a remarkable upsurge in dramatic activity,
even within the confines of the patent monopoly. This belated
Silver Age may be termed the "High Georgian" period. Goldsmith and Sheridan are the luminaries, but as I have shown in
detail elsewhere, they actually inherited a flourishing comic tradition.[8] Macklin's *Love A-la-Mode* (1759), Murphy's *The Way to
Keep Him* (1760) and *All in the Wrong* (1761), Foote's *The Minor*
(1760) and *The Lyar* (1762), Colman's *The Jealous Wife* (1761)
and *The Deuce is in Him* (1763), and Garrick and Colman's *The
Clandestine Marriage* (1766) are all highly successful laughing
comedies that predate the appearance of Goldsmith's *The Good-
Natur'd Man* in 1768. These and a flock of 1770s plays have long
been well-regarded by specialists, but even among eighteenth-

century scholars the curious myth persists that Goldsmith and Sheridan are an isolated flicker of light in the midst of numberless and depressing sentimental comedies. In truth this was an era of good writing and fine acting, and one offering the scholar-reader many pleasant surprises. And in fairness, one must say that the example of the *comédie larmoyante,* first really influential in England in the 1760s, stimulates English writers to thought and experiment—and to attempt more subtle and sympathetic character portrayal.

The High Georgian period has no sharply defined end. One could point to Garrick's retirement in 1776 as the close of an era, especially as his departure brought the Sheridan-Linley management into control of Drury Lane. Thomas Harris had taken over as manager of Covent Garden two years earlier. (Sheridan and Harris were to dominate management until 1809.) Arbitrarily, one might point to 1780 as a terminus. By then Garrick, Colman, Macklin, Foote, Murphy, Goldsmith, and Sheridan himself were dead or lapsing into silence, and a new generation of writers was taking over. Holcroft and Inchbald have very different interests and styles. One could even make a case for concluding the High Georgian period in 1794, when the opening of the mammoth new Drury Lane playhouse marked the end of the eighteenth-century theatre as Garrick had known it. I prefer to consider the years 1780-1794 a fifth phase, a *fin de siècle* epilogue in which we see a move toward the norms of the nineteenth century—a move accommodated in the rebuilding of Covent Garden in 1792 and the construction of Sheridan's Drury Lane. A few figures will show why theatre architecture had a decided—and unfortunate—influence on comedy. In the Restoration the Drury Lane theatre probably held no more than 800 people. In 1733 it was estimated to hold 1,000. By 1790 a series of revampings had expanded the capacity to about 2,300. The new Drury Lane of 1794 held more than 3,600 people—with disastrous effects on the audibility of dialogue. Covent Garden was likewise inflated—from a capacity of some 1,400 in 1732 to about 3,000 in 1792. The Licensing Act prevented the erection of more theatres, and in consequence the patent houses bloated themselves on their monopoly.[9] Given the difficulty of hearing dialogue clearly in such barns we cannot be surprised that ranting melodrama flourished while wit comedy languished.

The point is obvious. The eighteenth-century theatre is anything but monolithic, and one simply cannot make blanket statements. From the standpoint of the practicing dramatist, different
periods offered radically different circumstances and markets.
The writer whose every semiprofane wisecrack would be blue-
penciled by an efficient and arbitrary censor is not going to
indulge in the hijinks of the 1730s.[10] And a writer struggling to
sell his play to the cautious managers of ever bigger playhouses
was well advised to use proven formulas.

II

When we ask how "comedy" was conceived in the eighteenth
century (leaving subperiod distinctions aside for the moment), we
are confronted immediately with a conceptual difficulty. Is
comedy defined by its subject and its treatment of that subject (as
Aristotle suggests), or by an intrinsic structure—a movement
from adversity to prosperity (as Northrop Frye tells us)—or by
reference to its designed effect upon an audience (as Samuel
Johnson implies when he says that She Stoops to Conquer
achieved "the great end of comedy—making an audience
merry")?[11] Subject is the most common criterion: Comedy is "that
branch of the drama which adopts a humorous or familiar style,
and depicts laughable characters and incidents" (OED). But the
happy-ending structure is almost always assumed: "a stage-play
of a light and amusing character, with a happy conclusion to its
plot" (OED). Johnson's Dictionary definition ("A dramatick
representation of the lighter faults of mankind") stresses subject
and implies moral point. The difficulty of justifying a happy
ending for "low" or flawed characters causes eighteenth-century
dramatists no end of grief. And the reward of virtue is seldom
funny.

A large part of the difficulty is terminological, and reflects
confusion about exactly what the critic is trying to define and
discuss. Consider M. H. Abrams's well-known account of the
elements of criticism. The *world* is selectively imitated by the
author, who creates the *work,* which affects the *audience.* (In the
case of drama we have an added complication: actual performance demands middlemen between work and audience.) An

astonishing amount of the criticism devoted to eighteenth-
century comedy has focused morbidly and reproachfully on the
world-author relationship. Writers are accused of a sentimentalism that falsifies the world they show and leaves the resulting
work a saccharine invitation to tears and empathy. Though
"sentimental" comedy is always assumed to be affective in design,
most studies have treated it as a result—a deplorable result—of
the author's world view. The concept of authorial benevolence is
central to Bernbaum's seminal interpretation. He tells us that the
drama of sensibility "implied that human nature, when not, as in
some cases, already perfect, was perfectible by an appeal to the
emotions. . . . It wished to show that beings who were good at
heart were found in the ordinary walks of life."[12] Such ideological
study can certainly be valid and fruitful. One should not, however, take the *work–audience* relationship for granted. This is
especially true in works written for a conservative commercial
theatre. I shall try to pay the *work–audience* relationship proper
attention in the final section of this essay. At the moment I merely
make the point that eighteenth-century theorists seldom get
beyond claiming that comedy should amuse its audience—or
objecting to the inadequacy of such a view. Some of the objectors
assume that vice should be lashed; others that reform should be
shown, or virtue exhibited and rewarded. A moment's reflection
will tell that no one concept of comedy could possibly encompass
such diverse ends.[13]

What aims do eighteenth-century writers consider open to the
author of comedies? At the beginning of the century a remarkable
spread of possibilities finds critical warrant. The writer "could
evoke anything between contempt and admiration for the lead
characters; emphasize plot, character, or discourse; and work
with radically different balances of wit, humour, satire, and
example."[14] At any point during the century one can more or less
duplicate this spread of views. Early in the period Addison calls
ridicule "trivial" and argues that it is often used "to laugh men
out of virtue" (*Spectator* #249), though Francis Hutcheson—a
follower of Shaftesbury—accepts ridicule as a positive moral
force.[15] Traditional views by no means disappear in the course of
the century. William Cooke considers comedy a means for curing
vice by ridicule—a commonplace in magazine pronouncements
right into the nineteenth century.[16]

Eighteenth-century pronouncements on comedy are complicated by two major changes. First, as Draper and Gray correctly observe, writers come increasingly to "make character the essence of comedy."[17] This is true both in theory and in practice. Plot is treated as secondary. A concomitant rise in concern for "passion" encourages the rise of highly emotional *drames* and melodramas in the second half of the century. But what is the author to do with his characters? The more prominent they are in his design, the more we need to know how the author regards them. The second change — a much more visible one — comes in the way characters are viewed. Edward Niles Hooker long ago pointed out that in the Restoration period "Humours . . . were follies and vices to be lashed. Though the term *humour* occurred in diverse senses during the lifetime of Dryden, still the thing in whatever guise was likely to provoke a single attitude: disapproval or contempt."[18] As Hooker noted, this attitude was changing even by 1700. Increasing sympathy for singularity and eccentricity breeds a gentler view of potential objects of ridicule. The "mighty chasm" that yawns between Swift and Sterne has been well studied by Stuart M. Tave,[19] and the whole shift from hostile to sympathetic humor needs no recounting here.

The effect of this enormous change in sensibility is still underestimated and misunderstood. Tave was little concerned with the drama, and in part we may agree with Hooker's observation that comedy failed "to adapt itself to the new interests of the age." That Tave has to take his illustrations from art and the novel does tell us something about the drama. Theorists of comedy (as opposed to theorists of humour) stuck doggedly to the notion of ridiculing vice and folly, and to a remarkable degree writers of comedies persist in "satirizing" stock figures. The jealous husband or lover, the fop, the miser, the social climber, the country booby — all offer easy and inviting targets. But there is seldom any bite to such portrayals, which are "satire" only in a technical sense. By late seventeenth-century standards practically every writer of comedy after 1740 is "sentimental" — not because they all accept benevolent Shaftesburyite principles, or aim to evoke tears (few do), but because of a more subtle and more pervasive change in prevalent views of humours and human nature.

The chasm that yawns between Swift and Sterne likewise separates Goldsmith and Sheridan from their Restoration forebears. One simply does not find in eighteenth-century comedy the sort of harsh, ugly, bitter criticism of society and the human condition which is to be found in the comedies of Otway and Southerne. An Aristotelian traditionalist like Thomas Twining can say in 1789 that comedy is to ridicule vicious characters,[20] but in practice this meant no more than potshots at long-established sitting ducks. Foote, Murphy, and Macklin can occasionally muster some sting, but most writers — Goldsmith and Sheridan included — are robustly genial, even about their "satirized" characters. Mrs. Hardcastle is not a portrait etched in venom, nor is Lady Sneerwell.

To confuse amiable humor and "sentimentalism" is a terrible mistake. And neither can be equated with the "exemplary" bent that underlies Steele's theory of comedy.[21] I will try to sort out some of the differences in practice in the next section. The point I am trying to insist upon here is twofold. Theorists are chaotically diverse in their prescriptions — and practice by no means tidily illustrates theories. Horace Walpole's "Thoughts on Comedy" (completed about 1786) shows us the grab bag nature of thinking on the subject. Walpole likes "genteel" upper-class comedy; subordinates plot to character; can be very fussy about the working out of the "moral," but thinks *The Alchemist* Jonson's best comedy; likes the satire of *The Double-Dealer,* but delights in the feeling of *The Careless Husband.* Walpole diverges from popular taste in his scorn for obvious butts: "A Scot, an Irishman, a Mrs. Slipslop, can always produce a laugh, at least from half the audience."[22] The diversity of possibilities is evident. And whatever anyone thought comedy should be or do, William Jackson is very much to the point when he observes near the end of the century that comedies are merely amalgams of stage conventions.[23] What kinds of results such amalgamation could produce is the problem to which we must now address ourselves.

III

Discussions of eighteenth-century comedy have long been haunted by the peculiar idea that "sentimental" comedy overwhelmed and suppressed the "laughing" comedy tradition inherited from the seventeenth century. So fine a scholar as John Harold Wilson states that at the end of the seventeenth century, comedy "turned, like a penitent prodigal, to the comedy of tears." Writing in 1974 A. Norman Jeffares tells us that in the eighteenth century "cynicism bowed to sententiousness, worldly wit gave way to worthy wisdom, and the comedy of sex was completely swamped by a flood of sentimentality." Kenneth Muir says flatly that "when we come to the middle of the century . . . the new plays were all sentimental."[24] Such views are not tenable. Twenty years ago Arthur Sherbo provided statistics from Genest to prove the overall dominance of laughing comedy—results decisively confirmed by *The London Stage*.[25] Nine years ago I myself showed that there is no truth to Goldsmith's wails about the triumph of the sentimental muse in the 1760s.[26] Not wanting to repeat I refrain from any extended flogging of what ought to be a very dead horse—though I must admit that sentimental comedy has proved a remarkably durable corpse.

The whole concept of sentimental comedy is in fact merely a distraction and a red herring. Anyone who has read a reasonable number of the plays usually dubbed sentimental knows that in fact they are too disparate to constitute a definable genre. To imagine that there is "something absolute" to define—a type which exists as a kind of platonic form—is unsound and unhelpful, as John Loftis notes in a review of Sherbo's *English Sentimental Drama*.[27] None of the categories into which one can put eighteenth-century comedies remotely approaches the absolute. But granting this we will want to find categories that overlap as little as possible. On this ground we may conclude that Nicoll's long-influential choices are unsatisfactory.

Nicoll divides eighteenth-century comedy into (1) comedy of manners; (2) comedy of intrigue; (3) comedy of humour; (4) comedy of sensibility—dubbed "sentimental comedy" in his account of the second half of the century; and (5) farce. Shakespearean adaptations and ballad opera he sets in separate categories altogether. The problems are obvious. As Stone observes, "Shakespearean, humours, manners, intrigue, and sentiment, prove categories of some use—yet what comedy of sentiment fails to call heavily upon intrigue and manners to make it go at all?"[28] As Stone says, one may dub *The Clandestine Marriage* a comedy of manners for its satire on Lord Ogleby and the Sterlings, or a comedy of sentiment for its use of Fanny. Any decision is arbitrary. Most twentieth-century writers call *The Provok'd Husband* a sentimental comedy, yet to Samuel Johnson it seemed one of the best laughing comedies of the century. Nor should we forget that a "comedy of manners" can be as harshly critical as Fielding's *The Modern Husband* or as warmly affectionate as Goldsmith's *The Good-Natur'd Man*. A ballad opera may be as tart as *The Beggar's Opera* or as saccharine as Bickerstaff's *The Maid of the Mill*. Messy borderlines are one thing; fundamental vagueness about categorization quite another. A large part of Nicoll's problem is that some of his distinctions are based on subject (manners, humours, intrigue — or source!), others on treatment (pathetic or musical), which are altogether different matters. About thirty years ago John Harrington Smith tried to escape such tangles, and simultaneously free himself from the bogs of sentimentalism, by describing the change in drama between 1675 and 1710 as a transition from "cynical" to "exemplary" comedy. His study remains one of the best treatments of this drama ever written, but though it is useful, the concept of exemplary comedy is much too narrow to serve as a characterization of eighteenth-century practice in general. To say that "comedy should devote itself to recommending . . . higher ideals by framing characters who . . . exemplify them and by punishing or chastening their opposites"[29] describes well the modus operandi of what I am about to define as reform and exemplary comedy, but is largely irrelevant to a majority of the plays in the period. And the distinction between positive example and reform is one that seemed important to Steele — rightly so, for very different kinds of plays and characters can be involved. The difference is obvious when one compares the treatment of an errant wife in Charles Johnson's *The Masquerade* (1719) with the didactic display of exemplary propriety in *The Conscious Lovers* (1722).

To find descriptive terms that will work satisfactorily we need to look for a single basis on which to determine them. To look simultaneously at subject and at treatment simply breeds confusion. My very modest proposal is that we abandon the world-author nexus for the moment and turn instead to the work–audience relationship. Comedies are designed to elicit a reaction: let us categorize on that basis. For the Augustan period we might divide as follows.

Type	Reaction to be elicited	Example
farcical	amused contempt; benevolent indifference	Johnson's *Love in a Chest* (1710)
satiric	superiority; disdain	Baker's *The Fine Lady's Airs* (1708)
humane	benevolent good will	Centlivre's *The Busie Body* (1709)
reform	strong approval; relief	Johnson's *The Generous Husband* (1711)
exemplary	outright admiration	Steele's *The Conscious Lovers* (1722)

A few notes and observations are in order. Both satiric and genuinely exemplary comedy are a rarity between 1708 and 1728. Bits of satire may be found in some farces—*Three Hours After Marriage,* for example—and in many of the humane comedies that are the norm in this period. By contrast with the "hard" Carolean comedy, almost all of these works are "soft." One may quibble over whether a given Centlivre play is humane or reform comedy, but in comparison with the norms of 1675 a decisive shift has been accomplished. Obviously a given play may comprise plot lines that would be classified differently. In *The Provok'd Husband* the Townly plot is a high-life reform; the Lady Grace-Manly plot is purely exemplary; and the Wronghead plot is a sharp satire on country "gentry." Because reform is a crucial part of the two most conspicuous story lines, it seems to me to characterize the play.

The principal types of Augustan comedy are humane and reform. Humane comedy is the dominant type right through to 1780.[30] After that, under increasing pressure from musical comedy, it gradually evaporates and changes: Its humorous and farcical elements are carried on in the afterpiece tradition, and its more serious concern with its characters is absorbed into serious comedy and the *drame.* Humane comedy is characterized by its essential good humor, even where it is satiric. As an extreme instance of the contrast we may take *The Country Girl,* Garrick's 1766 adaptation of Wycherley's *The Country-Wife* (1675). Wycherley's play leaves the impression that the author is showing up the hypocrisy dominating London life: Margery learns that lying is necessary to survival. Garrick's version leaves the audience to delight in a traditional romantic plot in which youth and love triumph over age and avarice. Unlike the old "hard" comedy of the Carolean period, the humane comedy never presents bitter or cynical acceptance of an unsatisfactory status quo. Even *The Beggar's Opera,* with its strong satiric leanings, has no essential bite and ugliness. Its incipient despair is offset by an essentially comic perspective. The indignation and contempt which Southerne, Wycherley, or even Congreve can elicit is lacking. This distinction need not imply a value judgment. Cynicism can be cheap and true humanity profoundly moving. To take noncontroversial instances we might contrast the raucous political satire of *Eastward Hoe!* with the blithe pastoralism of *As You Like It.*

The *Beaux Stratagem* (1707) is a quintessential example of humane comedy. Its sunny country air and affectionate treatment of its characters put it a world away from *The Country-Wife* or *The Souldiers Fortune.* Aimwell's celebrated volte-face and confession in Act V have been denounced as sentimental mush, and the fairy-tale solution of genuine and ugly marital problems between the Sullens removes any semblance of social realism. But do we want to see something else happen? I think not. Centlivre's long-popular *The Busie Body* (1709) is an excellent illustration of a play whose characters and plot devices simulate those of Carolean plays, but whose cheery high spirits rob it of the gritty ugliness an earlier writer might have found in similar elements. Addison's *The Drummer* (1716) was considered an important sentimental comedy by French and German writers later in the eighteenth century,[31] but has been largely ignored in this century. The play is in fact an enjoyable and farcical romp, set off from other such works only by the seriousness and affection with which Addison presents Sir George Truman (presumed dead), his loyal wife, and his devoted steward, Vellum. Such sentiment as the play may be said to possess consists in genuinely virtuous characters and a lack of "studied Similes and Repartees," as Steele terms them in his 1716 preface. The joking use of a fake ghost, and the gusto of Addison's satire on the fortune-hunting Tinsel, give the play a tone far from the saccharine ponderousness one might expect from most critics' dismissive descriptions. Three of the characters are exemplary, but by no means is this a sentimental play in the terms defined by Sherbo: it does not exaggerate sentiment or invite excessive emotional response from the audience.

Critics have often called humane comedies sentimental if the successful dénouement relies on the voluntary yielding of the blocking figure. Colman and Garrick's *The Clandestine Marriage* (1766) is an excellent illustration of such a response. If Lord Ogleby's heart were not genuinely and honorably touched by Fanny, he would not intervene to set all right. Critics often ridicule such presumption of the essential goodness of the human heart (to paraphrase Bernbaum) — but are we to assume that the illustration of disinterested feeling automatically renders a play contemptible? Or even sentimental? Surely the way in which the author uses this feeling to affect the audience is a far more significant indicator of the nature of his play. John Kelly's *The Married Philosopher* (1732) has a design very similar to Garrick and Colman's play, and has likewise been condemned for sentimentality. Young Bellefleur's firmness and nobility under the threat of disinheritance by his ranting uncle is the sort of thing people sneer at in Cumberland, and the uncle's giving way at the end, though not pat, does presume some essential decency. But the play as a whole, despite its over-long speeches, presents lively contretemps and amusing characters.

The conventions of the humane comedy, and the ways it could be viewed in its own day, are well summed up in Dr. Benjamin Hoadly's *The Suspicious Husband* (1747) and the controversy it stirred.[32] Almost always dismissed as sentimental, this immensely popular play is full of racy intrigue, bedroom encounters, and bawdy propositions. Mr. Strictland's jealousy is sharply satirized, but Ranger's exuberant womanizing is left unpunished. At the play's end he remains an "extravagant rake" on the loose. Hoadly leaves no doubt that Ranger's dissipated ways are foolish and unsatisfying — indeed he has Ranger tell us so in the soliloquy with which he opens the play.

Let me reflect a little — I have set up all Night. I have my Head full of bad Wine, and the Noise of Oaths, Dice, and the damn'd tingling of Tavern Bells; my Spirits jaded, and my Eyes sunk into my Head: and all this for the Conversation of a Company of Fellows I despise. . . . Honest *Ranger,* take my Word for it, thou art a mighty silly Fellow.

Steele might have suggested that he be brought to an appropriate state of penitence, and rewarded with a virtuous heiress.[33] Hoadly is satisfied to let us enjoy the rake's schemes—frustrating them for the duration of the play—while letting us see that though Ranger is no model, neither is he a liar or a scoundrel. Mrs. Strictland is indeed an exemplary character, and the two pairs of young lovers are virtuous enough, but nothing in the play invites emotional excess. "No Tears, I beg. I cannot bear them" says Mr. Strictland at the height of the reconciliation scene. Garrick, we may note, scored a great and highly profitable triumph in this play—acting the insouciant Ranger. And it appears that the author had the actor in mind as he wrote the part.[34]

If a basic dichotomy is to be drawn, it must rest not on the presence of virtuous characters but rather on the kind of action presented and the sort of response it seems designed to elicit. The standard pattern of the humane comedy generally involves a romance plot. Reform comedy most often presents a marital situation. In the case of *The Suspicious Husband* we do see a satire on jealousy, concluded with the cure of the offending party. One might say the same of a great many "Restoration" comedies, which conclude with the rake mending his ways and receiving his heiress. In most such cases, however, the reform is essentially pro forma. As Dryden remarks in his preface to *An Evening's Love* (published in 1671): Poets "make not vicious persons happy, but only as heaven makes sinners so: that is by reclaiming them first from vice. For so 'tis to be suppos'd they are, when they resolve to marry." What makes the end of Shadwell's *The Squire of Alsatia* (1688) remarkable, and prophetic of eighteenth-century forms, is the serious didactic and emotional weight placed upon the reformation.[35] Plays that make reform prominent and crucial in their basic design seem to me to fall in a special category.

Reform comedy may be as tidily facile as Cibber's *The Careless Husband* (1704) or as ponderous and preachily didactic as his *The Lady's Last Stake* (1707). Such plays tend to be unrealistically optimistic marital tracts,[36] though Steele's *The Lying Lover* (1703) and Centlivre's *The Gamester* (1705), for example, make similar points in romance plots. Charles Johnson's *The Generous Husband*, *The Wife's Relief*, and *The Masquerade*, and the

Cibber-Vanbrugh *Provok'd Husband* are well-known instances of this kind of play. By no means, however, can we say that reform comedy is sentimental comedy, if by that designation we mean a work that presumes the goodness of human nature. Hildebrand Jacob's *The Prodigal Reform'd* (1737 Part 1 of *A Nest of Plays*) is an instructive illustration. Young Severn must be reclaimed from a life of dissipation: fortunately his heart "is yet sound and uncorrupted." Told that his father has died at sea and that he is now a pauper, young Severn quickly learns that his loving mistress is a heartless and mercenary whore, his bosom friends a pack of sneering spongers. His distress is of course artificial, and his father soon reappears, bearing a rich heiress. But young Severn has learned his lesson: other people are *not* necessarily as kind, decent, and honest as he is. Quite a sentimental moral! Reform comedy is indeed as various as humane comedy. It grows out of Shadwell's late didactic humours comedies, and in it we may discern the roots of the serious comedy of the latter half of the eighteenth century.

The humane and reform types I have been illustrating are dominant in the Augustan period and indeed persist well into the second half of the century. During the 1730s boom they are joined by a flock of relatively topical political, social, and literary satires—a set of works well illustrated by Fielding's *Historical Register, Modern Husband,* and *Author's Farce.*[37] Such works were successfully squelched by Walpole, and throughout the Low Georgian period the standard types are repeated with minor variations. Many of the best plays are afterpiece farces by Foote. In the High Georgian period some alteration in terminology becomes necessary. The influence of *comédie larmoyante* and rising concern with social and moral problems produce plays that cannot always be properly discussed as "comedy." For want of a better term I will refer to it as "serious comedy," but some account of the checkered history of its classification is necessary to indicate the nature and complexity of the subject.

Serious comedy has been little studied. Many of the relevant plays have been called sentimental, and most students of sentimental drama have been hostile to it. Indeed one of the best of them, Arthur Sherbo, says explicitly that sentimental drama "is a debased literary genre"; consequently his whole study is a history of what he terms artistic degeneracy. Nicoll (whose categories were followed by Sherbo) is almost alone in trying to discern subtypes in sentimental comedy—surely a necessary proceeding, when we consider the diversity of the works so categorized. It is evident, he says, "that three distinct tendencies are to be traced in the comic literature of this type. There are the relics of the Cibberian genteel comedy, . . . there is the often mawkishly pathetic theatre of Cumberland, intent upon raising a sigh and calling forth a tear; and there is the more revolutionary humanitarian drama which is seen at its best in the plays of Mrs. Inchbald and of Thomas Holcroft."[38]

This division seems awkward and incomplete. To begin with, the whole idea of "genteel comedy"—plays that depict the manners and conversation of an upper-class world—is muddled and largely irrelevant. Many critics assume that a genteel comedy must be an exemplary comedy. This assumption is easy to make for several reasons. Traditional comedy invites us to laugh at or despise low characters. Presented with graceful, witty, often wealthy persons of rank, we tend to be favorably impressed and take them as models. Steele certainly suggests in *Spectator* #65 that this is what happens when we see a Dorimant in *The Man of Mode,* and he bitterly denounces the play as a tempting picture of an altogether false ideal. Horace Walpole, for whom the play "shines as our first genteel comedy," reminds us that "when Addison [to whom he attributed *Spectator* #65] . . . anathematised this play, he forgot that it was rather a satire on the manners of the court, than an apology for them."[39] As Walpole here suggests, genteel comedy must thus be distinguished from exemplary. As the class, wealth, and gentility of the characters rise, we cannot easily view them as we do the rogues of Alsatia—but we are not to presume that the author is giving us a model. *The Man of Mode, The Careless Lovers,* and *The Conscious Lovers* are all genteel comedies—and they are, respectively, satiric, reform, and exemplary comedy. "Genteel" refers to subject and presentation, not to designed response, and is therefore not a category in the classification I am proposing.

Nicoll's second category—the "mawkishly pathetic theatre of Cumberland"—is both unduly hard on that much abused writer and simplistic, for it runs together emphasis on delicate feelings (of the sort used and satirized by Hugh Kelly) and the use of distress to evoke suspenseful empathy—the basis for what becomes the nineteenth-century *drame*. Nicoll's third category—humanitarian drama—again confounds semidistinct types, running together the moral and social concerns that seem to me to separate a play like Holcroft's *Duplicity* from Inchbald's *Every One Has His Fault.*

The inadequacy of traditional terminology is manifest. We may even ask whether reform and exemplary plays, past a certain point, are properly to be discussed as comedy at all. To move the pity and empathy of the audience—let alone its admiration—is sufficiently distinct from the traditional aims of comedy conceived in Aristotelian terms to make the resulting works essentially distinct in kind. If we appeal to the plays of Shakespeare, a theorist like Elder Olson will tell us that *As You Like It, Twelfth Night,* and even *Much Ado* are not comedies but romances.[40] The influence of *comédie larmoyante* after 1760 is a further complication. Earlier writers sometimes speak with pride of eliciting tears from an audience, but the sensibility to be found in the plays of Frances Sheridan, Hugh Kelly, and Cumberland is new and distinctive. Their work blurs the differences in subject and sensibility which separate comedy from tragedy—and it definitely aroused the hostility of writers with more traditional views of comedy. Goldsmith and Sheridan, among others, do certainly react against a heavy emphasis on sensibility, a reaction perhaps most delightfully embodied in Foote's *The Handsome Housemaid, or Piety in Pattens* (1773).[41]

English theorists never altogether caught up with the developments of theatrical practice, but Diderot offers us some useful distinctions in his essay "On Dramatic Poetry" attached to *Le Père de famille* (1758). "Gay comedy . . . has for its object ridicule and vice; serious comedy . . . has for its object virtue and the duties of man." To these types he adds tragedy dealing with domestic affliction and that grander tragedy that presents "public catastrophes."[42] Diderot's defense of *comédie sérieuse* is impassioned. He urges the attractions of serious concernment with the subject on the part of the audience, and emphasizes sincerity, sensitivity, and the goodness of human nature. We need not suppose, however, that only a benevolist can write *comédie sérieuse.* The association of eighteenth-century "sentimental" comedy with belief in the goodness of human nature is a matter of historical fact, but Diderot makes a terribly obvious point: Comedy and tragedy are not absolutes. In *Le Fils naturel* he attempted to write a drama "between comedy and tragedy"; in *Le Père de famille* he splits the difference between that midpoint and comedy.[43] One can easily find English precedent for late eighteenth-century ventures into *comédie sérieuse*. A number of late seventeenth-century plays that merely designate themselves "A Play" on the title page anticipate this pattern. Southerne's *The Disappointment* (1684) and Durfey's *The Banditti* (1686) are obvious examples. Despite this early move to get away from the designation "comedy," no satisfactory terminology evolved by which the efforts of serious but nontragic dramatists could be properly distinguished.

Had Horace Walpole's little essay possessed the catchiness of Goldsmith's, our inherited views of eighteenth-century comedy might be very different indeed — and a good deal more in line with reality. Walpole fully comprehends the difference between what he terms "merry comedy" and "serious comedy," pointing to *Le Misanthrope* as "a pattern" for the latter. Sentimental comedy — or as he specifically calls it, *comédie larmoyante* — Walpole understands as a deliberate attempt to create a new, intermediate form.

I do not take the *comédie larmoyante* to have been so much a deficience of pleasantry in its authors, as the effect of observation and reflection. Tragedy had been confined to the distresses of kings, princesses, and heroes; and comedy restrained to making us laugh at passions pushed to a degree of ridicule. . . . I should therefore think that the first man who gave a *comédie larmoyante,* rather meant to represent a melancholy story in private life, than merely to produce a comedy without mirth. If he had therefore not married two species then reckoned incompatible, that is tragedy and comedy, or, in other words, distress with a cheerful conclusion; and, instead of calling it *comédie larmoyante*, had named his new genus *tragédie mitigée,* or, as the same purpose has since been styled, *tragédie bourgeoise*; he would have given a third species to the stage.[44]

Some forty years ago Fred O. Nolte argued that pathetic comedy and domestic tragedy are both part of a *drame bourgeois* movement which grew throughout Europe during the eighteenth century.[45] I am suspicious of the tidiness of Nolte's ideas about evolution, but his perspective does put *comédie sérieuse* in more comfortable company than it usually enjoys. Voltaire, Kotzebue, and Lessing (who was quite hostile to *pathetic* comedy) make more interesting comparisons for Cumberland and Holcroft than do some of their English contemporaries.

If we ask what types are commonly tried in the High Georgian and *fin de siècle* periods we will see that though the English drama has changed slowly, the change is real. Farce, satiric, and humane comedy are all flourishing (examples are *Piety in Pattens,* Murphy's *The Way to Keep Him,* and Burgoyne's *The Heiress* respectively). However, in place of the reform and exemplary categories which suffice early in the century we must distinguish at least four types of English *comédie sérieuse.*

Type of serious comedy	Emotion sought	Example
Drama of sensibility	exhibition of genteel feeling to rouse delicate empathy	Inchbald's *Lovers' Vows* (1798)
Pathetic drama	happy-ending exhibition of distress to rouse suspenseful empathy	Holcroft's *The Deserted Daughter* (1795)
Moral melodrama	exhibition of folly or error to rouse didactic distress	Holcroft's *The Road to Ruin* (1792)
Humanitarian problem drama	exhibition of social problems to rouse didactic empathy	Cumberland's *The Jew* (1794)

There are two basic tendencies within serious comedy. They are not mutually exclusive, but as a rule one or the other predominates. One is a stress on feelings (whether pathos in *The Deserted Daughter* or generosity in *The West Indian*); the other is a drive toward the arousal of an explicitly moral response. The difference is well illustrated in a comparison of Edward Moore's *The Gamester* (1753, technically a bourgeois tragedy) with Holcroft's *Duplicity* (1781), a work that, as its author admits in his preface, is significantly indebted to Moore's play. What one remembers about *The Gamester* is the harrowing misery of Beverley and his wife. They are made sympathetic characters, and though one certainly recognizes Beverley's culpability, one cannot help sympathizing with him in his woe. Upon reflection one may indeed conclude that gambling is bad, but the play itself is a vehicle for the presentation of affecting distress. In *The British Theatre* Mrs. Inchbald severely criticizes it on precisely these grounds. To make gambling repulsive, she says, Moore should have made his gamester not "an object of pity" but one "of detestation."[46] Holcroft contrives a happy ending after teaching his gamester a lesson. (In design his play is very close indeed to Mrs. Centlivre's *Gamester* of 1705, itself indebted to Shirley's *Gamester* of 1633. *Plus ça change* . . .) Holcroft leaves us good will toward the erring Sir Harry Portland, but he is careful not to distract our attention from the potentially dire results of the vice he is attacking. Because of the rather gratuitous demise of Beverley we must call Moore's play a bourgeois tragedy—but the difference we see here is between pathos and what Dougald MacMillan has termed sentimental satire.

The rise of the social form of serious comedy is a crucial factor in differentiating the dominant type of the High Georgian period from that of the *fin de siècle* years. This rise of "social" concern in comedies usually dismissed as sentimental has been well discussed by Dougald MacMillan in an important and neglected article.[47]

The course of serious comedy, however, began to turn more and more toward the representation of situations and persons from everyday life. The tone of genteel sensibility characteristic of Kelly and the sentimental pathos played up by Cumberland . . . *began to give place to an attitude of sentimental satire,* if such a term can be used. (P. 336; emphasis added)

This point, implicit in Nicoll's excellent account of Mrs. Inchbald, is of great importance for any true understanding of the so-called sentimental comedy. In the work of Inchbald, Holcroft, and Frederick Reynolds (to cite the best-known cases) we see serious criticism of genuine social and moral evils. Critics' reluctance to concede much merit to these works seems odd, when one considers the relative esteem in which Kotzebue's problem plays are held. The sentimental satire on which many of the serious comedies rely has been little studied and poorly understood. By the standards of those accustomed to the angry, biting satire of Wycherley, Otway, or Southerne, or the witty, cutting criticisms of Congreve or Vanbrugh, sentimental satire seems ponderous

and preachy. Satire that lacks the spice of "Tory gloom" discon-
certs us: the sentimental satirists are basically optimists about
human nature, however severely they show up vice and evil.

Why did the lighter forms of mainpiece comedy languish
toward the end of the century? A large part of the answer lies in
the tremendous appeal of musical comedy. Ballad opera enjoyed
a major revival in the 1760s, and the concomitant rise of the
burletta gave legitimate comedy stiff competition. The direction
in which audience taste was tending is obvious in figures supplied
by Charles Beecher Hogan.[48] Of the twelve most frequently
staged mainpieces in the years 1776–1800 four were Shakespeare
plays (*Hamlet, Macbeth, The Merchant of Venice,* and *Romeo
and Juliet*). Only two were contemporary legitimate comedies:
Sheridan's *The School for Scandal,* and Hannah Cowley's *The
Belle's Stratagem* (1780). The other six (in descending order of
popularity) were all musical comedies of one sort or another: *The
Beggar's Opera,* Bickerstaff's *Love in a Village* (1762), Sheridan's
The Duenna (1775), the younger Colman's *Inkle and Yarico*
(1787), the elder Colman's *The Spanish Barber* (1777), and
Cobb's *The Haunted Tower* (1789). Caught between the delights
of musical comedy and the continuing appeal of farcical afterpieces, traditional mainpiece comedy stagnated.

At this point it is well to reflect briefly on the ground just
covered. The account of differing types of serious comedy just
concluded should serve as a reminder of precisely what I mean by
"multifarious." Not only are several quite different sorts of
comedy written during each period of the century, but each one
has its own set of diverse potentialities. The longstanding tendency—dictated by inherited terminology—to categorize as
laughing or sentimental has largely obscured the diversity of play
types actually common in the period. Within this rather confusing spread of possibilities, however, we find dramatists after
the Licensing Act extremely conservative. Despite the hundreds
of new plays, shifts in common types occur so slowly that they are
perceptible only when they are considered against at least a
decade of time, and often much longer. As Joseph Donohue
observes, "the first instinct of the English repertory theatre is to
rely on the tried and proven. Its second instinct is to seek out the
new, especially if only slightly different. . . . A glance through
any season . . . reveals the dominance of the known commod-
ity."[49] Indeed the sheer unoriginality of almost all eighteenth-

century comedies is so striking, and the theatrical reasons for it so evident, that we can scarcely avoid inquiring exactly what our knowledge of the theatrical circumstances of these plays should do to our critical perceptions of them.

IV

Critics have almost unanimously preferred the harsh, sceptical comedy of the late seventeenth century to the "new" comedy that supplants it. Eighteenth-century comedy is not, on the balance, very "sentimental," though it is good-humored. The dominant humane comedy tradition is definitely grounded, in theory and in practice, in the concept of "laughing" comedy. And though some of the serious comedies do indeed play for bathetic emotion, many of the plays of that sort are honest, well-crafted works. The real ground of objection to eighteenth-century comedy is not to sentimentality or false emotion — rather, it is to unimaginative use of stereotyped elements.

Anyone who has read a hundred comedies from the High Georgian period should be painfully aware of just how essentially unoriginal even the plays of Goldsmith and Sheridan prove to be in type, characters, and comic devices. The repertory theatres mounted new plays grudgingly and exercised extreme caution in what they chose. Of course the Licensing Act is at least partly responsible for the problem. "Great comedy" (in Bonamy Dobrée's phrase)[50] can be hostile, subversive, and genuinely obnoxious to prevailing politics and mores. Scholars long spoke of the Grundyizing effect of the middle-class audience and the censor, but the really influential factor is the restriction to two patent theatres. A smaller, independent theatre could try to cultivate its own audience — perhaps one with minority tastes. The bloated patent houses naturally catered to the taste of the lowest common denominators. Television networks today make a legitimate parallel.

No period produces floods of great works. One may fairly say in defense of eighteenth-century comedy that it offers us many excellent plays of all types — if we are allowed to judge by the standards of the theatre for which they were written. Eighteenth-century comedy is nonelitist, and in truth it is not very literary. Lack of interpretive complexity and profundity characterizes humane comedy, reform comedy, farce, and the various sorts of serious comedy alike — and it has been a perpetual irritant to scholars, who like to be able to get their teeth into something substantial. The delightful farce tradition which flourishes in this period, always alive and well in afterpieces, offers the literary scholar little to do. Farce can be chronicled, and its constituent elements pointed out, but even a Leo Hughes cannot really bring it to life on the page. At the other extreme serious comedy tends to date badly. Social mores and contemporary issues quickly lose their fascination for an audience, especially when handled in a quasi-realistic setting. The very seriousness and realism for which Dougald MacMillan commends late eighteenth-century comedy now work against it. Moral earnestness is no substitute for the delights of literary technique in the eyes of a scholarly interpreter.

We must face an unpalatable fact bluntly. Though there are many fine eighteenth-century comedies of diverse types, interpretive studies of them have usually been depressingly sterile. Most of the comedies simply need no explication — a fact which has left scholars doing the unnecessary, or trying to place comedies in relation to largely imaginary concepts of sentimentalism. The complexities and ambiguities which allow critics to bicker endlessly and happily over Wycherley and Congreve are lacking even in Goldsmith and Sheridan. Sheridan's language has delighted scholars, partly because it makes him far more readable than, say, Murphy. But what else are we to do with Sheridan? He can be praised (falsely) for returning to Restoration norms, or for doing battle against overwhelming tides of sentimentalism — and has been, ad nauseam. Heaven knows I do not mean to dispraise Sheridan, whose plays delight me both as a reader and as theatregoer. But I as a literary critic find him an unappealing subject. *The Rivals* is a wonderful play, and one which has maintained its appeal for me through the four productions I have seen. But I have no doubt what it "means," or how to respond to it. The only really fruitful criticism I have seen of it is Mark Auburn's recent article — a study that looks to stage history and promptbooks as a key to possible meanings in *performances*.[51]

This brings us to a question. To what extent are these plays properly considered written literature? Certainly they were almost always published, and the reading demand for a popular play "was virtually inexhaustible," as Hogan remarks.[52] Ten editions of *The Road to Ruin* were called for in 1792; *Lovers' Vows* achieved eleven in 1798. Older plays were steadily reprinted, and the popularity of Bell's British Theatre and other such collections is solid evidence of the enormous demand for reading texts. Some authors did revise for publication: the 1710 edition of Congreve shows a systematic attempt by the author to present his plays in literary rather than theatrical form. Much later in the century the availability of Larpent MSS allows us to determine differences between acted and printed texts. Richard W. Bevis points out, for example, that a great deal of the sentimentalism which cloys Kelly's *The School for Wives* (1773) was in fact not spoken in performance, but was evidently considered welcome by the novel readers of the day.[53] We cannot safely assume that what we read in play quartos was always what the audience saw in the theatre.

Despite the obvious popularity of published play texts, most of them now seem to lie pretty dead on the page. This is, I think, a function both of the theatre system that bred them and of the way we go about reading them. The poetic richness of Shakespeare, the plot intensity of Jacobean city comedy, the linguistic polish of Vanbrugh, and the verbal gags of Wilde all work to satisfy the reader. So do the character depths of Ibsen, and Shaw's quasi-novelistic descriptions — the latter obviously designed for reading. But eighteenth-century comedies do not develop the features which make for good reading, and in consequence we see them at a crushing disadvantage.

Just as Styan would have us visualize Shakespeare in performance, so we need to recreate the circumstances of eighteenth-century theatrical performance as we read. Even many teachers of this drama seem disturbingly vague about the physical characteristics and operation of eighteenth-century playhouses. The way the changeable scenery worked, the size of a particular theatre at a particular date, and the identity of the actors for a given play are facts readily available to anyone.[54] Drury Lane of 1710 is not Drury Lane of 1780, and the importance of understanding the physical characteristics of the theatre is painfully evident if one reads Harley Granville-Barker's grumpy account of Wycherley.[55]

The reader should not forget that the text he is reading was in fact merely the largest element in what often amounted to a mixed-bag variety show. A normal night included preliminary music, a prologue, a mainpiece, entr'acte singing and dancing, and an afterpiece. From the very start of the century the managers were forced to supplement dramatic offerings with anything they thought might help the theatre. In April of 1703, for example, Drury Lane offered Southerne's *Oroonoko* with the following additions:

> . . . several Italian Sonatas by Signior Gasperini and others. And a new Entertainment of Instrumental Musick compos'd by Mr. *Keller,* in which Mr. *Paisible,* Mr. *Banister,* and Mr. *Latour* perform some extraordinary Parts on the Flute, Violin, and Hautboy, with several new Dances by Mr. *Du Ruel,* and Mrs. *Campion.* Likewise the famous Mr. *Evans,* lately arriv'd from *Vienna* . . . will Vault on the manag'd Horse, where he lyes with his Body extended on one Hand in which posture he drinks several Glasses of Wine with the other, and from that throws himself a Sommerset over the Horses head, to Admiration. (*Daily Courant*)

The atmosphere of the eighteenth-century theatre was closer to Barnum and Bailey than to Bayreuth.

Aware of this carnival atmosphere, the reader should try to see the play as it was originally mounted. We might liken the imaginative effort involved to reading music. A passably skilled musician can "hear" a work in his head as he reads the printed page, even when dealing with a complex orchestral or operatic score. A work like Bach's *Art of the Fugue* has technical fascinations that a Schubert quartet does not, however delightful to hear. But in either case, to enjoy "reading" the work, one must actively recreate the piece. Likewise the reader of a play needs to see and hear, at least in his head. We should block out the action as we go along, moving the actors about, and imagining the costumes and changeable scenery which are so important in this theatre. A reader can "see" stage movement and scene shifts, hear the speeches as they would be spoken, and respond to the personality and technique of well-known and pleasing actors. In a repertory theatre one sees the same actors again and again, and there is a special pleasure in seeing how they will adapt themselves to different roles, and in returning to savor the details of an interpretation one knows well. To read a playtext from this period without an appreciation of the actors who mounted it — and for whom it was usually specifically tailored — is to rob oneself of one of the best ways of understanding the potentialities of the roles.

Know the actors is an excellent piece of advice for readers.

Such visualization is of course much easier if one has examples to work with. The cinemagoer who has seen Max von Sydow in a dozen parts has a great advantage in recreating a sense of the cinematic experience from the scrappy bits of the published screenplay of *The Seventh Seal.* Or consider another parallel. First read the score and libretto of *The Magic Flute.* Then listen to a recording. Then watch the Bergman film two or three times. Then return to the score and libretto. They should come to life. Similarly, when one has seen a fine performer in a shallow role — Martyn Greene as the Lord Chancellor in *Iolanthe* — it should electrify one's sense of the part. We have ample testimony that Garrick did this for a host of roles — Ranger in *The Suspicious Husband* among them.

We cannot bring the eighteenth century back to life, and most of us would not want to. But we can cultivate a sense of theatrical circumstances and a producer's eye. So doing we can understand why these plays worked so well in the theatre — and also help ourselves enjoy them. My final point may prove controversial, but I think it important. To read eighteenth-century comedy without regard for the actors' "subtext" is to leave most of it at an uninteresting level. What we find in these play scripts is seldom profoundly meaningful; rather, we see here vehicles that offer good theatrical potentialities for skilled performers to elaborate on. Literary interpreters must deal with intrinsic and demonstrable meanings. But a performance that does so will be leaden indeed. A production I saw of *The Way of the World* in 1976 was precisely that. It played what was on the page — giving the effect of a note-perfect and quite expressionless musical performance. No competent director would want to restrict his actors to the letter of the page. As readers — not as interpreters — we need to cultivate the kind of imagination which goes into production. Only then will these comedies regain for us the vitality that made them such effective stage vehicles in their own setting.

NOTES

1. Hume, *The Development of English Drama in the Late Seventeenth Century* (Oxford: Clarendon Press, 1976), chap. 10.

2. *Memoirs of the Life of David Garrick,* 2 vols. (London: Printed for the Author, 1780), I, 208.

3. *The London Stage 1660–1800*, Part 3: 1729–1747, ed. Arthur H. Scouten (Carbondale: Southern Illinois University Press, 1961), I, cxxxviii–cxxxix.

4. For a discussion, see *The London Stage*, ibid., cxxxix–cxlix.

5. *Comedy and Society from Congreve to Fielding* (Stanford: Stanford University Press, 1959), chap. 5.

6. *The London Stage*, Part 4: 1747–1776, ed. George Winchester Stone, Jr. (1962), II, 741.

7. See, for example, Edward Purdon's *Letter to Garrick on Opening the Theatre*, a pamphlet published by I. Pottinger in October 1759, and an article in the *Weekly Magazine* (1 January 1760) deploring lack of competition.

8. "Goldsmith and Sheridan and the Supposed Revolution of 'Laughing' Against 'Sentimental' Comedy," *Studies in Change and Revolution: Aspects of English Intellectual History 1640–1800*, ed. Paul J. Korshin (Menston: Scolar Press, 1972), pp. 237–276.

9. For a discussion of theatre size and finances, see the Introductions to the five parts of *The London Stage;* and Harry William Pedicord, *The Theatrical Public in the Time of Garrick* (New York: King's Crown Press, 1954; rpt. Carbondale: Southern Illinois University Press, 1966), chap. 1.

10. For a good account of this subject see L. W. Conolly, *The Censorship of English Drama 1737–1824* (San Marino: Huntington Library, 1976).

11. *Boswell's Life of Johnson*, 6 vols., ed. G. B. Hill, rev. L. F. Powell (Oxford: Clarendon Press, 1934–1950), II, 233.

12. Ernest Bernbaum, *The Drama of Sensibility* (Boston: Ginn & Co., 1915; rpt. Gloucester: Peter Smith, 1958), p. 10.

13. I have demonstrated this point at length in "Some Problems in the Theory of Comedy," *JAAC*, 31 (1972), 87–100.

14. *The Development of English Drama in the Late Seventeenth Century*, p. 62. For a detailed survey of theories of comedy 1660–1710, see chap. 2, passim.

15. *Reflections upon Laughter* (Glasgow: R. Urie for D. Baxter, 1750), pp. 32 ff.

16. *The Elements of Dramatic Criticism* (London: Kearsly and Robinson, 1775), p. 145.

17. John W. Draper, "The Theory of the Comic in Eighteenth-Century England," *JEGP*, 37 (1938), 207–223. Quotation from p. 218. Charles Harold Gray, *Theatrical Criticism in London to 1795* (New York: Columbia University Press, 1931; rpt. New York: Blom, 1971), p. 19. On the presentation of character in this drama the reader may wish to consult Joseph W. Donohue, Jr.'s excellent *Dramatic Character in the English Romantic Age* (Princeton: Princeton University Press, 1970).

18. "Humour in the Age of Pope," *HLQ*, 11 (1948), 361–385. Quotation from p. 363.

19. *The Amiable Humorist: A Study in the Comic Theory and Criticism of the Eighteenth and Early Nineteenth Centuries* (Chicago: University of Chicago Press, 1960).

20. *Poetics of Aristotle* (London: Payne, 1789), Part I, Section viii.

21. See Shirley Strum Kenny, "Richard Steele and the 'Pattern of Genteel Comedy,'" *MP*, 70 (1972), 22–37.

22. "Thoughts on Comedy," in *The Idea of Comedy*, ed. W. K. Wimsatt (Englewood Cliffs: Prentice-Hall, 1969), p. 203.

23. *Thirty Letters*, 3d ed. (London: T. Cadell, 1795), Letter #14.

24. John Harold Wilson, *A Preface to Restoration Drama* (Boston: Houghton-Mifflin, 1965; rpt. Cambridge: Harvard University Press, 1968), p. 129. A. Norman Jeffares, ed., *Restoration Comedy*, 4 vols. (London: Folio Society, 1974), I, xx. Kenneth Muir, *The Comedy of Manners* (London: Hutchinson, 1970), p. 156.

25. Arthur Sherbo, *English Sentimental Drama* (East Lansing: Michigan State University Press, 1957).

26. "Goldsmith and Sheridan" (n. 8 above).

27. *MLN*, 74 (1959), 447-450.

28. *The London Stage*, Part 4, I, clxi.

29. *The Gay Couple in Restoration Comedy* (Cambridge: Harvard University Press, 1948), chap. 8, esp. p. 226.

30. I should explain that I am employing the term "humane" in a sense slightly different than that proposed by Shirley Kenny ("Humane Comedy," *MP*, 75 [1977], 29-43. Her definition is postulated on matters of character, dialogue, and plot; mine on reaction elicited. And she considers substantially all early eighteenth-century comedies humane, including those I define as reform and exemplary types. I entirely agree that vis-à-vis Carolean norms all of these plays may be called humane, but beyond that basic distinction my reform and exemplary categories are designed to supply necessary subdivisions.

31. See Allardyce Nicoll, *A History of English Drama 1660-1900*, rev. ed., 6 vols. (Cambridge: Cambridge University Press, 1952-1959), II, 199.

32. For a hostile contemporary response, see Macklin's *The New Play Criticiz'd* (Huntington Library, Larpent MS #64).

33. Foote addresses precisely this point in *The Roman and English Comedy Consider'd and Compar'd. With Remarks on the Suspicious Husband* (London: T. Waller, 1747), pp. 29-30. "Could not . . . the Author throw this Youth, in the Course of his Nocturnal Rambles, into some ridiculous Scene of Distress, which might, with Propriety, have reclaim'd him[?]" His reply is that the "amiable Beauties" of Ranger's character allow us to overlook "Blemishes in his Conduct" without tempting us to emulate his follies.

34. *The London Stage*, Part 3, II, 1287.

35. I have discussed this subject in "The Myth of the Rake in 'Restoration' Comedy," *Studies in the Literary Imagination*, 10 (Spring 1977), 25-55.

36. I have analyzed a number of such works in "Marital Discord in English Comedy from Dryden to Fielding," *MP*, 74 (1977), 248-272.

37. Fielding's plays remain astonishingly neglected — in large part because of their social and political topicality. For some account of his comic and satiric theory and strategy, the reader may consult W. R. Irwin, "Satire and Comedy in the Works of Henry Fielding," *ELH*, 13 (1946), 168-188; A. E. Dyson, "Satiric and Comic Theory in Relation to Fielding," *MLQ*, 18 (1957), 225-237; William B. Coley, "The Background of Fielding's Laughter," *ELH*, 26 (1959), 229-252; and J. Paul Hunter, *Occasional Form: Henry Fielding and the Chains of Circumstance* (Baltimore: Johns Hopkins University Press, 1975), chaps. 2, 3.

38. Nicoll, III, 153-154.

39. "Thoughts on Comedy," p. 198.

40. *The Theory of Comedy* (Bloomington: Indiana University Press, 1968).

41. Extant as Larpent MS #346 and Folger MS D. a. 48. First printed by Samuel N. Bogorad and Robert Gale Noyes in *Samuel Foote's "Primitive Puppet-Shew" Featuring "Piety in Pattens" A Critical Edition,* published as a special issue of *Theatre Survey,* 14 (1973), no. 1a.

42. Denis Diderot, "On Dramatic Poetry," appendix to *Le Père de famille* (1758). Translation by John Gaywood Linn in *Dramatic Essays of the Neoclassic Age,* ed. Henry Hitch Adams and Baxter Hathaway (New York: Columbia University Press, 1950), pp. 348-359.

43. Burgoyne's popular *The Heiress* (1786) is a lightened adaptation of this play. In type it is really more a humane than a serious comedy, but its style delighted the fastidious Horace Walpole, who declared it "the best modern comedy" (Letter to Lady Ossory, 14 July 1787).

44. "Thoughts on Comedy," p. 204.

45. *The Early Middle Class Drama (1696-1774),* New York University Ottendorfer Memorial Series of Germanic Monographs, no. 19 (Lancaster, Pa., 1935).

46. Elizabeth Inchbald, ed., *The British Theatre,* vol. 14 (London: Longman et al., 1808).

47. "The Rise of Social Comedy in the Eighteenth Century," *PQ,* 41 (1962), 330-338. MacMillan was evidently unaware of Nolte's study, which covers some of the same ground.

48. See *The London Stage,* Part 5: 1776-1800, ed. Charles Beecher Hogan (1968), I, clxxi-clxxiii.

49. *Theatre in the Age of Kean* (Oxford: Blackwell, 1975), p. 84. Donohue provides a useful account of the repertory ca. 1800, explaining the way serious comedy shades into the nineteenth-century melodrama—a subject beyond my scope here.

50. Bonamy Dobrée, *Restoration Comedy* (London: Oxford University Press, 1924), chap. 1.

51. "The Pleasures of Sheridan's *The Rivals:* A Critical Study in the Light of Stage History," *MP,* 72 (1975), 256-271.

52. *The London Stage,* Part 5, I, clxxv.

53. "The Comic Tradition on the London Stage, 1737-1777" (Ph.D. diss., Berkeley, 1965), p. 109.

54. Richard Southern's *Changeable Scenery* (London: Faber and Faber, 1952); Donald C. Mullin's *The Development of the Playhouse* (Berkeley and Los Angeles: University of California Press, 1970); and Richard Leacroft's admirable *The Development of the English Playhouse* (London: Methuen, 1973) are extremely helpful.

55. Harley Granville-Barker, *On Dramatic Method* (London: Sidgwick & Jackson, 1931; rpt. New York: Hill and Wang, 1956), chap. 4.

TRAGEDY
Editor's Headnote

Tragedy, though less frequently played than comedy in the century, triumphed in the performance of Shakespeare's serious plays. The course of newly created tragedy just before the 1740 decade could go each (or one) of three ways to hold audience interest: heap up *to new pinnacles the stimulants of sex and violence (which it did in some shows);* engage itself *with serious treatments of the political currents of ideas in the time (which it did, not so much by presenting propaganda for this or that cause, as by treating timeless issues somewhat ambiguously, so that all persuasions in the audience could identify and enjoy); and/or* rejuvenate *both old and new plays by a new kind of acting that moved away from attitudinal presentation of universal passions (jealousy, anger, love, fear) to individualized treatments of the same, which the Macklins and the Garricks ushered in. Professor Loftis here develops the second area by discussing the multitude of relevances which lay within the pages of James Thomson's popular* Tancred and Sigismunda *—so well acted in both the* old *mode by Goodfellow, and in the* new *mode by Garrick and Mrs. Cibber. He notes that its continued success, however, depended upon stage performance by the superb actors Garrick, Mrs. Cibber, and Thomas Sheridan. Although the rebellion of 1745 led Thomson to suggest political parallels, and audiences to perceive them, critical opinion of the time dwelt upon the power of performance. Professor Loftis reminds us, in his survey of other ambiguously political plays, that audience response to text and performance is, in the end, what drama is all about.*

2. Thomson's *Tancred and Sigismunda* and the Demise of the Drama of Political Opposition

John Loftis

Bailey Professor of English, Stanford University

The London newspapers of 1745 record a series of public events that, though very different from one another, have relevance to Thomson's *Tancred and Sigismunda:* to the nature of the tragedy as well as to its reception in performances at Drury Lane Theatre. In the hours before dawn of the day of its premiere, 18 March 1745, the Earl of Orford—better known as Sir Robert Walpole—died, some three years after having accepted a peerage that marked the end of his long dominance of British political affairs. Present at the performance of Thomson's play was a man who, as much as any single other person, has been responsible for Walpole's resignation of his places in government, William Pitt. Pitt as well as several of his friends and political allies including George Lyttelton applauded the play vigorously. Pitt and Lyttelton had personal reasons to applaud: they had assisted Thomson in preparing the play for the stage and had attended rehearsals, giving instructions to actors.[1] The audience at the premiere was aware of the possibility of an event that came to pass four months later, when Prince Charles Edward landed in Scotland to assert the claims of his father to be acknowledged King James III. Any hope of success Charles Edward might have had depended on support from Irish, Scottish, and English Jacobites much more than on support from France, then allied with Spain in a war against Britain which Walpole earlier had attempted to avoid. The great world of international rivalries, and political antagonisms in Britain, found a parallel in the small world of Drury Lane Theatre.

For reasons in theatrical, dramatic, and political history,

Tancred and Sigismunda has an importance in Georgian tragedy which may be unique. It was a very popular play, holding the stage to the end of the century. Garrick alone played the role of Tancred more than twenty times.[2] The large number of editions reveal that it was popular with readers as well.[3] The formal, declamatory dialogue in blank verse, in a tragedy that in the eighteenth century moved the emotions of audiences, provides a reminder that altered dramatic conventions impose a major barrier to our aesthetic response to Georgian tragedy. Furthermore, this play, with a focus on the tragic frustration of young lovers, signals clearly and emphatically the end of an era of anti-ministerial tragedy that had its beginnings in the 1720s. Whereas in most of the earlier tragedies, by Thomson as well as other dramatists, loosely disguised comment on current political issues is a liability, in *Tancred and Sigismunda* the political comment—multifaceted and susceptible to conflicting interpretations—contributes intellectual and emotional subtlety. Finally, the play poses a question about the early career of one of England's greatest statesmen, the elder William Pitt. Why did he ostentatiously patronize a play, first performed in March 1745, that includes passages that can sustain a Jacobite as well as a Hanoverian interpretation?

Tancred and Sigismunda was Thomson's fourth tragedy, followed by only one other, an adaptation of *Coriolanus* produced posthumously in 1749. His first three tragedies include, with varying levels of emphasis, themes that may be interpreted as critical of Walpole—whose policy of maintaining peace with Spain Thomson had implicitly criticized as early as 1729 in a poem, *Britannia*.[4] The first of his tragedies, *Sophonisba* (1730), can be described only with qualifications and with attention to established habits of political rhetoric as an opposition play. At a time when English merchants and their Parliamentary spokesmen deplored Walpole's failure to take more vigorous measures to protect English shipping, Thomson's reference (in his dedicatory epistle addressed, by permission, to the Queen) to Britain as "more powerful at sea than *Carthage* . . . more flourishing in *commerce* than those *first Merchants*" would have carried political innuendo. In the context of the tragic drama of the previous decade, the determined effort by Queen Sophonisba of Carthage to defend the liberty of her nation would have had a subtle political meaning.

The relevance of this to the political opposition to Walpole, who was accused of political "corruption," requires elucidation. It will be useful to quote a brief passage from a cogent modern formulation of assumptions in that era about the structure of English political society. Referring to the " 'Country' vision of English politics as it appears in a multitude of writings in the century that follows 1675," J.G.A. Pocock differentiates that vision from the court or ministerial conception of the subject:

> The business of Parliament is to preserve the independence of property, on which is founded all human liberty and all human excellence. The business of administration is to govern, and this is a legitimate activity; but to govern is to wield power, and power has a natural tendency to encroach.

Pocock describes some of the means employed by administration in preventing Parliament from performing its function of preventing the enlargement of the powers of the executive: "it seduces members by the offer of places and pensions, by retaining them to follow ministers and ministers' rivals, by persuading them to support measures—standing armies, national debts, excise schemes—whereby the activities of administration grow beyond Parliament's control"—measures "known collectively as corruption."[5] Although the specifics of this analysis of "corruption" have an inevitable application to the propaganda of the opposition to Walpole, it is apparent that they have an application as well to other ministers in the century following 1675. From 1721 until 1742 Walpole provided but a conspicuous target for the expression of long-held grievances. Because many dramatists drew on a common body of political thought, we need not assume in reading their tragedies that they acted in concert—though some no doubt did so.

It will suffice to mention but a few tragedies produced in the 1720s that celebrate "liberty" and noble defiance of tyranny—or "corruption." In *The Briton* of 1722 Ambrose Philips turns to the reign of the Roman emperor Claudius for a dramatic fable enabling him to assert the independent spirit of his remote ancestors. A "Carnavian" prince replies indignantly to an unjust demand made by a Roman tribune (III):

Were I a Villager, the meanest Freeman
In all your State; and *Claudius* should presume. —
Or any *Caesar,* — to abuse his Power,
And authorize enormous Crimes; I would not, —
No! — were his Anger Death, — I could not bear it!
But would oppose him to my stretch of Power.

In the same year William Philips employs a locale in ancient
Ireland for his *Hibernia Freed,* dramatizing the Irish reconquest
of their nation from the Danes and reestablishment of their
"Liberty." Philip Froude writes about ancient Spain in his *The
Fall of Saguntum* of 1727. The besieged city falls to the army of
Hannibal, but not before the daughter of its governor has
addressed to its patron goddess an appeal for aid in the name of a
"glorious Love of Liberty and Truth! [II]" The generic resemblance of these tragedies to Thomson's *Sophonisba* and Addison's
Cato of 1713 will be apparent. Opposition to encroachments on
constitutional rights by a powerful political or military force
animates dialogue and conditions dramatic action. It would be
inaccruate, and in some instances anachronistic, to regard all
such plays as critical of Walpole.

Some of them, including *Sophonisba*—which followed publication of Thomson's *Britannia* by only a year—probably were so
intended by their authors. Sophonisba's lament for her country
and continent, in a play produced at a time when many political
writers expressed fear for the British constitution, would have had
a double meaning for those who chose to find it (I.ii):

> . . . All *Afric* is in chains!
> The weeping world in chains!

So too her reference to Rome as "the scourge/ Of the vext world"
(III.iii):

> . . . While fair *Carthage*
> Unblemish'd rises on the base of commerce.

The final phase and the demise of the drama written in opposition to Walpole may be illustrated by Thomson's *Agamemnon*
of 1738, *Edward and Eleonora* published in 1739 after the
Examiner of Plays had refused it a license, and *Tancred and*

Sigismunda of 1745. It is sufficiently obvious that Thomson was a poet and a dramatist of a higher order of genius than most of the writers of the era who wrote tragedies with partisan political themes. Yet in the two earlier of these tragedies he followed familiar patterns of opposition drama.

All three of them are dedicated either to the Princess or Prince of Wales, who in 1737 broke definitively with his parents and formed an alliance with the leaders of the opposition. Through the intercession of his secretary, George Lyttelton, the Prince granted a pension to Thomson. *Agamemnon* and *Edward and Eleonora* can be read, in their political dimensions, in only one way: as supporting the Prince, to whom the opposition looked with hope as successor to his father. In *Agamemnon* Thomson drew on Aeschylus for the triangular relationship among Aegisthus, the evil courtier, who represents Walpole; Clytemnestra, the queen under the malignant influence of the courtier, who much less obviously represents Queen Caroline (who died in 1737 while Thomson was at work on the play); and Agamemnon, the king who returns from the wars only to be murdered. The tragic catastrophe could not sustain an allegorical reading, though the concluding prophecy that the king's son Orestes would take revenge on Aegisthus no doubt carried overtones of the hostility the Prince of Wales felt for his father's chief minister. In *Edward and Eleonora* Thomson drew on a legend of King Edward I as Prince of Wales for a fable celebrating the courage and the devotion to one another of both Prince Frederick and his wife. He includes in his opening scene an admonition spoken by a wise nobleman to Prince Edward, representing Prince Frederick, to displace wicked ministers in the councils of his father. The implied political doctrine is akin to that of Bolingbroke's tract *The Idea of a Patriot King*.[6]

The political passages in *Agamemnon* and *Edward and Eleonora* are aesthetical liabilities, patently intrusive, and damaging to the structures of the dramatic fables. In contrast, the political themes of *Tancred and Sigismunda* add strength to the play.

In the years since the publication of *Edward and Eleonora* the alliances and allegiances that controlled political life had changed fundamentally and so had the political themes of Thomson's drama. It had become irrelevant to attack Walpole, and in fact his successor, Lord Granville (Carteret), had given place in 1744 to Henry Pelham as the King's chief minister. George Lyttelton and William Pitt had left opposition, and in doing so had become alienated from the Prince of Wales. Although Thomson maintains a focus in *Tancred and Sigismunda* on the love of the title characters for one another, he no longer writes as a supporter of the political opposition and the Prince of Wales (notwithstanding his dedication of the published play to him).

Before turning to relationships between national and theatrical affairs, I will refer to *Tancred and Sigismunda* and — so far as surviving records permit — the audience's experience of it during its first run. If the play is, as is now generally believed, the best of those written by Thomson, the enthusiasm it generated in March 1745 can be attributed only in part to the author. "Everybody agrees that no play was ever so much improved in acting," wrote a member of the first audiences, Catherine Talbot, "at least since the Booths and Bettertons."[7] And more than the excellence of the acting enhanced its popularity.

It would be difficult to think of any other play of the eighteenth century, with the possible exception of Addison's *Cato,* in which so much high talent was expended in preparation for its performance. I have already alluded to Pitt's and Lyttelton's advice to the performers at rehearsals as well as their assistance to Thomson in completing the play. A more capable group of actors and actresses, well suited to their roles, could scarcely have been assembled. The title characters were played by David Garrick, already famous though still in his youth, and Susanna Maria Cibber, described in her role of Sigismunda by Arthur Murphy as "harmony itself."[8] Thomas Davies emphasized their compatibility as the young lovers; in fact he attributed the success of the play chiefly to them.[9]

We can believe Davies's assertion that Garrick and Mrs. Cibber, in their roles as lovers entrapped in a fatal dilemma, contributed to the success of the tragedy without accepting his comment that the success was attributable to them. Two actors, Thomas Sheridan as Siffredi, Lord High Chancellor of Sicily and father of Sigismunda, and Denis Delane, as Earl Osmond, Lord High Constable, whom her father forces Sigismunda to marry, had already earned notable reputations. Sheridan's and Delane's roles were but slightly less prominent than those of Garrick and Mrs. Cibber in this tragedy with an intensity of focus on the changing relationships among a few characters reminiscent of Racine.[10] Garrick was becoming increasingly prominent, but in 1745 he had not reached the eminence he later achieved that put him above competition. A latent professional rivalry among Garrick, Sheridan, and Delane probably contributed to the excitement aroused by *Tancred and Sigismunda.*

The nature of Thomson's dramatic verse — the formality of his diction, the superlatives in which his characters so often speak, the frequency with which they turn from the rapid interchange of conversation to long speeches reminiscent of French and even Spanish dramatic convention — required a skill and style of delivery of which the actors and the actress in the principal roles were capable. Neander's complaint, in Dryden's *Of Dramatic Poesy,* that the French dramatists wrote for their characters "declamations, which tire us with the length,"[11] might have been applied to *Tancred and Sigismunda* if actors of lesser ability had played the central roles. Thomson made strong demands on the performers, but demands that they could meet. Garrick, Sheridan, and Delane could speak with formality and dignity, and yet avoid pomposity. Mrs. Cibber, in her appearance as well as in her mode of delivery, could render the pathos of Sigismunda's sufferings without distasteful sentimentality. "There is a Delicacy in her Deportment," Samuel Foote wrote two years after the premiere, "and a sensible Innocence in her Countenance, that never fails to prejudice the Spectator in her favor, even before she speaks."[12] The critics of the time consistently alluded to her ability to move an audience to tears.

Garrick's role required formality of delivery, a more formal style than we customarily associate with him. Let us remember, however, Alan Downer's valuable caution against overstatement of Garrick's departure from the older style of acting: the style, for example, we associate with Barton Booth's performance of his most famous role, Cato, in Addison's play. "David Garrick in fact," Downer writes,

was more of a refiner than a reformer of previous acting techniques. From Macklin he took the natural speech and the broken tones of utterance, from the older school he took the fire of romantic acting and the careful attention to grace and posture and gesture, and a certain method of delivery which even his most loyal supporters decried.[13]

Because *Tancred and Sigismunda* came early in his career, presumably his style was closer to that of his predecessors than it later became.

Thomas Sheridan was a theorist and in time a teacher of oratory — and extraordinarily successful teacher of oratory in at least one instance, that of his son, Richard Brinsley Sheridan. Reading Samuel Foote's dramatic caricatures of Thomas Sheridan and reading about him in Boswell's *Life of Johnson,* we can easily underestimate his abilities. He was petulant and easily angered. His personal relationships with Garrick were difficult. But on stage in *Tancred and Sigismunda* they achieved a harmonious and forceful accommodation of their styles of acting. "That first scene especially, where Siffredi discovers to Tancred who he is," wrote a person who saw them in performance, "pleased me almost beyond anything I ever saw."[14] In reading the scene — and we can scarcely expect to see it in performance even by actors trained in the different traditions of the twentieth century — we are tempted to concur in the criticism of Thomson's dialogue written by his younger contemporary, Samuel Johnson, that "his diffusive and descriptive style produced declamation rather than dialogue."[15] Perhaps so, but that style succeeded in the theatre.

Like Sheridan and Garrick, Denis Delane in the role of Osmond could render "declamation" to advantage. Having established his reputation in tragic roles such as Alexander in Nathaniel Lee's *The Rival Queens* — the role in which he was best known — he spoke in a voice that was, as Thomas Gray put it, "deep-mouth'd," "like a Passing Bell." As Osmond, a husband who believed himself betrayed, he had an opportunity to exploit what a contemporary (perhaps but not certainly Henry Fielding) described as a "loud Violence of Voice . . . useful to him when Anger, Indignation, or such enrag'd Passions are to be expres'd."[16]

The skills of the performers, as well as the stage tradition in which they acted, made possible the representation of the tragedy to the best imaginable advantage. Let us remember that we cannot hear Garrick, Sheridan, and Delane recite their lines, and that they were trained in a mode of delivery to which their audiences were accustomed. Modes of delivery change with the passage of time as well as passage over national borders to such prominent countries in the history of drama as France and Spain.

If extra-literary circumstances, such as the abilities and renown of the performers and the ostentatious enthusiasm for the play shown by Pitt and Lyttelton, contributed to the warmth of the reception in March 1745, the history of subsequent performances reveals that the play could please eighteenth-century audiences with qualities for which Thomson was responsible. He was a poet of genius and, although his reputation derives from his non-dramatic poetry, *Tancred and Sigismunda* is written in blank verse that is often much more than competent.

Despite the political innuendo, the tragedy turns on the mutual love and the misfortunes of the title characters. Indeed, the emotional intensity of their love evoked criticism from at least one perceptive contemporary. "The loves of *Tancred and Sigismunda*," Arthur Murphy wrote, "are exquisitely tender, but too poetical in the expression."[17] Although an attentive and well-informed spectator in 1745 could scarcely fail to perceive the relevance of certain passages to problems of succession to the English throne, the spectator would have found the balance of interest elsewhere.

Thomson's expository first act is busy, conveying complex dynastic relationships as well as portraying the intensity of Tancred's and Sigismunda's devotion to one another.[18] The young lovers have grown to maturity amid the pastoral surroundings of the estate of Sigismunda's father, Siffredi, the Lord High Chancellor of Sicily. From Siffredi comes the news, first to Sigismunda and then to Tancred, of the quiet and natural death of the old king of Sicily. In a private conversation Siffredi tells Tancred that he, whose parentage had not been known, is "the lineal offspring of our famous Heroe/ ROGER the First" and the legitimate heir to the throne, so designated in the will entrusted to Siffredi by the late king. Siffredi counsels Tancred to marry the sister of the late king, Constantia, previously thought to be heiress to the throne, in order to prevent threatened civil violence. When Tancred vehemently rejects the counsel because of his love for Sigismunda, Siffredi expresses apprehension. Yet he does not then inform Tancred that the king's will includes, as a necessary condition for Tancred's succession, his marriage to Constantia. Soon Tancred tells Sigismunda the momentous news, renewing his pledge of devotion to her. Summoned to a public assembly, Tancred signs a blank document and tells her to give it to her father and report to him his royal command that on it be written his, Tancred's, "solemn Marriage-Contract" to Sigismunda.

The remainder of the play depicts the consequences of Siffredi's determination to perform what he regards as his duty to his country even at the cost of his daughter's happiness—and, in the event, her life. Like the late king, who had determined that Tancred should marry Constantia to prevent hostilities between supporters of the two dynasties they represent, Siffredi believes the hostilities to be a present danger. In his unyielding effort to prevent civil war, he consents to the suit of Earl Osmond, a leader of the faction that had supported the claims of Constantia, to marry Sigismunda. Sigismunda reluctantly consents to the marriage, which is performed though never consummated. Although he loves Sigismunda, Osmond even before the ceremony expresses in soliloquy apprehension lest Siffredi's and Sigismunda's consent might arise from some dark motive. His suspicion of a secret relationship between Tancred and Sigismunda grows when, after a confrontation with the young king, he is arrested as a prisoner of state. Granted temporary leave from prison, he comes upon Tancred and Sigismunda together, innocently so, though he does not know the circumstances that led to the meeting. In the fight that ensues, Tancred wounds Osmond fatally, though Osmond retains sufficient strength to kill Sigismunda before his death.

In a curtain speech addressed to the audience, Siffredi deplores his own actions that have resulted in the death of his daughter and her husband, in lines that have the ring of an authorial pronouncement on his own conduct. Insofar as he acted by subterfuge, Siffredi's self-condemnation may be warranted. Yet the decisive events of the play, as they are consecutively depicted, reveal that had King William's will and the true identity of Tancred become known and had Tancred married Sigismunda rather than Constantia, a civil war would have been the probable consequence. The catastrophe results from irreconcilable claims placed on a sovereign by his rank and his natural affections; only secondarily from Siffredi's disingenuous but well-intentioned stratagem to avert a civil war.

Even in the first act, when Tancred tells Sigismunda what he has just learned from her father and passionately expresses his determination to make her his Queen, she responds in fear and prophetically alludes to the possibility that Tancred may be compelled to marry Constantia. A few moments before, Tancred had ordered Siffredi to summon the Council, where King William's will should be opened, and thereafter to convene the Senate, where the Sicilian barons should attend to pay their homage to

> Their rightful King, who claims his native Crown,
> And will not be a King of Deeds and Parchments.

Siffredi disobeys Tancred, in doing so employing the blank document Tancred had given Sigismunda after having signed it. In a soliloquy at the beginning of Act Two, Siffredi explains his intended stratagem:

> Here is the Royal Hand—
> I will beneath it write a perfect full
> And absolute Agreement to the Will;
> Which read before the Nobles of the Realm
> Assembled, in the sacred Face of *Sicily,*
> CONSTANTIA present, every Heart and Eye
> Fix'd on their Monarch, every Tongue applauding,
> He must submit.

Siffredi's neatly but treacherously conceived plan succeeds, and Tancred is indeed forced to submit, at least to the extent that he loses Sigismunda.

Thomson wrote *Tancred and Sigismunda* and revised it with the assistance of two leading political figures at a time when there was danger of a Jacobite invasion, conceivably one supported by French military and naval force, and furthermore at a time when British internal political allegiances were changing rapidly. Although he had vigorously and for a long time supported the Prince of Wales and the opposition to the King's Ministry, he includes in *Tancred and Sigismunda* a passage of dialogue that can be read as praise of the elderly King George II (I.iv). His loyalty to Pitt and Lyttelton, who were no longer in opposition, remains firm. He includes a transparent defense of their recent change in political alliance—and we have Benjamin Victor's word for it in a published letter that the passage was interpreted by the first audiences as Thomson, as well as the two politicians themselves, intended.[19] In the second act, Earl Osmond, previously a counselor to Constantia, addresses the assembled barons of Sicily. He speaks first of the reconciliations made possible by the projected marriage of Constantia and Tancred, the legitimate heir to the throne (II.iv):

> We meet to-day with open Hearts and Looks,
> Not gloom'd by Party, scouling on each other,
> But all the Children of one happy Isle,
> The social Sons of Liberty. No Pride,
> No Passion now, no thwarting Views divide us:
> Prince MANFRED's Line, at last, to WILLIAM's join'd,
> Combines us in one Family of Brothers.

Osmond's speech to this point, though curiously bold in its susceptibility to a Jacobite interpretation, articulates the early eighteenth-century conception of rival political groups, familiar to us in the writings of Swift and Bolingbroke, as disruptive factions. In the latter part of his speech, however, in lines that Benjamin Victor quotes and explicates, Osmond sounds as though he were William Pitt or George Lyttelton speaking from the floor of the House of Commons:

> I here renounce those Errors and Divisions
> That have so long disturb'd our Peace, and seem'd,
> Fermenting still, to threaten new Commotions —
> By Time instructed, let us not disdain
> To quit Mistakes.

Benjamin Victor's comments on these lines merit attention. He refers to Lyttelton, "a very remarkable new Lord of the Treasury," and his friends, "all very lately most flaming Patriots!" present with him at the premiere, applauding Osmond's lines announcing his determination "By Time instructed" "To quit Mistakes." Victor writes that a more accurate interpretation of the motive for change in allegiances could be expressed as "by PLACE instructed"; and he amplifies his hostile interpretation of the motive for the change in allegiance, alluding in sarcasm to the bequest of £10,000 to Pitt by Sarah, Duchess of Marlborough, who had died in October 1744:

Did not all these Gentlemen very lately act quite counter to this very
Doctrine when they acquir'd the amiable and Distinguish'd Character
of Patriots? . . . Did not a late Duchess leave a very large Legacy to one
of those Patriots for his honest opposition? — Well, Sir, this opposition
was, at last, attended with success; and most of these Patriots are in the
Administration of Affairs.

Victor's accusation is without ambiguity, though the historical
realities of the reasons for the ministerial changes late in 1744 are
by no means so simple as he implies.

Thomson's defense of Pitt and Lyttelton in *Tancred and Sigismunda* is consistent with his friendship with, admiration for, and
gratitude to them. More difficult to reconcile with what is known
of his own political convictions and allegiances are the passages
that lend themselves to a Jacobite as well as a Hanoverian interpretation. In *London in the Jacobite Times,* published in 1877,
John Doran writes in detail about the play and the audience's
response to it. In consequence of Pitt's and Lyttelton's interest, he
remarks, the play "had a certain political significance, and Whigs
and Jacobites sat in judgment on it. Thomson's cunning, however, enabled him to please both parties." Doran continues, with
every appearance of working from contemporary sources, to
describe the passages that the separate parties applauded. Unfortunately, he provides no documentation[20] — though the political
resonance of the passages he isolates lends credibility to his
analysis.

Earl Osmond, in his speech to the Barons (II.iv), alludes to a
prospect of reconciliation of factions in the Kingdom by a marriage of the legitimate heir, Tancred, to the sister of the late King
William "the *Good,*" who had been the son of the usurping King
William "the *Bad.*" In historical fact a matrimonial reconciliation between Stuart and Hanover was manifestly impossible. Yet
few in the first audiences could have been unaware that the Old
Pretender was the brother of Queen Anne and that, in accordance with traditional principles of succession, he was the legitimate heir; whereas the reigning sovereign was the son of King
George I, whom an act of Parliament had placed on the throne.
Tancred's vehement declaration, upon learning his true identity
(I.iv), that he would "not be a King of Deeds and Parchments"
could be interpreted as a reference to the Parliamentary Act of

Settlement of 1701. Thomson may not have written "parallel
history," as in limited measure he had done in *Agamemnon* seven
years earlier. But he exploited the public interest in the dynastic
rivalry that reached a climax a few'months later in the "forty-
five."

The political double-entendre appears at its boldest in
Siffredi's revelation to Tancred of his identity as heir to the
throne: in Siffredi's exposition of the relevant historical events
and in Tancred's response. Siffredi's praise of King William II of
Sicily could have been interpreted — and in view of George Lyttelton's recent break with the Opposition and with the Prince of
Wales was presumably intended to be interpreted — as praise of
George II, elderly but with fifteen years of life ahead. Siffredi's
allusion to the King's adherence to the rule of law has Hanoverian
rather than Stuart overtones (I.iv):

> He sought alone the Good of Those, for whom
> He was entrusted with the sovereign Power:
> Well knowing that a People in their Rights
> And Industry protected; living safe
> Beneath the sacred Shelter of the Laws,
> Encourag'd in their Genius, Arts, and Labours,
> And happy each as he himself deserves,
> Are ne'er ungrateful.

Emphasis on a sovereign's obligation to respect the laws of the
kingdom had been commonplace since the Revolution of 1688.
Although King William III of England had been the husband of
the Stuart Queen Mary, who in turn had been the sister of the
Old Pretender, the passage could scarcely be interpreted as
hostile to the Hanoverians, who derived their claim to the throne
from the Act of Settlement. They recognized constitutional limits
to their authority, as James II notoriously had not.

Yet the interchange between Siffredi and the young King
Tancred includes lines that will bear a Jacobite interpretation.
Before the Chancellor reveals to Tancred his identity, he tells him
that a prince lives in Sicily, "the lineal Offspring of our famous
Heroe,/ ROGER the First," of whom the prince is a great
grandson. Alternative parallels with English history invite appli-
cation. George I was the great grandson of James I. Prince
Charles Edward was the great grandson of Charles I, who, like

Roger I of Sicily, had been deprived of his throne, imprisoned, and finally murdered. Emphasis in the passage falls on lineal descent, and hence on the claims of the Stuarts.

Tancred's response to Siffredi has an even stronger Jacobite ring. Referring to the prince descended from Sicily's ancient "Norman" line, Tancred declares his loyalty to him: "The Right is clearly his," he says, and he adds:

> There is no ground for Fear. They have great Odds,
> Against the astonish'd Sons of Violence,
> Who fight with awful Justice on their Side.
> All *Sicily* will rouze, all faithful Hearts
> Will range themselves around Prince MANFRED's Son.

The chance of success on which the Jacobites gambled in the invasion a few months later turned on their anticipation of massive defections of Britons from loyalty to the Hanoverians to support the Stuarts. French support of Charles Edward was uncertain and in the event proved to be minimal; even in March 1745 they could scarcely be expected to provide sufficient strength for him to depose King George unless many Scots and many Englishmen "range[d] themselves around" the Prince. To be sure, the Sicilian Prince to whom Tancred and Siffredi refer could be identified with the Prince of Wales or his father George II. The lines could not have been spoken from the stage of Drury Lane had they carried in allegory an unambiguous Jacobite burden. It is indeed surprising that, even with the precautions Thomson took to avoid overt political reference, the play was not banned or drastically altered by order of the Examiner of Plays.

The text of the first edition and that of the manuscript submitted for licensing[21] are almost identical, a circumstance suggesting that the Examiner had little if any part in making changes in the play. The first edition does not include passages marked by inverted commas, a typographical method employed in some plays of the era to designate lines not to be spoken from the stage. (The concluding lines of the prologue to Thomson's *Agamemnon*, written in the most vigorous idiom of the literary opposition, are marked in this manner.) The manuscript of *Tancred and Sigismunda* submitted to the Examiner reveals both cancellations and substitutions, to be sure, some of which look as though they were politically motivated, but from what we know of the play's composition it would seem more likely that Thomson himself or his political patrons were responsible for the alterations than that they were enforced by censorship. In any event, it is the fable of the play in its entirety, about the tragic consequences of the dynastic rivalry for the title characters, which is the primary vehicle for the political burden of the play. Furthermore, contemporaries who saw it in performance mention two of the sensitive passages. We know from Catherine Talbot, who praises the scene "where Siffredi discovers to Tancred who he is," that the dynastic rivalry received emphasis in performance;[22] we know from Benjamin Victor that Earl Osmond's defence of a change in political allegiance (II.iv) was spoken and furthermore that it was vigorously applauded, by Pitt among others.[23]

Yet as performed on 18 March 1745 the text of the play was not identical to that of the first edition. In his letter to the *Daily Post,* 26 April, Victor writes that three hundred lines were deleted after the first performance. To the published play, Thomson prefixed the following "Advertisement".

This play is considerably shortened in the performance; but I hope it will not be disagreeable to the reader to see it as it was at first written; there being a great difference betwixt a play in the closet, and upon the stage.

Although the statement lacks detail, Thomson's emphasis falls on aesthetic considerations. The absence of any complaint about censorship is worth noting. Certainly the leisurely dialogue, in which single speeches sometimes require more than a page in print, provided sufficient motive for omitting many lines.[24]

Like Dryden's heroic plays, Thomson's tragedies are easy to burlesque. Yet Thomson's tragedies are not to be dismissed with a casual laugh. The best of them, *Tancred and Sigismunda,* merits — at least by students of drama — close attention. It is difficult to read in our time with an awareness of the force it carried, when performed by actors trained in a declamatory tradition for audiences accustomed to a declamatory mode of delivery. The political and military circumstances of 1745 contributed to the warmth of its reception in its first run. But the revivals even in the later years of William Pitt the Younger during the Napoleonic era testify to the tragic intensity of Thomson's representation of the conflict between the responsibility of supreme rank and irrepressible affection.

The danger of civil war that Siffredi foresaw if Tancred married Sigismunda was real, as we are repeatedly reminded. Osmond, having been released "on my parole" from the prison to which Tancred had committed him, goes by night to the house of Siffredi, to whom he confirms the accuracy of Siffredi's often-expressed fears of civil war (V.ii):

> Know then, the faithless Outrage of To-day,
> By him committed whom you call the King,
> Has rouz'd CONSTANTIA's Court. Our Friends, the Friends
> Of Virtue, Justice, and of Publick Faith,
> Ripe for Revolt, are in high Ferment all.
> This, this, they say, exceeds whate'er deform'd
> The miserable Days we saw beneath
> WILLIAM the *Bad*. This saps the solid Base,
> At once, of Government and Private life;
> This shameless Imposition on the Faith,
> The Majesty of Senates, this lewd Insult,
> This Violation of the Rights of Men.

Osmond adds that the late King's will provides that, if Tancred "make not CONSTANTIA partner of his Throne," he be excluded from succession and she be given in marriage to the King of the Romans, who seeks her alliance. This passage like others invites multiple and conflicting applications to British history—but within the limits of the play it provides a reminder that Siffredi is a political realist and not a legalistic eccentric. Siffredi fails: his daughter is killed; Tancred, broken in spirit, remains king at play's end, but with a grave threat to him and the nation presented by the dynastic rivalry unresolved.

In an age in which sovereigns retained great power, even the sovereigns of eighteenth-century England whose prerogatives were constitutionally restricted, princes in line of succession could not marry as they wished. In many respects they lacked freedom of choice that even the humblest of subjects possessed. The dynastic wars of the first half of the eighteenth-century—the War of the Spanish Succession and the War of the Austrian Succession

— in which the government of nations and empires seems super-ficially to have been regarded as inherited property, analogous to the inherited property of private persons, turn out on close examination to have been wars of religious and economic compe-tition, in which royal persons were cyphers — sometimes vocal and influential cyphers — not competing masters of destiny. *Tancred and Sigismunda* is a tragedy about frustrated young love, but it is also a political tragedy including a depiction of the limitation of freedom to which sovereigns and their heirs were subjected. The recent history of England provided numerous instances of kings and their heirs who, as a responsibility inseparable from their rank, had chosen wives for reason of state.

The emotional conflicts and political dilemmas faced by the leading characters of *Tancred and Sigismunda* had parallels — leaving out of account, to be sure, the lyricism of young love so prominent in the play — in the lives of royalty. Frederick, Prince of Wales, to whom Thomson dedicated it, was as unamiable a person as we are likely to encounter in the great world of mid-eighteenth-century Britain. Yet his father had arranged his marriage and, though he may have regarded himself as leader of the opposition, he was in fact a tool used by much abler men, some of whom, including Lyttelton and Pitt, deserted him in 1744 and 1745. Of course he, and less conspicuously Prince Charles Edward, lacked the personal qualities of the Tancred of Thomson's play. Yet their experiences remind us that Thomson wrote about subjects that touched men's lives.

It is doubtful that a play including passages as susceptible to a Jacobite interpretation as *Tancred and Sigismunda* could have been licensed after Prince Charles Edward's invasion in the summer of 1745. So much is implied by the fate of William Shirley's *Electra,* completed by the author in the spring of 1745.[25] *Electra,* like Thomson's *Agamemnon* of 1738 written in support of the Prince of Wales and in opposition to Walpole, derives from Aeschylus, but in this later play the fable derived from the *Oresteia* carries a Jacobite burden. Orestes, representing Charles Edward, returns from exile to depose the usurper Aegisthus, representing George II. To be sure, the "parallel history" lacks the subtlety and ambiguity of *Tancred and Sigismunda.* It is not surprising that Shirley did not attempt to have the play produced, or published, during the season of 1745-1746. Yet the length of time that elapsed before Shirley could persuade a proprietor of a theatre to present the play, in 1763, eighteen years after it was written, is surprising, and even more so is the fact that after it was accepted for production two successive Lord Chamberlains forbade performance of it, long after the Jacobite threat had vanished. Confronted with an unyielding governmental ban, Shirley published the play in 1765. The London theatres were no longer receptive to drama critical of the government or of the structure of English society.[26]

Thomson's final and posthumous tragedy, a version of *Coriolanus* more accurately considered an original play on Shakespeare's subject than an adaptation, provides an apt illustration of the new political temper of the theatres. I know of no evidence external to the play, apart from Lyttelton's continuing assistance to and encouragement of him,[27] that Thomson in *Coriolanus* intended to comment on public affairs. Yet I think it unlikely that he would have turned to the story of Coriolanus's treasonous warfare against his own country, as he did in the latter part of 1745[28] when many Britons were in arms against their sovereign, without an awareness of a relevance of the story of the Rebellion. Not performed until January 1749 after the author's death the preceding August, the tragedy closes with what must be regarded as an authorial admonishment against the crime of which Coriolanus was guilty.

> Whatever private views and passions plead,
> No cause can justify so black a deed:
> . . . .
> Then be this truth the star by which we steer,
> *Above* ourselves *our* COUNTRY should be dear.

The relevance of these lines to the events of 1745 and 1746 could not be mistaken. Nor could Thomson's declaration of allegiance to the reigning dynasty. He closed his dramatic career in a spirit of loyalty to government that would be typical of the drama performed in London for the rest of the century.

NOTES

1. Thomas Davies, *Memoirs of the Life of David Garrick, Esq.* (London: Printed for the Author 1780), I, 79.

2. Comment by the William Andrews Clark Professor, George Winchester Stone, during the seminar at which this essay, in an earlier version, was read, May 20, 1977. The play had a life on stage of 50 seasons, lasting for 98 performances until May 22, 1794.

3. Carl J. Stratman, *Bibliography of English Printed Tragedy* (Carbondale: Southern Illinois University Press, 1966), pp. 658-660, lists twenty-four eighteenth-century editions, apart from collected editions of Thomson's work. Several of these may have been variant "issues" rather than separate "editions," but the number was certainly very high.

4. Bertrand A. Goldgar, *Walpole and the Wits: The Relation of Politics to Literature, 1722-1742* (Lincoln: University of Nebraska Press, 1976), pp. 85-86.

5. Pocock, *Politics, Language and Time: Essays on Political Thought and History* (New York: Athenaeum, 1971), pp. 124-125.

6. On Thomson, Bolingbroke, and the Prince of Wales, see Isaac Kramnick, *Bolingbroke and His Circle: The Politics of Nostalgia in the Age of Walpole* (Cambridge, Mass.: Harvard University Press, 1968), pp. 33-35.

7. Letter of Catherine Talbot, mistakenly dated 2 March 1745. In *A Series of Letters between Mrs. Elizabeth Carter and Miss Catherine Talbot* (London, 1809), I. 90. (Quoted in Arthur H. Scouten, ed., *The London Stage*, Part Three [Carbondale: Southern Illinois University Press, 1961], p. 1160.)

8. Murphy, *The Life of David Garrick, Esq.* (London: Printed for T. Wright 1801), I, 103.

9. Davies, *Garrick*, I, 79-80.

10. Thomson admired Racine and, it would appear, looked to the French dramatist's plays as formal models. In the preface to *Sophonisba,* he quotes a passage from Racine on the "unity of design" in drama, remarking that it *"contains all that I have to say on this head."*

11. *The Works of John Dryden*, XVII, ed. Samuel Holt Monk and A. E. Wallace Maurer (Berkeley, Los Angeles, London: University of California Press, 1971), p. 47.

12. Foote, *The Roman and English Comedy Considered* (London: T. Waller, 1747). (Quoted from Philip H. Highfill, Jr., Kalman A. Burnim, and Edward A. Langhans, *A Biographical Dictionary of Actors, Actresses, Musicians. . . .,* III [Carbondale: Southern Illinois University Press, 1973], 274.)

13. Downer, "Nature to Advantage Dressed: Eighteenth-Century Acting," *PMLA,* LVIII (1943). Reprinted, John Loftis, ed., *Restoration Drama: Modern Essays in Criticism* (New York: Oxford University Press, 1966), pp. 339-340.

14. Letter of Catherine Talbot cited above, p. 39.

15. Johnson, "Thomson," *The Lives of the English Poets,* ed. George Birkbeck Hill (Oxford, 1905), III, 293.

16. My account of Delane is based on Highfill et al., *Dictionary of Actors,* IV, 286-290.

17. Murphy, *Garrick*, I, 103.

18. In a letter of 29 December 1744, Garrick identified the source of the plot: "Thompson has a Tragedy ready for Us, upon the Tapestry Story in The Second Vol. of Gilblas—." David M. Little and George M. Kahrl, eds., *The Letters of David Garrick* (Cambridge, Mass.: Harvard University Press, 1963), I, 46.

Garrick referred to Alain-René Le Sage, *Gil Blas*, Livre IV, Chapitre IV: "Le Mariage de vengeance." Boccaccio had earlier included a version of the story in *Il Decamerone*, Giornata Quarta, Novella Prima. Dryden had translated this story in his *Fables*: "Sigismonda and Guiscardo," the latter name being the one Boccaccio had used for the character corresponding to Tancred.

19. Victor's letter, about the play and the audience's reception of it, appears in the *Daily Post*, April 26, 1745. The letter is reprinted in Alan Dugald McKillop, ed., *James Thomson (1700–1748): Letters and Documents* (Lawrence: University of Kansas Press, 1958), pp. 178-181.

20. Doran (London, 1877), II, 108-110. I have been unable to find the sources he presumably used.

21. The manuscript is in the Larpent Collection of the Huntington Library, San Marino, California.

22. See above, p. 41.

23. See above, p. 44-46.

24. An edition of the play printed in 1776 includes inverted commas to indicate "the Passages omitted in the Representation at the Theatres." Although this edition, printed thirty-one years after the first, is too late to be regarded as a reliable guide to the performance at the première, it is suggestive that the deletions seem to have been made for aesthetic reasons—to reduce the redundancy that often is a corollary of Thomson's expansive imagery. (This edition was called to my attention by Professor Gwendolyn W. Brewer.)

25. L. W. Conolly, *The Censorship of English Drama, 1737–1824* (San Marino, Calif., The Huntington Library, 1976), pp. 73-74.

26. Ibid., passim.

27. Douglas Grant, *James Thomson: Poet of the "Seasons"* (London: Cresset Press, 1951), p. 246.

28. In addition to other expressions of esteem for Thomson, Lyttelton wrote an affectionate prologue about the late poet which was spoken at the première of *Coriolanus*.

FARCE
Editor's Headnote

The comic muse, as noted, enjoyed a particular heyday in performances during the eighteenth century. A basic type of comedy was, of course, comedy of situation, or farce. Many of the most creative stage pieces of the century—those by Foote, Garrick, Murphy, and Fielding—lay in this general category. Increasingly through the century a special place was made for them in the much-called-for brief afterpiece following the main play of the evening. The afterpiece, however, provided a field for wide experimentation in all sorts of presentation: pantomime, procession, elaborate ballet, or skits on contemporary taste. Professor Hughes traces the history and development of this portion of a night's entertainment in the century, noting how this element of the "whole show" attracted enthusiastic attention from duchesses and literati to sober citizens and tradesmen, from liberal clergy to apprentices and footmen. Some of them still amuse on the page; all of them brightened their evenings on the stage.

3. Afterpieces: Or, That's Entertainment

Leo Hughes
Professor of English, University of Texas

Sometime late in 1676 Thomas Otway, not yet twenty-five but with two plays already performed, tried out a novelty on the London audience: a French playbill. I am not alluding to a poster in a foreign language but to a combination of two plays in one evening: Racine's *Bérenice*, retitled *Titus and Berenice* and squeezed down from five acts to three, plus Molière's *Fourberies de Scapin*, which, though somewhat shortened, was allowed to remain in three acts. Downes tells us that the play—he obviously thinks of the tragedy as the main event of the evening, the farce as a mere appendage — was "well acted and had good success." Precisely what the last phrase signifies remains unclear. Certainly *Titus and Berenice* did not become a staple in the London repertory; in fact it seems to have sunk without trace. Molière's farce, on the contrary, was revived on occasion throughout the coming century. Of interest here, however, is not the fortunes of the individual plays but their being used in combination, the double-billing. Otway's experiment proved at the time quite untransplantable to regular London fare.

Why this should prove true requires no profound search or speculation. Theatrical tradition accounts for much. The evening's bill had never been a double one. Nothing but the whim of an individual accounts for the experiment, which, it may be stressed, was not repeated by Otway. If he was impelled by an urge to follow the French in their insistence on the separation of genres he fails to say so. The only reference in dedication or prologue to French customs is a sneer at English fops who return from France with "a very little French breeding" and "heels [which] abound with dance." His later practice, especially in the notorious "Nicky-Nacky" scenes in *Venice Preserved,* suggests no strong antipathy to mixing. The English principle of simultaneity as it has been dubbed in recent critical parlance is so well established that it hardly requires the eloquent defence it got from Samuel Johnson in his *Preface to Shakespeare,* though a bit of that defence seems eminently quotable here:

The interchanges of mingled scenes seldom fail to produce the intended vicissitudes of passion. Fiction cannot move so much, but that the attention may be easily transferred; and though it must be allowed that pleasing melancholy may be sometimes interrupted by unwelcome levity, yet let it be considered, likewise, that melancholy is often not pleasing, and that the disturbance of one man may be the relief of another; that different auditors have different habitudes; and that, upon the whole, all pleasure consists in variety.

By citing the case of Otway's failed experiment I am not maintaining that an afternoon or evening's performance had always been barren of supplement, especially of song and dance, even mimetic song and dance. Samuel Pepys is our ever faithful reporter. On 2 May 1668 he did not care for Shadwell's *Sullen Lovers,* thinking the little boy who "for a farce, do dance Polichinelli" much superior. On the following 19 January he thought Katherine Philips' tragic *Horace* and John Lacy's "farce of several dances—between each act one" both silly. Of some interest on both occasions is Pepys's use of *farce* in the literal French meaning of *stuff* and his report of entr'acte material utterly foreign to the mood of tragedy, however silly it might have been. On other occasions Pepys refers to *jigs* though these seem always to be within the play and therefore hardly independent as well as less mimetic and sustained. In other words the term may have taken on a different meaning from the one it had in the Elizabethan theatre, though I have never been persuaded by Baskervil's enormously detailed treatise that the Elizabethan jig was ever an afterpiece in the sense used here.

If then the afterpiece as an independent segment did not come by direct import from France, where it had been a fixture for decades, where did it come from? Perhaps the best way to answer that question would be to turn to a familiar passage in one of the world's masterpieces, *Faust*. In Goethe's "Prelude in the Theatre" three principals argue over what would be best to offer the public. The poet, a man of great soul and exalted views, wants nothing to do with the rabble; he is willing to await the judgment of posterity, *die Nachwelt*. The comedian, much less exalted, could not care less about the *Nachwelt;* his concern is with the *Mitwelt*. The manager takes the middle road, the received view:

> Wie machen wir's, dass alles frisch und neu
> Und mit Bedeutung auch gefällig sei?

Or, as the whole relevant passage is Englished by Philip Wayne for Penguin:

> How can we manage something brisk and new,
> Not only smart, but edifying too?
> For, frankly, nothing pleases me much more
> Than sight of crowds, when they begin to pour
> In daylight through our strait and narrow door;
> Or when they shove and fight towards the wicket,
> And nearly break their necks to get a ticket.

Tradition in the English theatre, stubbornly resistant as it was, eventually yielded to the pressures of the box office. I have sketched some part of this story before, in a book now long out of print.[1] The editors of *The London Stage* have provided ample, even overwhelming, detail with which to document the story. Perhaps a brief resume will be useful in showing the main events in the theatre which led, in the space of a quarter century, to the establishing of much the same bill the French had long had, and which made for a varied "whole show."

The efficient cause, the restoration of theatrical competition brought about by the revolt of Betterton and his veteran colleagues in 1695, did not lead *immediately* to the effect I speak of but that effect came in good time. If the revolt had occurred in response to a demand from a burgeoning audience things would no doubt have been different. The new company was not responding to any demand but mutinying against a manager whom they considered insufferable, Christopher Rich. For a time their new venture was a great success. They represented, after all, the great strength of the United Company. They started in a new theatre with a new play by the leading playwright of the day, *Love for Love,* still considered the most theatrically effective of Congreve's plays. Meanwhile the neophytes and secondary actors who remained with Rich fell upon hard times. By the beginning of the new century the rival companies had approached something like an equilibrium that amounted to a sharing of hard times and the development of vigorous, even cutthroat, competition and, more to the point, of offerings which they hoped would seem brisk and new but which often proved merely bizarre. To the customary bill they began to add all sorts of attractions: acrobats, ropedancers, freaks. Virtually no playbills survive from the very first years of the century and newspaper accounts in the brief period before the first London daily, in 1702, give us few details, but a chorus of commentators leaves us in no doubt. One remarked in a letter of September 1699:

But tho' Bartholomew-Fair is dead and buried for a twelvemonth, yet it is some consolation to us, that it revives in both the play-houses. . . . One would almost swear, that Smithfield had removed into Drury-lane and Lincolns-Inn-Fields, since they set so small a value on good sense, and so great a one on trifles that have no relation to the play. By the by, I am to tell you, that some of their late bills are so very monstrous that neither we, nor our forefathers, ever knew anything like them: They are as long as the title-pages to some of Mr. Prynn's works; nay, you may much sooner dispatch the *Gazette,* even when it is most crowded with advertisements. And as their bills are so prodigious, so are the entertainments they present us with: For, not to mention the Bohemian women, that first taught us how to dance and swim together; nor the famous Mr. Clinch of Barnet, with his kit and organ; nor the worthy gentlemen that condescended to dance a Cheshire-rounds at the instance of several persons of quality; nor t'other gentleman that sung like a turky-cock; nor, lastly, that prodigy of a man that mimick'd the harmony of the Essex lions.[2]

As the informant says nothing about actual plays perhaps one should look at some complete performances as listed by Emmett Avery in *The London Stage.* At the turn of the century Drury Lane was depending rather heavily on Farquhar and Steele, just entering the lists, and on older playwrights like Shakespeare, Jonson, and Fletcher. Lincoln's Inn Fields relied on Congreve, on the point of retiring, and Dryden, about to go into complete and permanent retirement, plus older playwrights as well. But Mr. Clench is here too with his one-man band and his animal imitations. The "turky-cock" is here too or something very like. The bill for 22 December 1702 at Lincoln's Inn Fields calls for *The Country Wife* with miscellaneous dancing, principally *"The Mad-Man's Dance.* A new dance perform'd by 16 Persons in Grotesque Habits, in which a Black will perform varieties of Postures to Admiration. *Roger a Coverly,* by Weaver, as it was done originally after the Yorkshire manner." A couple of songs, one in dialogue, appear, and finally *"The Turkey-Cock Music.* An Entertainment performed before The Doge and Senate of Venice at this last Carnival." More significant for my purposes than either Wycherley's play or the Turkey music is the dance material. The Weaver who did the Sir Roger a Coverly is almost certainly John Weaver, who was soon to become choreographer at the rival theatre and who in the next few decades was to have a large share in the development of pantomime and even early ballet and to become a self-appointed spokesman and historiographer for mime and dance. As late as 1728 Weaver looked back on these years for the first clear sign of mimetic dancing and singled out an even earlier performance, one in August 1702 at Lincoln's Inn Fields. Avery gives us details. On Saturday the twenty-second Betterton's company performed Brome's *Jovial Crew,* followed by the inexhaustible Mr. Clench, by "vaulting on the horse," and a "Night Scene by a Harlequin and Scaramouch, after the Italian manner, by Serene and another Person lately arrived in England. The last time of acting till after Bartholomew Fair."

Even with their own best entr'acte dancing and singing and with some highly promising recruits like Robert Wilks and Anne Oldfield, the rival company at Drury Lane found the going hard. Avery quotes Cibber under date of 26 November 1702, the premiere of *She Wou'd and She Wou'd Not:* "The Kind Imposter [subtitle of the Cibber play] did not pay the charges on the Sixth day."

By December we find Lincoln's Inn Fields venturing a step farther on the road toward double-billing. On the eleventh it gave *The Indian Emperor* followed by *Acis and Galatea,* not to be sure the splendid baroque opera by Handel — that was to come thirty years later and constitute a full bill in itself. This was some sort of masque about which we know very little except for a few interesting details supplied by Roger Fiske, who tells us that Acis was sung by Mrs. Bracegirdle in breeches and that, unlike his Handel-Gay counterpart, he was allowed to survive.[3]

After this tentative beginning things moved more rapidly. By February 1703, at Drury Lane, a one-act *Fairy Queen* appeared, Settle's elaborately mounted opera from Shakespeare with music by Henry Purcell, first performed ten years earlier, followed by a two-act version of *Marriage à la Mode.* On the last day of April that year is recorded what would appear to have been a modest enough offering, a double bill of Otway's old *Cheats of Scapin* and Cibber's *The School Boy,* both of which became in time stock afterpieces. But so much miscellaneous singing and dancing was added to the bill that, we are told, acting began at 5:00 P.M. "so that all may be done by nine."

The movement toward a regular double bill, toward the use of a main piece and briefer afterpiece, did not maintain the pace set in these early years. Other devices were tried to reduce competition. In the fall of 1707, for example, an agreement was reached whereby one company, Drury Lane, was to have a monopoly of plays whereas the other, at Vanbrugh's new theatre in the Haymarket, with its baroque decor and impossible acoustics, was to do musical pieces. With the reduction of competition there was a similar reduction in added attractions. Double-billing declined.

By the beginning of the 1714-1715 season, the first when competition was resumed, the afterpiece had almost disappeared. From September 1714 when Drury Lane opened the season without rivalry to January 1715 just two afterpieces were scheduled. From January through the summer there were one hundred. The sharp increase has an obvious cause: the opening just before Christmas of the Rich brothers' new house in Lincoln's Inn Fields.

With this opening the future of the afterpiece was assured. Not that it was all clear sailing for John Rich. His first seven or eight seasons were bleak indeed. He had a new theatre, a callow set of actors, and formidable competition from the people at Drury Lane, who were now the popular veterans. So Rich, hard put to keep his doors open, resorted to added attractions. Most of the 100 afterpieces appearing for the spring and summer of 1715 were offered by Rich. Most of the innovations or the resort to what had seemed innovative a decade earlier were Rich's. Frequency of comic dancing, "comic masques," such as the "*Pyramus and Thisbe,* [with] Lyon, Moonshine, and Wall," picked up in April 1716. And in spite of the futility of most of his efforts — some nights receipts dropped below £10 — Rich had a curious impact on his more successful rivals. Just a week preceding the tradesmen's masque at Lincoln's Inn Fields, Cibber and his associates brought back from Paris the pair who had entertained Drury Lane audiences with their Italian night scenes fourteen years earlier, Sorin and Baxter. This international pair had in recent years been heading — or lending their names to as ostensible proprietors — a Parisian troupe called "le Theatre de bel air" which played at the Parisian fairs just such a piece as they now offered Londoners, *The Whimsical Death of Harlequin.*

Rich's good fortunes, of which for the first seven or eight years there seemed destined to be none, are in some sense closely tied to the development of the supplementary bill. By 1722-1723 Rich's fortunes had reached their lowest ebb. Early in the season, on October 9, the receipts dipped to £9 10s. Drury Lane, by all reports thriving though comparable detailed information is lacking, had even begun to dispense with afterpieces once more. Steele's *Conscious Lovers* started on its highly successful career in early November. By Christmas the company had performed just one afterpiece, an *Escapes of Harlequin,* left over from the preceding season. But their complacency was shattered in February by the unexpected but enormous success at Rich's theatre of Fenton's *Mariamne*. The receipts for the author's first benefit were £224. The *British Journal* reported "the greatest audience ever known at either theater" and predicted that Fenton would eventually garner "upwards of a thousand pounds." Though this estimate proved too high, the solid success of *Mariamne* turned Rich's fortunes directly around.

The impact on his rivals was startling but predictable. Though they had given only six afterpieces between September and mid-March they made up for their neglect during the rest of the season, which ran till August, by giving twenty-seven. Rich had closed his season on 7 June, presumably to count his money.

Another event of the 1722–1723 season, though not as significant as the success of Fenton's tragedy, had at least symbolic effect, which warrants brief recounting. During the seasons I passed over, specifically beginning with 1716–1717, Rich had tried his hand at some of the old Italian night scenes his rivals had reintroduced the preceding fall. But instead of importing Parisian exotics he determined, possibly in the interest of economy, to play Harlequin himself. On 22 April 1717 Rich made his debut, under the stage name of Lun, in "an Italian Night Scene" entitled *The Cheats; or, The Tavern Bilkers*. His success, though it did not match the triumph he was to enjoy six years later with *Mariamne,* was enough to encourage him to repeat the attempt on occasion in succeeding seasons on up to that of 1722–1723. The Drury Lane company, doubtless frustrated over their rival's success, determined in March 1723 to jeer at the new Harlequin-impresario. On 16 March they performed *Love for Love,* with a splendid cast, incidentally, and added a new afterpiece called *Blind Man's Bluff,* "perform'd by eight Harlequins!" *The Weekly Journal* reports the unexpected result:

The Managers of Drury-Lane Theatre observing how successful Lincoln's-Inn-Fields has been in several Entertainments, in which the character of Harlequin has the principal Part, were resolv'd to cut them out, and therefore prepared . . . *Blind Man's Bluff,* to be perform'd by no less than eight Harlequins; for, in their way of Reasoning, eight Harlequin's must divert better than one; the Thing was so ridiculous there was no Musick to be heard but Hissing.

Having found the multiplication of Harlequins abortive, the managers of Drury Lane shifted their strategy from ridicule to imitation. They set their pantomimist, John Thurmond, to work on a piece that would beat Rich on his own grounds. On 26 November they produced "A new grotesque entertainment," the current term for pantomime, entitled *Harlequin Doctor Faustus,* "the whole concluding with a Grand Masque of the Heathen Deities, (viz.), Apollo, Mars, Bacchus, Mercury, Diana, Ceres, Flora, and Iris. All the Scenes, Machines, Habits, and other Decorations being entirely new."

The result of the new strategy was less dramatic than the earlier one involving the burlesque harlequinade but in the long run even more significant in the history of pantomimic afterpieces. For Rich retaliated in just under a month with his own panto-mime exploiting the adventures of the legendary German magician. This piece, *The Necromancer; or, Harlequin Doctor Faustus,* was played scores of times throughout the next couple of generations. The last performance listed in *The London Stage* is for the Christmas season of 1773. Meanwhile it was followed by others, some of them even more successful, especially several by Lewis Theobald. *The London Stage* lists for Covent Garden on 14 October 1778 a pastiche afterpiece by James Messink of three of Theobald's greatest successes.

Pantomime did not replace the short play as the staple after-piece in spite of its strong showing in the 1720s and 1730s. In the season in which Rich's fortune turned, 1722-1723, a total of 82 bills list an afterpiece, dialogue, or pantomime. A decade later, 1735-1736, shortly before the Licensing Act cut back sharply on the number of theatres springing up in London, some 220 panto-mimes were put on but 280 nonpantomimes matched them for a grand total of 500. The day of the afterpiece had indeed arrived. Popular demand had made it economically feasible, and necessary.

By the time of Garrick's appearance in 1741, farce became the staple offering for the century. So commonly were farces used as afterpieces that the terms came to mean much the same thing. Of the some thirty to forty pieces credited to Garrick, more than half admittedly adaptations, a quarter were farces. Of these some six, *The Lying Valet, Miss in Her Teens, The Guardian, The Irish Widow, Bon Ton or High Life Above Stairs,* and *Catherine and Petruchio,* became fixtures in the repertory, being played season after season on to the end of the century and beyond. The term farce was almost universally applied to all such plays when they appeared. A brief glance at a few will indicate their qualities. Most of them were derivative though derivative in various ways. The last named, *Catherine and Petruchio,* was, of course, a shrinking of Shakespeare's play to three acts by a concentration on the boisterois *Taming of the Shrew* scenes. The first piece listed, *The Lying Valet,* has a different source, the French clever-servant farce, heavily exploited by Molière's successors, such as Dancourt, Regnard, Hauteroche. This last-named writer provides the source for Garrick's very clever and fast-moving play in which the servant becomes the central figure, like the innumerable Crispins, Merlins, and the rest of that ilk on the French stage. Henry Fielding had anticipated Garrick in the type by providing two of the most popular afterpieces in the century: *The Mock Doctor,* from Moliere's woodcutter-turned-physician, and *The Intriguing Chambermaid,* borrowed from Regnard and drastically altered to fit the valet part to the talents of Fielding's favorite actress, Kitty Clive. Garrick was much more likely, especially in his early years, to write the best parts for himself. He had played the valet, Sharp, at Goodman's Fields within six weeks after making his first bow in London in the fall of 1741. He played the even giddier role of Fribble in *Miss in Her Teens,* borrowed from Dancourt's *Parisiènne,* to scores of delighted audiences.

Bon Ton, or High Life Above Stairs is more likely derivative in a different way. At the time of its first performance, almost at the end of Garrick's career, Hopkins, the Drury Lane prompter, noted that it had been written "15 or 16 years ago." Since another of the century's most popular afterpieces, James Townley's *High Life Below Stairs* was first performed between fifteen and sixteen years before, I conjecture that Garrick had decided to get into the upstairs-downstairs business himself but later changed his mind and shelved his piece for a time. Both plays ran well into the next century and, ironically, both were long ascribed to Garrick.[4]

Other dramatic types appeared in the afterpiece category, such as the short comic piece with music, variously called comic (or ballad) opera, musical entertainment, musical farce, or what you will. Garrick's chief musical afterpiece appeared in October of his last season. *May-Day; or, the Little Gipsy,* with music by Arne, was written to introduce a new singer, Harriet Abrams, to the London audience. Its success was quite modest, but by this date the afterpiece composed of dialogue and songs had been firmly established for some two generations. The vogue of the ballad opera, given its initial propulsion by Gay's enormous success in 1728, affected the afterpiece almost instantaneously. Within a season several of the most popular fixtures in the repertory were turned into ballad operas by the addition of new lyrics to popular tunes. A *Hob's Opera,* retitled in a few seasons *Flora* soon appeared, plus a *Stage Coach Opera,* and a *Contrivances* (Henry Carey's popular farce of 1715, revamped as a ballad opera in June 1729). Many new afterpieces obviously designed on Gay's pattern and named to cash in on his success came forth: a *Beggar's Wedding,* a *Cobler's Opera,* a *Lover's Opera,* a *Sailor's Opera.*

Not all of these earned a lasting success but others in the new fashion did. One of the most successful of all was *The Devil to Pay,* written as a full-length ballad opera in the manner of *The Beggar's Opera* in spring 1731, then, cut down to a one-act afterpiece and with a Miss Raftor — soon to be known as the famous Kitty Clive — in the part of Nell, launched in the fall of 1731 at Drury Lane on one of the most successful careers in theatrical history in England, America, France, and Germany. As I noted in editing the play twenty-nine years ago, the most recent performance was in 1945 on the campus of UCLA under the direction of Dr. Walter Rubsamen. Having cited the nonpareil of afterpieces one hesitates to risk an anticlimax of less successful ones. The list goes on and runs into scores, with or without songs, in one act, two acts, and three, original or, much more commonly, cobbled from earlier pieces.

Louis Riccoboni, not only a leading actor in the company of Italian comedians but also a student of theatrical history, published a study of Molière's work in 1736, *Observations sur le comédie, et sur le Genie de Molière.* His fifth chapter is devoted to a play of a kind comparatively rare on the English stage, what he calls *"farce ou petites scénes détachees."* His chief, in fact only, example is *Les Facheux* to which, incidentally, he never again applies the term *farce* but always *comédie.* My interest, however, is in the alternate term for which there really was no English equivalent though there were examples of the "kind" going back as far as Thomas Randolph's *Muses' Looking Glass* in 1638. A more familiar and more recent example would be Vanbrugh's *Aesop,* December 1696. The fact that Vanbrugh's play was the main, and only, piece in the bill, the fact that it was followed in March by an *Aesop, Pt. II*, plus Cibber's *Schoolboy*, and, finally, the fact that C. B. Hogan records a two-act *Aesop* as afterpiece at Drury Lane on December 19, 1778[5] — all add up to a fairly clear suggestion of what Riccoboni means by *scènes détachées*. *Aesop* provides occasion for the fabulous fabulist to be approached by a whole series of persons representing this or that specific human folly. We might well translate the French term as "open-ended play" and reflect gratefully on Vanbrugh's restraint in stopping with only two parts.

Garrick's very first play was an afterpiece of this sort. On 15 April 1740 William Giffard, then with the Drury Lane company, chose for his annual benefit Cibber's *Careless Husband* in which he acted Sir Charles Easy. For an afterpiece he graciously accorded a chance to a young friend in the wine trade whose *Lethe: or, Esop in the Shades,* with the help of actors like the tenor Beard, Charles Macklin, Woodward, and Kitty Clive, was started on its long road to success. There are several other afterpieces of this type though not a host. Dodsley's *Toy Shop* and *King and Miller of Mansfield* are almost sermonettes using similar devices.

A kindred but separate kind is the burlesque, of which *The Rehearsal* rather than earlier pieces like *The Knight of the Burning Pestle* is probably the real forerunner. Though a full-length play, *The Rehearsal* provided the model for numerous afterpieces in rehearsal form such as Garrick's *Peep Behind the Curtain, or the New Rehearsal.* A far better play was Sheridan's *Critic;* far more satirical were some of Fielding's brief pieces in rehearsal form, though the ones which succeeded in pulling the house down on their author's head, *Pasquin* and *The Historical Register,* were usually, not always, played as main pieces. Still other variants were the highly popular but good-natured rather than acerbic spoofs of Handel by Henry Carey, *The Dragon of Wantley* and its sequel *Margery.*

Still another form of afterpiece, destined by the end of the century to become highly popular, was the occasional play, often in the form of a ceremonial procession. One of the most famous, or notorious, was *The Jubilee,* 1769, a questionable enterprise into which Garrick threw himself with almost pathetic zeal. It was, after all, in celebration of Shakespeare's birth and no extravagance seemed too much for such an occasion. The chief feature of this celebration was a great procession of characters from the bard's plays, not a new thing on the London stage, of course, for such De Millean displays had long been popular, perhaps the best known being the elaborate coronation procession first attached to *Henry VIII* back in 1727 at the time George II was crowned but later detached and presented as an afterpiece to miscellaneous plays. Another such extravaganza by Garrick was offered two years after the *Jubilee,* an enormously expensive thing called *The Institution of the Garter; or, Arthur's Round Table Restored,* about which little need be said. For a sample of the great popularity of this sort of thing late in the century I might give the titles—eloquent enough—of half a dozen for May and June of 1794, supplying first a reminder of two circumstances which would explain much: (1) the great swell of nationalism brought on by the French Revolution, and (2) the existence of new and greatly enlarged theatres with "lakes" far upstage designed initially for security from fires but useful for sea battles or nautical panoramas. The titles are self explanatory: *The Sailor's Festival; or All Alive at Portsmouth* ("with a representation of the Grand Fleet at Anchor in Portsmouth Harbor"); *British Fortitude and Hibernian Friendship; or, an Escape from France; Naples Bay; or, The British Seaman at Anchor; The Soldiers Festival; or the Night before the Battle; The Fall of Martinico; or, Brittainia Triumphant;* and finally, by Sheridan himself with help from James Cobb, *The Glorious First of June,* which played to a first-night house of 1300 guineas.

I am not suggesting that Garrick be held responsible for this outburst of patriotic fervor. I am saying that he contributed to the movement toward a greater and greater expansion of the bill with the inevitable result of its being opened up at times to productions of questionable taste and value.

One must bring this list of the great actor-manager's wide-ranging offerings to a close with no more than a brief note on his activities directly in rivalry with Rich, his pantomimic contributions. In *The Drama's Patrons* I quote a passage from a pamphlet published quite early in Garrick's career in which high hopes were expressed that "a young hero" was busy in the "discouragement of pantomime," and in the restoring of Shakespeare, a suggestion faintly echoed by Johnson's famous prologue of 1747, from which

I purloined my own title, and far more forcefully announced in Garrick's occasional prologue opening Drury Lane's season of 1750-1751:

> Sacred to Shakespeare, was this spot design'd
> To pierce the heart, and humanize the mind.
> But if an empty house, the actor's curse,
> Shews us our Lears, and Hamlets, lose their force;
> Unwilling, we must change the nobler scene,
> And, in our turn, present you Harlequin.[6]

Garrick did not prove so resolute in the long run, in the very short run as a matter of fact, but was soon competing with Rich on the latter's terms, largely by using the talent in both the composition and acting of pantomime of Henry Woodward. But when, at the Christmas season of 1759, Garrick decided it was time for a new pantomime, Woodward had deserted to Ireland, and Garrick set about writing his own pantomime, *Harlequin's Invasion*, vastly different from anything his rival had ever produced. It was "after the manner of Italian comedy," that is, it was a "speaking pantomime," and therefore some half century ahead of its time. True, Richard Bentley wrote a similar piece which was acted at Drury Lane some sixteen months later, *The Wishes; or, Harlequin's Mouth Opened*, but except for a brief revival at Covent Garden some twenty years later, it proved no match for Garrick's piece, which was still being played in the next century.

Garrick did not write any ballets but he did make a valiant attempt to advance the cause of ballet in England. The expansion of London bills had made serious, professional dance more easily possible. There had been ballet in the English theatre since 1717 according to Felicitee Forrester, who designates John Weaver's *Loves of Mars and Venus* as the first *ballet d'action* in England.[7] Garrick's share in this story is not altogether happy, through no fault of his. After extensive preliminaries and at great expense he attempted in 1755 to introduce Jean George Noverre, commonly thought of as the father of modern ballet, to the English public in a "New Grand Entertainment" called *The Chinese Festival*, but the English public was not prepared to accept this troupe of supposed light-heeled Popish Frenchmen and eventually became so violent that Garrick was obliged to give up the project. It is comforting to give a happier sequel, for Noverre returned just over a quarter of a century later with great success in what the bills list as pantomime-ballet at the King's theatre, where the more select audience of opera-goers were ready for ballet by Frenchmen or dancers of any or no nationality.

What, finally, was the long-term effect on this deference to the Mitwelt, some substantial part of which would have passed for rabble in the more exalted view? The establishment of the after-piece as a fixture in the bill was, to be sure, an effect in itself but might not that effect in turn have produced still others? The first of these would have been the great increase in the variety of forms. The English theatre never settled into the rigid molds of the French new-classical theatre but for generations it did face a limited set of expectations. Take the simple matter of the number of acts. Horace had said quite firmly that the number was five, no more, no fewer, and as late as midcentury we find Henry Fielding puzzling over the rationale of that requirement in one of his critical discourses in *Tom Jones*. We need not take the novelist too seriously of course, for, as he very well knew, there had been a number of assaults on the strict Horatian limit, not the least effective being his own. Before the century was over the supposed rule was in bad repair, for plays—tragical, comical, farcical, pastoral, of all varieties—came in a number of lengths. Tragedies in five acts, four acts, three acts show up, as well as comedies in all three of these forms plus a few in one act or two. Several years before Fielding's query, in fact, a bill was posted for the Little Haymarket consisting of *The Beggar's Wedding* followed by an afterpiece, destined to remain unpublished, entitled *The Vintner's Escape*, which the newspaper bill describes as "a farce in one act and a half."[8]

Speculatively I contend that the extension and variation of the theatrical bill we call the afterpiece helped in some small way to break down the neoclassical interpretation of that more signifi-cant dictum of Horace we heard from Goethe's impresario: *"Und mit Bedeutung auch gefällig sei."* Horace had indicated a willing-ness to accept either *pleasing* or *instructing* but the critical tradition in England, at least as early as Sidney, had put the stress on instruction. Of the vast florilegium of pronouncements one could collect in the period let me give just two or three sprigs. My first would be John Weaver's disapproval of the Italian night scenes of the early eighteenth century as tending to stress entertainment over instruction. My second would be from the sober soul who in a long treatise on *The Present State of the Stage* published in 1753 still hoped that the stage could function as a "school of instruction." My irritating favorite is from Voltaire when he disdains Marivaux' weighing flies' eggs in scales of gossamer. Without even hinting a personal preference I point out that Marivaux's gossamer still lives, on the French stage at least, whereas Voltaire's stilted preachments have long since expired.

I trust the stage has said goodbye to all that, that our received position is one eloquently expressed by Shaw in his preface to *The Six of Calais:*

Now a playwright's direct business is simply to provide the theatre with a play. When I write one with the additional attraction of providing the twentieth century with an up-to-date religion or the like, that luxury is thrown in gratuitously; and the play, simply as a play, is not necessarily either the better or the worse for it. What, then, is a play as a play? Well, it is a lot of things. Life as we see it is so haphazard that it is only by picking out its key situations and arranging them in their significant order (which is never how they actually occur) that it can be made intelligible. The highbrowed dramatic poet wants to make it intelligible and sublime. The farce writer wants to make it funny. The melodrama merchant wants to make it as exciting as some people find the police news. The pornographer wants to make it salacious. All interpreters of life in action, noble or ignoble, find their instrument in the theatre; and all the academic definitions of a play are variations of this basic function.

NOTES

1. *A Century of English Farce* (Princeton: Princeton University Press, 1956).

2. *The London Stage, 1660–1800* Pt. 1, ed. William Van Lennep (Carbondale: Southern Illinois University Press), p. 515.

3. *English Theatre Music in the Eighteenth Century* (London: Oxford University Press, 1973), p. 14.

4. As recent a work as the *CBEL,* with a great show of impartiality, or diffidence, ascribes Townley's play to both authors.

5. *The London Stage 1660–1800,* Part 5.

6. *The Drama's Patrons* (Austin: University of Texas Press, 1971), p. 108.

7. *Ballet in England: A Bibliography and Summary* (London: Library Association, 1968), p. 63.

8. *The London Stage,* Pt. 3, I, ed. A. H. Scouten, p. 299.

Part II

FUNDAMENTALS OF STAGE
AND THEATRE STRUCTURE,
AND OF SCENIC DESIGN

STAGE STRUCTURE
Editor's Headnote

The familiar genres—tragedy, comedy, farce, and pantomime—took place in the century on rather similar stages whose structures and accompanying auditoriums varied mainly in size only. Acting space and audience relationship to actors in various models have concerned both dramatists and performers from remotest times. Professor Mullin in his "Theatre Structure and Its Effect upon Production" distinguishes theatre of celebration and theatre of visitation, then points out how lighting, scenery, stage form, and audience positioning are, as they always have been, pertinent to the aesthetic effect of effective drama.

4. Theatre Structure and Its Effect on Production

Donald C. Mullin
Professor of Dramatic Arts, University of Guelph

Since architecture does reflect public interests, or lack of them, we may examine buildings from previous eras and determine with some accuracy the life habits and states of mind of the peoples who erected them. This is no less true of theatres than it is of palaces and cathedrals. In fact it is possibly more true, as theatres have been closer to public daily life than either seats of government or seats of bishops.

Theatre decoration may change with the whim of fashion, but theatre form does not. Changes in form come about rarely, are introduced slowly, and then only as the feelings of the public change in regard to the world in which they live. The architectural historian may suggest that a particular change in form was stimulated by the discovery of a special aspect of mechanics, or of iron trusses, whereas the social historian attributes those same changes to improved drains or to the growth of democracy. The historian of ideas knows better. Theatres like cathedrals and sometimes even palaces have always taken forms directly related to what takes place in them. The true nature of the theatrical event has not yet been established with satisfactory accuracy, but we at least suspect that it has more to do with man's instincts than with his daily preoccupations. For this reason, in many ways, Shakespeare's theatre differed little from that in which Garrick made his debut, even though the decorative treatment of one bore small resemblance to that of the other.

The things, of course, which matter most in the theatre are the actor and the audience, a proposition with which few would disagree. More argumentative is the corollary that the playscript runs a poor third and serves little purpose if it cannot promote easy cooperation between the first two. An effective exchange may take place between an actor and his audience with a poor script or with none at all, for such an exchange is accomplished through technical proficiency and serves a purpose quite unrelated to scripts. If that purpose is understood and is properly served by the design of the playhouse, the design is good. If the playhouse fails to encourage that exchange the design is bad. It is, to be sure, possible to combine good relationships with an eccentric house plan, but the occurrence is rare. For the last century and three quarters, at least, most theatres have been designed to accommodate the large amounts of scenery necessary to the production of spectacle or realistic drama. They have seldom been designed especially to maintain any particular actor–audience relationship.

The theatres in which Garrick and his contemporaries worked seem, on the surface, to present us with few difficulties. A multiplicity of data has been gathered by theatre historians about Drury Lane, Covent Garden, and the opera house then operating. But even with all the gathered information it is still not entirely clear why the seventeenth- and eighteenth-century English playhouse, in particular, assumed the form it did; why this form is associated almost exclusively with British theatres; and what effect, if any, this difference had upon production.

We are familiar with the phrase "English Stage" and understand it to refer to something clearly distinguishable from the

"Continental Stage." In the eighteenth century one of the characteristics associated with this distinction was the large forestage
thrust forward into the audience chamber, while in the nineteenth century the differences turned more on methods of
handling scenery and machines. The platform stage was never
exclusively English, of course. A cursory examination of the old
Schouwburg Theatre in Amsterdam or of the Thèatre du Marais
in Paris will tell us that. It is only that the development of the
public playouse in Britain differed somewhat from similar developments in most of Europe, and physical arrangements also
differed as a consequence.

The continued British preference for the large forestage seems,
at first, to be something of a puzzle. The French had a similar
acting space, which they referred to as the *avant scène,* which
remained common in public theatres well into the nineteenth
century. Influenced as we are by numerous reproductions we have
seen of Renaissance scene designs made for *intermezzi,* we usually
think of the continental theatre as having an audience chamber
divided sharply from the scenic area by a proscenium. Such a
division was common in the early temporary stages rigged for
festival productions in court halls, but was not a common
arrangement in seventeenth- or eighteenth-century public
theatres. Playhouses intended for the continued production of
drama required a sounding board to project the actors' voices into
the house. This consisted of a sloped ceiling placed between the
area reserved for scenery and the open auditorium. The space
below the sounding board was neither scenic nor public, but an
intermediate area, decorated as an architecturally distinct
portion of the building, fancied up with statues in niches and
with columns in order to connect it aesthetically with the auditorium. Although the *avant scène* was in front of the scenery, the
space did not seem thrust forward, as did the English forestage,
neither was it provided with practicable doors to the sides.

The English development included both thrust and doors,
continuing a practice of Elizabethan times, with antecedents
going as far back as we have record. The French forestage seemed
like a proscenium-in-depth, whereas the English forestage did
not. Decorated divisions between stage and audience were few in
England. The ill-favored Dorset Garden Theatre had something
of a mixture of proscenium and platform. Vanbrugh's Opera

House had a platform dressed up with monumental columns. In Christopher Wren's Drury Lane of 1674, however, there was nothing of the kind, and it was Wren's theatre that was to serve as the model for most other public theatres built in the eighteenth century. In Wren's playhouse there was no special demarcation between boxes and scenic area other than a variation of the old-fashioned "frontispiece," or what might be referred to today as tormentors: a two-dimensional framework, painted, if one pleased, to look like permanent construction, and meant to mask the side scenes. This was not dissimilar from the decorated framework thought to have been used on pageant wagons, or from the elaborately engraved borders found on any contemporary print.

The decorated *avant scène* lacked doors, and in their stead were placed *balcons,* or small sets of bleachers. These were separate from the boxes and distinct from the standing pit. The *balcons* were substitutes for the stools for gentlemen found on stage in Molière's and Shakespeare's time. Public theatres on the rest of the Continent appear to have been arranged principally in imitation of the French, whereas opera house construction copied the form developed in Venice, of horseshoe galleries surrounding a large *parterre,* with a fixed and decorated proscenium arch.

But why the platform stage at all? Why, once the Italian-style scenic stage was introduced, was the old forestage retained? After all, elaborate movable scenes are fascinating and entertaining in their own right, as anyone who has seen the film showing scenic operations at the Drottningholm Theatre in Sweden will attest. Perhaps retention of the old platform was due to some of the factors which prompted its introduction in the first place. Perhaps Garrick's perfection seemed to be so because his more "natural" method suited the theatres in which he performed, just as Quin's acting style seemed stilted and false because it was essentially alien to the stage available to him.

For centuries, or even millennia, there were two general types of performance and therefore of playing spaces arranged to accommodate them: what I shall refer to as the Theatre of Celebration and the Theatre of Visitation. Both had beginnings associated with religious exercises and both also had secular developments. The playhouse of the Theatre of Celebration is familiar to us in the large edifices constructed by the Greeks and Romans, dedicated to various gods, and used initially on days connected exclusively with high religious festivities, although not especially for what we would think of today as religious drama. This type of theatre was constructed for the benefit of the community at large out of the public purse, and could contain most of the adult population of free men. Events produced within such spaces were necessarily large in scale and frequently universal in theme. This applies loosely but equally to Greek tragedy and Old Comedy, Roman pantomime, and to the Roman circus. The principal architectural characteristic of the Theatre of Celebration is that the audience is seated above the principal action, and looks down on it. A few patrons, seated in the first rows, would regard the action more or less at eye-level, but the majority obtained a different perspective and therefore the feeling of the audience assembly was dictated by the majority relationship. The figures of the performers in such an arrangement necessarily are remote from most of the spectators. The distance and angle of view both encourage an objective response from those watching the performance, and reactions tend to be group identifications rather than individual ones. The death of Antigone or of a gladiator is not a personal calamity but is rather part of a moral or social lesson. The scale and rhythm of movement in such a context effectively removes the action from any connection with immediate daily life. Such a point of view is not determined by text so much as it is by circumstances surrounding production. The "medium" in this case is indeed the "message."

Theatre of Visitation is a term by which it is convenient to describe what originally were exclusively gymnastic, acrobatic, or gross farcical interludes, performed by itinerants travelling in small troupes. Thespis was of this group in his earlier days, as was, much later and under different circumstances, Vincent Crummels. In the Theatre of Celebration the audience is gathered in a precinct dedicated to a god in order to participate in a special event. The town leaves the dwelling place and moves en mass to the grove or hillside. In the Theatre of Visitation it is the players who go to the town, who bring the "message" to the local audience in the midst of their dwellings and domestic environment. The visitation may be inspired by religion or ancient tradition in a recognizable way, as in the case of the English mummers, or may degenerate almost entirely to secular entertainment of the type we associate with the Commedia dell'Arte. In either instance, however, those viewing the performance are not the whole or even a majority of the social unit, but are rather a fragment of it, a neighborhood, so to speak. For such a limited audience the itinerant troupe does not *present* moral lessons that are meant to be reacted to objectively and whose purpose is to establish or review the relationship of the community to forces outside it. Rather, they *represent* direct personal experience, meant to stimulate individual and immediate reaction to situations common within the social unit. The Theatre of Visitation, then, is by its nature personal, emotional, and domestic, whereas the Theatre of Celebration is intellectual and universal. The events portrayed in one affect the individual or family, while in the other they affect the community at large.

The ancient and traditional physical arrangement for the Theatre of Visitation differs from that of its more formal relative. In some instances, as in the case of the mummers, the players perform on the open ground, the audience gathering about in a circle. In the case of the more sophisticated itinerant troupes, the players position themselves on the back of a wagon or on a small platform laid over trestles, while viewers stand about in as large an area as is convenient, looking upward. This is precisely the arrangement found in the pit of the Elizabethan and early French public theatres, and one which was modified only slightly in the seventeenth and eighteenth centuries through the introduction of benches.

In order to obtain unified responses from an audience there must be uniform viewing conditions. When seating arrangements differ in various parts of the house then audience reactions also will differ. The box, pit, and gallery patrons in the British theatre in the eighteenth century each reacted differently partly because of the differences in audience perspective in regard to the actions of the players. The pit looked up; the box patrons, for the most part, looked across; while the gallery looked down. In the earliest public theatres the boxes and galleries were shallow affairs, accommodating only a few rows each. The bulk of the audience was therefore contained in the pit, below the eye-level of the performers. The principal feeling of the house was that of the Theatre of Visitation, an effect enhanced by the large forestage. If we are to credit contemporary observers, audience action and reaction was precisely that which could be expected from a social

fragment gathered together before a group of itinerants, identifying closely with the performers, watching them illustrate aspects
of daily life.

Alterations from such clear domination of the house change
the relationship at once, and also change the audience reaction as
well as the playing method of the actors. Enlargement of the
boxes and galleries tips the balance away from the pit, making
the different types of reaction from different kinds of audience
positions more important and more obviously felt. Different reactions create problems difficult to resolve, for a combination of the
effects associated with both Visitation and Celebration creates a
mixture which is awkward to handle. For financial reasons
Garrick caused Drury Lane to be expanded far beyond the size
and proportions originally laid down by Christopher Wren. An
enormous first gallery, with an upper gallery above that, was
hung over what were called "front boxes," or a raised and divided
series of benches located behind the pit, which contained as many
rows of seats as did the pit itself. The character of this arrangement (ca. 1775) was vastly different from that of Wren's of 1674.
It has always been explained that the reactions of gallery patrons
differed from those of patrons in the pit because the inhabitants
of heaven were rude and unlettered. That may indeed have been
the case, but it is an additional probability that the reaction
differed also because the relationship with the stage was different.
Pit patrons were always complaining that the insensitive gallery
would not be caught up easily in sentimental drama, and instead
preferred spectacle. Such a reaction cannot be attributed entirely
to rudeness, for it must have been difficult to wax sentimental
over a doll-like actor far below, bellowing in order to be heard
above the sobs in the pit. Distance alone, however, is only part of
the relationship. The position above is of especial importance.
Above, one understands that the violence or agony is at one's feet,
and therefore that one is safe from contamination. In the pit one
might easily be splashed by the blood or drowned in the tears,
and the sense of personal involvement or of immediate danger is
more acute.

If it seems that this point is stretched somewhat too far, one
need only regard what seems to be an instinctive reaction at the
present day. Children prefer to sit or lie below the television tube,
whereas adults prefer to sit or lounge slightly above.

In Shakespeare's theatre the pit dominated the house and the folk or visitation atmosphere prevailed. Hamlet did not understand that it was the pit and the effect of the Theatre of Visitation which shaped him and made his existence possible, and that mutterings about groundlings were in poor taste under the circumstances. Blackfriars, although still much of a puzzle, seems to have resembled the outdoor theatres in most respects, differing from them mainly in being enclosed and in having pit benches placed on graduated risers, thus effectively eliminating the folk atmosphere. Both the Great Hall and the later Banqueting House at Whitehall were fitted up for spectacles when the occasion required, with bleacher-type seating and no pit at all. The Cockpit-in-Court was reconstructed in a somewhat pale imitation of a Teatro Olimpico cum Globe, with rising tiers and galleries. Vanbrugh's Opera House of 1704, in which Betterton attempted to perform without much success, had orchestra seating rising in regular arcs in the antique style. These coterie or court theatres were appropriately designed for the functions and audiences to which they were intended to cater. The obvious differences between them and the public theatre may answer a few questions. The sharp distinction between the two types of theatres was maintained as long as theatrical presentations were given at court. By Garrick's time, however, the production of spectacles at court had long since died, and the sovereign was reduced to gracing the public theatres in Command visits. Modifications of the platform stage and the pit dominated house were made gradually; until, in the last quarter of the eighteenth century, the original relationships had been altered out of all recognition.

The London public theatres of most of the eighteenth century had a type of enclosure which affected audience and actor alike. It required a special acting style that differed from that of the formally arranged theatre typical of courts. In the Continental or celebratory style theatre, heroic drama and its associated formality of delivery could be admired and taken seriously; not as reality, but as conscious artificiality, artifice, or art. In the English visitation style, production of the same heroics could be, and was, attempted successfully, but the results were quite different. It was domesticated, being received not as artificial but rather as a heightened version of the domestic, with an emphasis placed on pathos and sentiment. The English style also encouraged a variety of entertainment given in a single performance. We marvel at the farces, rope artists, hornpipe dancing, and similar items on extended bills, but we should not do so considering the venerable antecedents of this type of entertainment and the popular audience upon which the theatres depended for their survival. What popular entertainment the theaters could not supply—which was precious little—was available with even greater variety and hoopla during the summer at such places as Bartholemew Fair. There, booths, platform stages, and all the paraphernalia of the itinerant performance were to be experienced in the more direct way. If we are tempted to look at extended variety bills as aberrations, we might compare them with the production of interludes. Interlude means, of course, "between plays," and comes to us from the days of the jongleur and the trouvere. In one manuscript a jongleur listed his accomplishments with satisfaction:

I can play the lute, the violin, the bagpipe, the syrinx, the harp, the gigue, the gittern, the symphony, the psaltery, the organistrum, the regals, the tabor, and the rote. I can sing a song well, and make tales and fables. I can tell a story against any man. I can make love verses to please young ladies, and can play the gallant for them if necessary. Then I can throw knives into the air, and catch them without cutting my fingers. I can do dodges with string, most extraordinary and amusing. I can balance chairs, and make tables dance. I can throw a somersault, and walk on my head.[1]

These accomplishments are not much different in substance from those learned by Edmund Kean when he played as a stroller when a child. That some of those same accomplishments were found exhibited on the eighteenth-century London stage is hardly to be wondered at. Variety of entertainment is characteristic of the Theatre of Visitation and of the folk tradition. Theatres built in that style could offer no less.

Following this, it is clear that the form of the English stage was not, as is sometimes suggested, the result of ignorance, provincial recalcitrance, or lack of money, so much as it was the result of a different point of view. European capitals commonly had several types of theatres, each built as a home for a particular type of entertainment or special audience, while court theatres were maintained for those divorced from the folk tradition. In eighteenth-century London there was but one type of public playhouse, accommodating all types of entertainment. Such a theatre necessarily had to be a compromise in design, and in it Italian-style scenes and machines did not wear very well. It is frequently suggested that such embellishments were avoided because of the expense, and the staggering costs of the court spectacles mounted by Inigo Jones are given in evidence. Such expenses occur only once in a theatre that uses machinery on a continuing basis, for such equipment lasts a lifetime, as does most of the scenery. Italian-style scenes were not fully developed in the public theatres because the public theatres did not require them. Italian operas were indeed occasionally produced at the patent theatres, but such offerings were not especially successful, being better suited to the arrangement and atmosphere of the Opera House. Much more popular with the theatre-going public was "English opera," being something of a musical version of a type of play long familiar to playgoers.

Playing in the English theatre required a large open platform close to a majority of the audience, for it was the fragmentary scene in the interlude style, that was of particular interest, not the larger world suggested by the more tightly organized script. The complicated and even eccentric English mixture was thought barbaric by the French, and some Jacobean and Restoration plays are thought to be almost unplayable even today because of their bewildering plot structures. Playwrights working with materials designed for platform stages did not concern themselves with the whole so much as they did with the parts. It is the scenes that are written to play well, and the whole pretty much takes care of itself. The Theatre of Visitation is actor-oriented, concerned not with the telling of a tale but with the teller; not with recitation but with conversation. Quin and his type survived only so long as the playhouse catered principally to courtiers familiar with Continental fashions. When the public at large began to enter in then the days of such actors were numbered. The visitation-style performance stressed personalities and internal complications, while the celebratory style emphasizes text and external framework. That is Garrick and Macklin on the one hand and Betterton and Quin on the other.

It is a commonplace that production on the London stage in most of the eighteenth century made use of scenery only for limited and specific purposes. For most scenes the proscenium doors offered sufficient entrance and exit of the domestic type. Domestic should be stressed, for Oedipus does not go about opening and closing doors. The scenic space, somewhat removed from the playing area, served as introductory and closing stations in a way that was familiar to older audiences from the days of pageant wagons, when Herod would go down and "rage." The characters are seen first against a background in order to establish themselves in a location or context. They would then move downstage where the serious acting was to be done. For special or prop business the scenic area is obviously necessary. It is usual to fall back on contemporary stage directions to support such statements, and I shall not be an exception.

In Otway's *Alcibiades,* stage directions required Betterton to enter "from the back part of the scenes." After eight lines of dialogue, presumably given center stage, he "goes to the door." Spectacular scenes requiring much stage space demanded the back scene to serve as something of a haven for characters who were needed to be present yet were not required to speak. Again in *Alcibiades,* Act II, Scene 1, "The scene drawn, discovers the tent of a Pavilion; in it an altar, behind which are seated the King and Queen, attended." Priests of Hymen dance about a bit in front of this, and other dramatic action follows, but the King becomes engaged in the action only after he "descends with the Queen."

Scenery was also useful for hiding or disclosing, especially pieces of furniture or floor-mounted decoration too awkward to have been brought onto the stage by theatre servants. In the last act, Scene 1, the scene opens and we see "An apartment, with a Chair of State, and by it a table, with the Crown and Sceptre." At the end of the act, "A glorious temple appears in the air, where the Spirits of the Happy are seated," and later still, "The scene drawn, discovers Timandra on a Couch, in the midst of her pains." These were from poison, not pregnancy.[2]

In Nat Lee's *Caesar Borgia,* the "Scene draws, and shows the Consistory: Borgia [Betterton again] comes forward." Dead bodies, which used to be carried off with sometimes ingenious excuses in Shakespeare's day, were now left on stage, to be swallowed by a closing backscene or a traverse curtain. In the last act of *Borgia,* Lee directs rather coldly that we "Draw here the curtain on 'em."[3] In *The Trip to Newmarket,* a Drury Lane piece of 1774, "Rivers retires to the back scene and sits down."[4] The character is present during the remainder of the scene but does not speak while action is going on downstage of him. In *No Song No Supper,* an upstage backscene is used somewhat more heavily, but a practical door is located in it which serves principally for much running in and out.

Scenes assumed importance in several ways. First, they performed the obvious function of providing visual excitement through the addition of color and spectacle, especially if they depicted exotic worlds different from that of daily life. Second, and equally as important, they served to vary the space available to the actor, defining the compass within which he moved and within which the dramatic value of the scene had to be compressed. The forestage was within the enclosure of the auditorium, in the same room as the audience. The scenes and related special effects were outside the audience chamber. The proscenium, for lack of a better word, marked the boundary between the closely observable world of daily life on the forestage and the world of exoticisms, surprises, or flights of fancy in the scenic space. To reveal a portion of a suspected but unseen world was to achieve one effect. To reveal more or all of it was another effect altogether. To reveal more than the audience knew the building could contain was startling indeed. The first Teatro di Tor di Nona, in Rome, was constructed with large doors in the back wall which could be opened on an outer courtyard in which additional scenery could be placed if the production required it. A smaller but similar door was present in the first Drury Lane, and in at least one instance was used for precisely this effect.

From the viewing of seemingly endless similar stage plans and of numberless elaborate stage designs we sometimes come to the conclusion that eighteenth-century settings were always large, requiring most of the available stage space. This perhaps was characteristic of the large continental opera house that lacked a forestage but was by no means common to the English stage. There, the forestage allowed the actors to be accommodated in a space reserved for them alone. The green baize curtain need only be lowered in order to allow the platform to live by itself, as in Shakespeare's day. Upon the raising of the curtain the scenes could be introduced. Although we know little about the actual rigging and arrangements common to the first half of the eighteenth century, it does seem as though there was but one set of backshutters. Thus, there was either a full set of scenes or none at all. Commencing in the 1760s, however, grooves for back-shutters were introduced at several additional locations in each of the patent theatres. These allowed the use of scenic backgrounds in any one of several degrees, reserving the full stage for the most demanding or most spectacular requirements. In any event, the full stage, with backshutters closed only in the last upstage position, would present a volume of space with which the actor on the forestage could compete with difficulty.

Compounding such aesthetic differences in volumes of space was the perennial problem of light. We are so used to electric lighting that effects that would result from different sources of illumination escape us. Garrick and his contemporaries depended at first on an arrangement that had been in common use well before his time, namely overhead chandeliers combined with a row of footlights at the front edge of the forestage. With a little ingenuity it was arranged so that the footlights could be raised and lowered, thus effectively dimming the forestage. With the overhead chandeliers little could be done. A constant fear was the drip of wax down the back of one's neck, and the constant snuffing and trimming required must have kept audiences amused during the duller portions of the plays. Behind the proscenium, on the other hand, a different set of circumstances prevailed. In the 1760s Garrick brought back from France an idea he really should have developed himself, that standards holding candles could be mounted behind the flats in each of the groove positions. By using these rather than chandeliers hanging overhead, light would then fall from the sides onto actors' faces, rather than light from overhead falling only upon the tops of wigs. With chandeliers alone, actors really could play only center, where the light was most intense. When lamps were placed at the sides, then the favored playing area must have moved with them, for the center no longer received the majority of light. The traditional arrogant lift of the chin—in order to get light on the face from overhead chandeliers—was no longer required. Lights placed behind the side wings also allowed the actor to increase emphasis merely by moving toward them, something he previously would have been unable to do with overhead chandeliers. This emphasis could in turn be varied by moving slightly up or down stage in relation to the nearest light standard. Games of this nature are interesting to imagine and, of course, are entirely conjecture. What the gloom must have been like before such an innovation is difficult to visualize. In any event, Garrick, with the help of his French friends, now had light. But of what kind?

Electric light is intense enough and white enough to remain more or less constant in appearance however it be located in reference to ourselves. In contrast, candle light, from its very lack of intensity, changes character. The yellow quality of the flame seems to increase the farther we get from it. A room illuminated by candle light may seem reasonably bright when we are in it, but it rapidly changes to a cavern lit by an unholy amber glow when viewed from a distance. The quality of the light in the backscene, then, differed from that on the forestage. This certainly posed problems for scene painters, especially so as interest in realistically depicted locales increased toward the end of the century. Painters must have had to rely more on suggestion than on detailed representation. The farther upstage the backscene, the more coarse the detail necessarily had to be, and therefore the more fanciful or exotic the effect it must have created. It is not surprising, therefore, that fancy scenery of the de Loutherbourg type found a home in pantomime and was not used with much effect in plays about daily life until candles were replaced with a better source of illumination. If we wonder why the forestage began to shrink we need only look to account books and to wishes of managers to crowd yet another row of benches into the pit. If we wonder why it disappeared altogether when it did, we must look to better sources of light. The scenic area could be lighted with greater and greater effectiveness, but with the poor forestage little could be done. It descended into greater gloom as the scenic area increased in brilliancy. The contrast was more than the old arrangement could withstand. This situation remained unaltered until the introduction of limelight, but by that time all the old forestages were gone.

There are other and less obvious reasons why the English stage had characteristics different from the continental variety. Those are more debatable in their particulars, although no less important in their generality. The English stage in Shakespeare's time was essentially medieval in character. We usually speak of the

Renaissance as though it occurred at the same time throughout Europe, knowing full well that to the sophisticated Italians it began with Petrarch, whereas in the culturally deprived northern countries it was not particularly noticeable until the seventeenth century. The nations whose development was delayed had a difficult and confusing time of it. They were required to assimilate ideas from the early Renaissance at the same time as those from the Baroque period. In Spain, the Netherlands, and especially in England, a confusing overlap of medieval and Renaissance culture is most apparent.

In the prebaroque Italian world, God was still the center of all things. The divinely inspired, symmetrical world, surrounded by the crystal spheres of the heavens moving to celestial music, was simulated by precisely ordered and equally symmetrical stage designs. The Theatre of Celebration was reintroduced in the court theatres, but the celebratory act revolved about marriage festivities and triumphal passages rather than God. The throne of heaven was displaced by that of the secular sovereign, ruling by divine right if not actually himself divine, and the system of order with its symmetrical scenes remained. This inspiration proved to be so strong that, in the earliest permanent public theatres, the point of view and scenic method of the courts was adopted by the citizen. Outside Italy, however, the medieval character of the public playhouse, with its disorderly folk atmosphere, simultaneous settings, and variety bills, gave way only slowly to the arrangements with which we are principally familiar today.

In the seventeenth- and eighteenth-century English playhouse the system of order, with its symmetricality, remained behind the players. Seldom did they move entirely within it. The practical reasons for this are relatively obvious and have been mentioned, but there are other reasons as well. Scenery located behind the acting area remained a suggestion of an understood but essentially ideal and therefore unreal world. An acting area within the scenery visualized an embracing and actual world to which the citizen should adapt. The symmetrical and ideal was foreign, heavily influenced by patterns, frameworks, and social discipline. The open stage platform was free of such suggestions. It was intensely native and regional rather than foreign and universal.

One characteristic of the baroque is that man is indeed the measure of all things. In the visual arts as well as in the theatre, everything radiated from man in the center. The world of God, in one-point perspective, gave way to the world of man, with its multiple points. Rather than an infinity of distance, with a "prospect," we find volumes of large but localized space. The distance from Serlio to the Bibienas is greater than can be measured in calendar years. The symmetrical scene was divine, or at the very least a symbol of divine right, whereas the asymmetrical scene replaced divinity with man. The English rejected both divine right and the essentially blasphemous proposition of Hamlet, that man was, even in apprehension, like a god. The Theatre of Visitation began in religion, it is true, but the local, folk, and domestic never attempt to glorify, much less to replace, God, but only to explain Him.

The arrangement of seats in a theatre has much to do with audience response, and should arise naturally from an understood relationship between actor and patron. In the first three quarters of the eighteenth century, at least, such an arrangement and understanding was apparent in the London theatre. The bulk of the audience, being in the pit, looked up at an immediate and practical world which, in most respects, reflected their own. At the same time other points of view were not excluded, although they took second place. The position below actor eye-level did not prevent differing types of response, but rather encouraged one at the expense of others. This was reinforced by the nature of the platform as well as its height. The thrust stage does not place man *in* an ordered world of his own contriving, from which all else radiates, but rather *on* a naked world without any compass other than divine prescript. An audience positioned around a platform stage places man on the spot, to be examined like a moth on a pin. In such an arrangement, man is not the "Measure of all things," but rather that which is measured. Faustus, Hamlet, and Lear grapple with God in a way in which contemporary French and Italian heroic protagonists do not.

Although not unique to the English, this view mentioned was characteristic of them until major alterations were made to the principal playhouses in the 1770s, and did not disappear entirely until the middle of the nineteenth century. By that time, in the rest of Europe, the platform had long since vanished, replaced by a world of increasing illusion, realism, delusion, and finally disenchantment. It would be too much to expect the English stage to have resisted entirely the plunge toward such an abyss. It did, however, manage to retain much of an older and more traditional point of view for almost a century after it had vanished elsewhere. We are the inheritors of that point of view. It is not the typical Broadway nor West End show, with its eight-thirty rise and eleven o'clock fall of the curtain which attracts and holds the mass audience. It is rather as it has always been; the music hall or vaudeville variety bill, the double-feature with cartoon and news-reel, or the present prime-time parade of pap on television. The element that is missing in the latest of these is the close relation-ship with the living performer, but perhaps the holograph will solve that. The other elements continue strongly. Camera angles and even set arrangements are calculated to place us in tradi-tional relationships. Given the strength of our British heritage we could react in no other way. We are quite aware that the single bill is a list of particulars about an artificially conceived world, whereas the "Whole Show" is nothing less than an interview with man.[5]

NOTES

1. Quoted in *Popular Entertainments Through the Ages,* Samuel McKechnie (London: S. Low, 1931), p. 7.

2. From the edition of 1758, printed in London for Dan Browne.

3. From the edition of 1734, printed in London for W. Feales et al.

4. From the edition of 1774, printed in Dublin for Messrs. J. Exshaw, etc.

5. For structures, architecture and scenic features see also Donald C. Mullin, *The Development of the Playhouse* (Berkeley and Los Angeles: University of California Press, 1970); Richard Leacroft, *The Development of the English Playhouse* (London: Methuen, 1973); Kalman A. Burnim, "La Scena per Angolo — Magic by the Bibienas," *Theatre Survey* (1961); and Richard Southern, *Changeable Scenery: Its Origin and Development in the English Theatre* (London: Faber and Faber, 1952).

SCENE AND DESIGN
Editor's Headnote

As all students of drama are aware, Aristotle placed "spectacle" at the foot of his six categories important in the art of dramatic composition, noting that it had more to do with stage carpenters than with creative dramatists. But spectacle became an element of major interest and special attention both to audience and manager (producer) in the eighteenth century. Professor Ralph G. Allen pays particular heed to stage innovations of Philip J. De Loutherbourg, whose scenic designs toward the end of the century tended to turn the rhetorical theatre to a pictorial theatre, and laid the foundations for the detailed realism in set and scene in which the nineteenth century reveled.

5. Irrational Entertainment in the Age of Reason

Ralph G. Allen
Professor of Speech and Theatre, The University of Tennessee

My subject is not the single texts that are frequently anthologized, and which form the official dramatic literature of the late eighteenth century. With a few exceptions, how unrepresentative those plays are of the tastes and enthusiasms of the rowdy, rough-and-tumble audience that Garrick and Rich lived to please, and pleased to live.

Drury Lane and Covent Garden were not subsidized theatres. There was no National Endowment for the Arts to rescue the managers from faulty assessments of the public taste. For every *Zara* there had to be a *Harlequin Fortunatus*. And what man of the theatre would have it otherwise? If drama as performed were responsive only to the enthusiasms of high-minded critics, it would smother in its own delicacy. I address, therefore, that element of drama considered least important by Aristotle. I refer, of course, to stage spectacle and to the so-called illegitimate entertainments in which spectacle plays so disproportionate a part.

The hero of an age of spectacle two hundred years ago is P. J. De Loutherbourg, the remarkable painter hired by Garrick in the season of 1772–1773 to supervise the scenery at Drury Lane. De Loutherbourg seldom receives more than a paragraph or two in any history of the stage, and yet, I would argue that he left behind him, for better or worse, a more enduring legacy to subsequent artists of the theatre than most of the playwrights and actors who are accorded whole chapters.

De Loutherbourg, more than any single individual, transformed the stage from a rhetorical to a pictorial art and prepared the way for the romantic and realistic revolution of the next century. He is one of the true innovators in the eighteenth-century theatre, and yet nearly all his great effects were achieved in connection with entertainments that were considered trivial by the most prominent of the self-appointed guardians of the public taste.

"Monstrous medlies," Pope called those earlier pantomimes that to his great disgust berattled the common stages. Paul Hifferman dismissed them as suitable only for the "vitiated and uncultivated." They are, he remarks, "the *Horrible* of comedy [and] are rejected by all elegant and noble minds with an innate disdain, that receives additional strength from a polished education."[1]

The remarks of Hifferman are echoed again and again in the journals of this period. But some of the worst carpers found secret pleasure in what they publicly deplored. After all, what man of sense would want to spend a whole evening in the leaden company of Cato or George Barnwell!

Certainly not the midcentury humorist who occasionally reviewed plays for the *Gray's Inn Journal*. I cannot resist quoting from him here. His sarcasm clearly masks a deep affection for the irrational entertainments, which on other occasions he pretended to despise.

I could wish I had lived in the days, when *Lun* was in his meridian Splendour; . . . Don't you think it must have given the quickest Sensations of Surprize to an Audience, to see him in the Character of Harlequin making his Escape into the Tub (the Tub, Sir, is the Box over the

Stage Door)—and when he was closely pursued by his Enemies, it must have been delightful to perceive him dart, as quick as an Arrow to its destined Mark, or with the Celerity of a Bird in the Air, from the Place, where the whole House imagined him destitute of the Means of an Escape, into the opposite Box, and there stand laughing at his Pursuers. . . . Perhaps you never would be able to guess how many Steps he made in running in a circular Manner round the Stage; three thousand Steps, Sir. . . . I believe there will be something done next winter; there is a Scheme on Foot to work the little Fellow. The thing is, we are to have an old Pantomime Entertainment, new vamped, with an additional Scene of a Scythian Winter-Piece, which I am convinced will draw the whole Town after it. There are already several Agents sent to Russia to purchase a sufficient number of Bears, and a large Quantity of Ice is now actually making. The Ice, Sir, will be disposed on the Stage in large Rocks, and the Beasts will be sent on shivering amidst the hoary Frosts; in one part of the Scene the Sun will be discovered, but shorn of his Beams, as Milton has it; the rigid Frost will be impervious to his Rays, and you will see the Lightning play upon the impassive Ice. There will also be exhibited at a Distance, a lofty Mountain, from whose Summit will come roaring down a tumultuous Cataract, loud, and impetuous in its course, and at the bottom will be placed a Reservoir to collect the rushing Torrent, where it will form itself into a smooth expansive River, which is to glide off in the Sight of the Spectators. There will also be situated on the Banks of the River a Man with a Fishing-Rod, intent upon catching the Tenants of the watery Plain, when on a sudden the Audience will perceive the Stream arrested in its Course by the Intenseness of the Frost, and the Fisherman's Line made a Prisoner for the Remainder of the Season. The Waterfall also will instantly be stopped by the gelid Season, and the Spectators will have the Pleasure of seeing the pendant Icicle. This, Sir, will be performed with Ease . . . as the Torrent is to come down in Sheets of Water, which will be represented with a glistening kind of Tin, it will be extremely practicable to stop the Tin all at once, and in that Case, the curious will admire the Wonders of the liquid Stone.[2]

As this passage indicates, spectacle of the most elaborate kind was the sine qua non of pantomimes and other "illegitimate" entertainments. And yet, before De Loutherbourg, displays of this sort were not distinguished by any unusual qualities of imagination or technical skill. There were no Bibienas or Servandonis working regularly at Drury Lane or Covent Garden. Praise for the achievements of a John DeVoto, a Thomas Lediard, or a George Lambert occasionally appear in the newspapers of the time. But for the most part, English designers worked out their careers in well-deserved anonymity. And except for pantomimes, related entertainments, and the occasional prestigious revival, only the most casual attention was given to the visual aspects of a production.

Indeed, the moribund state of the scenic arts can be deduced from an interesting pamphlet on theatre operations issued in Dublin in 1758. Basing his presumptions on current London practice, the author of the pamphlet lists as one of the first requirements for operating a successful theatre that "[i]t . . . be furnished with a competent number of painted scenes to answer the purposes of *all* the plays in stock." This number, he tells us, can easily be reduced to the following classes: "1st, Temples. 2dly, Tombs. 3dly, City walls and gates. 4thly, Outside of palaces. 5thly, Insides of palaces. 6thly, Streets. 7thly, Chambers. 8thly, Prisons. 9thly, Gardens. And 10thly, Rural prospects of groves, forest, desarts."[3]

Such a scenic prescription was not to the taste of a great many playgoers, and the newspapers of the time are filled with criticisms of theatre policy. Indeed, so the complaints tell us, even on the rare occasions when the decorations of a piece were costly and elaborate, they were mounted in a careless and haphazard fashion. An article describing conditions as they existed in 1750 is perhaps typical of the frequent dissatisfaction:

Theatrical amusements are so generally attended to, it must be the wish of all admirers of the stage to see it conducted with elegance and propriety, every thing which appears contrary to the *costume,* or the established laws of decorum and verisimilitude, cannot fail to raise the indignation, or at least displease the eye, of a judicious critic.

On this ground I mean to point out some actual inconsistencies, which are a direct opposition to common sense. The first to be noticed is the want of due order and regulation in the lower department of scene-shifters (who are complimented in France by the genteeler name of *machinistes*), by whose frequent inattention we are often presented with dull clouds hanging in a lady's dressing room, or overcasting an antichamber; trees intermixed with disunited portions of the peristyle; or a chief commander giving his orders for battle from a prison, instead of from the head of a camp, the stopscene not corresponding with the laterals, &c. Under such circumstances the gravity of the *drama* suffers considerably.[4]

A frequently quoted passage from Tate Wilkinson supports the impression created by the above article. Wilkinson, writing in 1790, was comparing the scenery of the time with the stock decorations of an earlier era:

Not any plays throughout were ever dressed as they are now—there the public enjoy a splendor indeed superior to their forefathers. . . . Except in Mr. Rich's pantomimes, the public then had seldom any scenery that proved to advantage so as to lure the eye:—But now frequently we have new scenery to almost every piece. It was very uncommon formerly for new plays to have more than what we term stock scenery:—There is one scene at Covent Garden used from 1747 to this day in the Fop's Fortune, &c. which has wings and flat, of Spanish figures at full length, and two folding doors in the middle!—I never see those wings slide on but I feel as if seeing my very old acquaintance unexpected.[5]

The kind of setting to which Wilkinson refers can readily be observed in many of the prints of Hogarth and later engravers. Almost inevitably, a scene was terminated by a pair of flats on which a monotonous architectural motif or equally conventional landscape had been painted. The wings, as often as not, were designed in an entirely different style from that of the back scene to which they were joined.[6]

And indeed, even in the new scenery created especially for a pantomime or related entertainment, the execution of the painting was often careless and inadequate. One of the most popular and successful spectacles of the entire century was Garrick's *Cymon,* produced at Drury Lane in 1767. One setting in this production, a transformation scene, was particularly applauded by the critics.[7] Yet to Thomas Malton, the author of one of England's earliest books on perspective, even that scene was a "jumble of inconsistencies, both in point of design and execution." As a result, Malton was led to conclude that "Few artists have made perspective so much their study, to know how to proportion one part to another on detached scenes, so as to make the whole unite in the proper point of view, whether the view be external or internal."[8]

Garrick himself professed some dissatisfaction with the scenery for *Cymon,* and the remarkable manager, who in 1762 abolished the practice of permitting spectators to sit on the stage during the performance of a regular play, and who in 1765 instituted a number of improvements in illumination (foreshadowing a time when actors would perform in the scenery not in front of it), is the same man who in 1772 recognized qualities of genius in a young Alsatian refugee whom he had met by chance at a friend's house. The refugee was, of course, De Loutherbourg, whose application of the principles of picturesque painting to scene design gave a new appearance of freedom and color to the Georgian stage.

Philip James De Loutherbourg was born in Strasbourg in the year 1740.[9] The son of a well-known painter of miniatures, he first began a study of mathematics and theology at the University of Strasbourg with every intention of pursuing a career either as an engineer or as a Lutheran minister. He had not advanced far in either discipline, however, before he abandoned both in order to study painting in Paris under Francesco Casanova and Carlo Vanloo.[10] Here, he attracted the attention of Diderot and his disciples, who took upon themselves the task of promoting his work.[11] So successful were their efforts that in 1762, the young artist was elected to membership in the French Academy. He was at that time twenty-two, eight years under the minimum age usually required as a candidate. Five years later, in 1767, he was elected to the Academy of Marseilles.[12]

De Loutherbourg's fame during this period rested principally on his abilities as a painter of rural scenes and domestic animals. It was this latter talent that attracted the attention of Etienne Fessard, who in 1765 was preparing his famous edition of La Fontaine. To this work De Loutherbourg contributed some excellent animal engravings as a counterpart to the human figures drawn by his friend, Monnet. The success of Fessard's book gained a new following for De Loutherbourg, and for a few years he was one of the most popular painters in France.[13] His restless disposition led him to experiment with a great many genres and styles, with the result that much of his early work now seems facile and imitative. His versatility, however, was greatly praised by contemporary critics. "He did not confine his pencil to portraits, landscapes, battles, still life, or sea pieces, but excelled, in each, so as to dispute the palm with those artists who have been deservedly eminent in either particular line."[14]

In the year 1769 or thereabouts De Loutherbourg left Paris with the intention of visiting "those parts of Germany, Switzerland and Italy, where he could observe the most perfect works of art, or the most picturesque views of nature."[15]

His observations were considerably abetted by an almost perfect visual memory, a gift that, according to John Williams, occasionally operated to his disadvantage "by feeding him with a vain inclination to despise those aids, which arise from a repeated contemplation of objects, and without which no man can design with precision, however eminently he may be endowed."[16] It was this memory that enriched many of De Loutherbourg's subsequent stage designs by enabling the artist to conjure up colorful and exotic images that he had first absorbed years before during his continental travels.

In 1771 De Loutherbourg's tour brought him to England with a letter of introduction to Garrick from their mutual Parisian friend, Jean Monnet.[17] The meeting between artist and manager occurred at the home of Henry Angelo, the fencing master, whose son recalled the event some years later.

It was at a dinner at his house in Carlisle-Street, that Garrick and De Loutherbourg became acquainted. After dinner, the conversation turning on the affairs of the stage, a common theme with the enterprising manager, though then far advanced in his popular career, Garrick feeling the value of De Loutherbourg's remarks, he soon determined to avail himself of his rare talents.[18]

The stage knowledge that Garrick so much admired in De Loutherbourg must have been acquired partly through practical experience. Perhaps during his stay in France the artist had studied under, and assisted, such designers as François Boucher and Luis René Boquet at the Paris Opera. Unfortunately, there is no record of this phase of his career.

Certainly, however, it was no novice who began work the next fall on a series of new machines and spectacles for Drury Lane. A part-time employee in 1772–1773, De Loutherbourg signed an exclusive contract at the beginning of the following term, a contract that was renewed each year until 1781, when a salary dispute with Sheridan forced him to resign. During his stay at Drury Lane, he painted scenes for almost thirty productions. After leaving that theatre, he designed settings for two more: one in 1781, an entertainment built around scenery and scenery alone at a small theatre of his own devising; and the other, a spectacular harlequinade at Covent Garden in 1785. Although De Loutherbourg lived in good health until after the turn of the century, he seems to have quit the stage permanently in 1786, just fourteen years after his debut as Garrick's protégé.[19]

De Loutherbourg's work for the theatre occupied only fourteen years of his busy life. But what a fourteen years it was! In that wink of time a century seemed to pass. For the first time stage space in the public theatres was organized romantically and realistically. De Loutherbourg used ramps, levels, transparencies, colored lights, constructed (as opposed to painted) scenery. He invented none of these devices, but he employed them with such flexibility and freedom that he was responsible for a revolution in taste and scenic style.

De Loutherbourg is sometimes described as a proto-realist, as the forerunner of Charles Kean and Clarkson Stanfield, and indeed his curious entertainment *The Eidophusikon* (1781) anticipates in its use of so-called organic materials the much more radical style of Antoine and Otto Brahm. But De Loutherbourg was no simple copier of nature. He had a special vision of the world, a Harlequin gift for making tame fancies seem unpredictable and strange. The same imagination that prompted his later search for occult secrets and magical cures created the possible-impossible world of his great Georgian entertainments.

Illustration of the range of the remarkable qualities of De Loutherbourg's vision — its sweep and complexity — may be seen in his contributions to a single season at Drury Lane. Not a typical season to be sure, but a season that forced the manager to make maximum use of his unpredictable but highly salable talent. The year in question is Sheridan's first winter at Drury Lane.

Sheridan's immediate problem in September 1776 was to find some way of compensating for the loss of Garrick, whose departure at the end of the previous season had deprived the theatre of its most dependable attraction. This problem was a pressing one, for, although King, Dodd, Reddish, Mrs. Yates and the other leading members of the now diminished company all had loyal supporters in London, those supporters were not sufficiently numerous to insure a steady profit from the ever-familiar plays that made up the greater part of the Drury Lane repertory.

To avoid a seemingly inevitable decline in the popularity of his theatre, Sheridan turned in the fall and early winter to De Loutherbourg. In 1776 De Loutherbourg was beginning the fifth season of his remarkable career at Drury Lane. His contract as chief scene painter had been renewed, despite the sale of the patent, on the same favorable terms that he had first negotiated with Garrick (£500 per annum). Five years later, in 1781, Sheridan was to revise his high estimate of the value of his principal artist.[20] In 1776, however, the manager had no second thoughts. During the first few months of Sheridan's stewardship, he presented no fewer than six of De Loutherbourg's entertainments. Three of these were revived and altered versions of the artist's most spectacular early successes. The other three were new productions: a fantastic romance in the style of *Cymon* and *A Christmas Tale*, an exotic historical tragedy, and a revival of *The Tempest*. This last is the only Shakespearean production to which we can assign De Loutherbourg's name with any certainty.[21] As such it has more than a passing interest for students of eighteenth-century scenography.

On October 11 an abridged version of *A Christmas Tale* was brought out, now altered into an afterpiece. This exotic supernatural romance had been written to order by Garrick during the artist's first season at Drury Lane. Based on Favart's *La fée urgèle*, *A Christmas Tale* concerns a good magician and his battle with the supernatural evil. The subject allowed De Loutherbourg the opportunity to create some startling transformation scenes and some elaborate picturesque paintings, vaguely oriental in subject. In Sheridan's revival all of De Loutherbourg's scenery was left intact, refurbished for the occasion by the designer himself. Its ability to delight and astonish an audience was undiminished by the years: "With its present judicious alterations," writes the critic of the *Gazetteer*, "[*A Christmas Tale*] is the most elegant and noble show we ever had in this country."[22]

A Christmas Tale is a perfect example of what we might call De Loutherbourg's exotic style. And his designs were the soul of the entertainment. Indeed, they were created in advance of the text that they were ultimately destined to illustrate. A note in Hopkins' *Diary* tells us as much: "This piece was written by Mr. G. which he wrote in a hurry & on purpose to shew some fine Scenes where were designed by Mons De Loutherberg."[23]

The play itself was greeted with contempt by the critics. Horace Walpole calls it a "dire mixture of opera, tragedy, comedy and pantomime." He praises De Loutherbourg's designs as "the most beautiful scenes next to those in the opera at

Paradise," but adds that "they have much to do to save the piece from being thrown to the devil."[24]

I will not attempt to recount all the delightful absurdities of this piece. The story concerns a good witch who masquerades as an ugly old fiend in order to test her lover's truth and fidelity. The climax of the play shows the sudden destruction of a palace and the instantaneous transformation was much admired and was mentioned favorably in at least one of De Loutherbourg's obituaries.[25]

Two other scenes are also worth our attention, for each shows us an aspect of De Loutherbourg's novel style. In Act III, Scene i, we are in a beautiful garden belonging to the heroine of the play, the good witch. She is worried about the constancy of her lover. The text of the scene clearly shows with what singleness of purpose and at what risk of logic Garrick arranged the action of his entertainment to display the talents of his designer. Camilla and Floridor are alone in the garden. Suddenly, Camilla says:

My fancy teems with a thousand apprehensions, all my senses are in disorder. I heard or thought I heard strange noises in the air, even now my eyes are deceiv'd, or this garden, the trees, the flowers, the heav'ns change their colours to my sight, and seem to say something mysterious which is not in my heart to expound.

The stage direction immediately following this speech confirms Camilla's apprehension, for indeed, *"The objects in the garden vary their colours."* This effect greatly impressed the critic for the *London Chronicle* (December 25-28, 1773) who reports with something approaching wonder: "that the trees change colour alternating from green to Red, resembling fire."

The importance of this scene is much greater than would first appear. The English audience was not accustomed to the spectacular possibilities of colored light, and the device created by De Loutherbourg had a sensational and startling effect. The novelty of the scene was remembered long after its inventor had retired from the stage. Indeed, one observer, writing in 1828, recalls it in detail:

It was a sudden transition in a forest scene, where the foliage varies from green to blood colour. This contrivance was entirely new; and the effect was produced by placing different coloured silks in the flies, or side scenes, which turned on a pivot, and, with lights behind, which so illumined the stage, as to give the effect of enchantment.[26]

The logic which connects this spectacular effect to Garrick's story is very faint indeed. Camilla sings a love song to Floridor in which she calls his boasted constancy into question. The song contains the following lines:

> Look round the earth nor think it strange
> To doubt of you, when all things change;
> The branching tree, the blooming flower,
> Their form and hue, change every hour
> While all around such change I see
> Alas my heart must fear for thee.

The other scene of interest is Act III, Scene iii, a scene described in the stage directions simply as "a prospect of rocks." The action at this point concerns a fight between the comic servant of the hero and a number of evil demons. The scene is important because a picture of it has survived, painted by De Loutherbourg himself, and serving as the earliest pictorial evidence of De Loutherbourg's use of the "broken scene"—of set pieces and ground rows irregularly spaced on the stage to provide an increased illusion of depth.

This painting is a perfect example of what the eighteenth century called a sublime or rugged landscape. It is, of course, an idealized picture of the setting, but it has a real, if limited value. There is, for example, an unmistakable indication of ramps and ground rows in the design. The scene is clearly broken up in the manner I have described. On one of the ramps downstage right, Tycho, the comic servant, is standing, sword in hand. Masking the ramp is a raking piece painted to resemble rocks. Literally, a new dimension had been added to the stage, or so it must have seemed to an audience accustomed to the monotonous platforms of the earlier eighteenth century.

Sheridan's revival of *A Christmas Tale* omitted nothing of importance, because, indeed, there is nothing of importance to omit once the integrity of the designs has been preserved.

Encouraged by the success of this condensed *pièce à machine*, Sheridan brought out another abridgment, this time an afterpiece based on Burgoyne's *The Maid of the Oaks*. Burgoyne's play had been created two years earlier for the express purpose of showing off some spectacular scenic effects—in this case, some topical scenes by De Loutherbourg of Lord Stanley's celebrated *fête champêtre,* including views of the pavillion designed especially by the brothers Adam for that most remarkable of social events.[27]

De Loutherbourg created many of these topical entertainments during his career, frequently attaching a scene depicting a recent battle or other important event to a hastily revived or newly created, but totally irrelevant, entertainment. This side of the eighteenth-century theatre has its distinct fascination. In a world that had no newsreels, no television replays, the stage became, in a very real sense, the abstract and brief chronicle of the time.

In the case of the revival of *The Maid of the Oaks,* despite what might be described as a diminished sense of occasion, the return of De Loutherbourg's designs was enthusiastically applauded. *"The Maid of the Oaks,"* [writes the fickle reviewer for the *Gazetteer*] is incontestably the most elegant and [splendid] entertainment . . . ever . . . exhibited on the English stage."[28]

Not surprisingly, the same critic was equally delighted two nights later, when a third revival was presented—this time a full-length version of *The Fair Quaker* containing one of De Loutherbourg's most famous designs—the representation of a naval review at Portsmouth in 1773 with accurate scale models of all the vessels which took part, each vessel distinct from the back scene.[29]

The grand Naval Review appeared much more elegant and splendid than heretofore. — Great encomiums are justly due to the spirited conduct of the present Managers: they have boldly launched out into the most expensive system, and are straining every nerve in order to deserve the encouragement of the public.[30]

The critic is perhaps too enthusiastic when he describes this series of revivals as a "most expensive system." The scenes for all these productions had been gathering dust for several years in the stockroom, and only a minimum of work was needed to prepare them for a second showing. Indeed, Sheridan's system, if it can be called that, was certainly designed to provide his spectators with a maximum of spectacle at a minimum of expense. Regardless of the cost, however, the temporary result was an appearance of opulence at Drury Lane unmatched during any other brief period in English stage history. In November it was almost impossible for a playgoer to visit Sheridan's theatre without seeing at least one of De Loutherbourg's major spectacles revived.[31]

As we might expect, not all the critics greeted this trend toward more spectacle with unalloyed delight. Of the condensed *Christmas Tale,* one observer writes:

> Though greatly shortened, it still contains nothing; and we were sorry to see the genius and abilities of Mr. Loutherbourg so misemployed. The scenes and machines were all admirable; and we could not help wishing that the talents of this man, instead of being used to save paltry things from dammnation, were united to those of a Shakespeare, to astonish or enchant into virtue.[32]

Much more emphatic are the objections of the reviewer for the *London Magazine.* In his savage two-part indictment of "the extreme degeneracy of the English stage," he devotes considerable space to "jubilees, processions, Christmas tales, mutilations, French translations, and . . . the long succession of noise, mummery and dulness infinitely beneath the detailed animadversion of the most patient or persevering critic."[33] His anger is directed particularly at Sheridan and his partners:

> They [the owners of Drury Lane] presented us alternately almost, The Maid of the Oaks and the Christmas Tale, altered from Mr. Garrick, till nearly the middle of the month; two of the vilest compositions, taking them in their different ways, that ever disgraced an English stage; and to compleat the whole of these repeated scenes of mummery, nonsense, and absurdity, the mere animal agility of a swarm of foreign caperers, was thrown in, in order to make this *managerial quackism* pass unnoticed. . . . It indeed may be said of the stage, we hope with more truth, as our violent patriots have often said of the nation, that it is on the *brink of ruin* if not *already* totally undone.[34]

Unfortunately for the critic, but fortunately for the average London theatregoer who had no time for such abstract concerns as the degeneracy of the stage, there was no immediate relief in sight from the mummery and nonsense which had so successfully possessed Drury Lane during November.

Indeed, on December 5, while the spectacular revivals were still attracting customers, Sheridan brought forward a new afterpiece with music by Linley (mostly stolen from Grétry) and elaborate scenes in De Loutherbourg's most extravagant manner. The piece was *Selima and Azor,* described by its author, George Collier, as a "Persian Tale in three parts." In mood, subject and style, Collier's entertainment strongly resembles *Cymon* and *A Christmas Tale,* and, indeed, the novice author may well have been inspired by Garrick's earlier efforts.[35] All three romances are adaptations from the French, Collier's source being a play of Marmontel, produced five years earlier at Fontainbleau.[36]

As a vehicle for spectacle, *Selima and Azor* is more than satisfactory. As literature, however, it leaves a great deal to be desired, and it is not surprising to discover that it was universally condemned by the critics. The reviewer for *Lloyd's Evening Post* writes: "As to . . . [its] . . . literary value, we boldly affirm that it is not possible to squeeze a drop of sense out of it nor is there any morality to be extracted from the Fable."[37] The *London Magazine* seconds this observation, adding that "the manager is too good a judge, to hope that this piece could stand a minute, but for the assistance of Mess. Loutherbourgh and Linley."[38] The editors of the *Biographia Dramatica* call the play "A pompous nothing, pilfered from the French. . . . By the assistance of Loutherbourgh's pencil, and Mrs. Baddeley's voice, it escaped the contempt to which on all accounts it was intitled."[39]

The story of *Selima and Azor* is a variation of the old tale of Beauty and the Beast. Azor, a handsome young prince, has been turned into a monster, as a punishment for his trifling behavior to women. He lives in an enchanted castle, in which Scander, a Persian merchant, together with his comic servant, Ali, take refuge during a thunderstorm. Azor refuses to let his guests go free until Scander promises to send his youngest daughter, Selima, to the castle in his stead. Eventually, Selima comes to Azor, and because he is kind and gentle to her, she learns to love him. Her devotion breaks the spell, and he is restored to his former shape. In traditional fashion, the fortunate pair live happily ever after.

The designs were, of course, executed in the exotic Eastern style that De Loutherbourg had already exhibited to great effect in *A Christmas Tale.* Although most of the stage tricks were predictable, at least one novel effect was introduced into the second act, a remarkable piece of transparent scenery which was used to conjure up a magical and somewhat sinister "vision."

The action of this part of the play is summarized as follows by the critic for the *Public Advertiser:*

In the second part . . . Selima is conducted to the enchanted palace by Ali. She sees in large gold characters "The Apartments of Selima." A curtain conceals the doorway, on her removing which, a group of Loves and Graces come forward and dance a ballet. During this dance Azor appears . . . Selima . . . swoons, but at length reviving . . . begs to see her father. Azor with a magic wand lets Scander and his two other daughters appear through a transparency; first cautioning her not to speak with him. . . . Selima is so enraptured that she cannot refrain, and begins addressing her father who . . . immediately disappears.[40]

Selima's magical vision is described in slightly different terms by the reviewer for the *Whitehall Evening Post:*

She . . . desires to see her father and sisters; upon which he [Azor] waves his talisman, and a long pier-glass divides, and discovers them in shade through it, who sing a trio, at the end of which she running up to embrace them, the glass closes, and the vision ceases.[41]

Is there any inconsistency in these accounts? Probably not. The transparency mentioned in the first review was undoubtedly hidden behind a pair of grooved panels, which had been built into the back scene. On the front of these panels the mirror or pier-glass was painted. At the moment when the vision was to occur, the panels were drawn aside, and light, thrown on the transparency from behind, revealed a shaded view of the concealed actors.

The only other notable scene is the transformation that concludes the action. A ubiquitous fairy who appears from time to time to assist the hero waves her magic wand, and a garden scene is suddenly transformed into *"a brilliant Palace [with] Azor . . . on a magnificent Throne."*[42] De Loutherbourg received his usual encomiums for this effect. The *Morning Post* calls the palace "striking" and describes it as "an illuminated temple . . . brilliantly diversified." The reviewer then qualifies his praise by adding that it "terminates too much like . . . *The Maid of the Oaks* to impress us with a proper idea of its originality."[43]

Even less original in conception was De Loutherbourg's fifth production of the season, *Semiramis,* a new tragedy, adapted from Voltaire and first produced at Drury Lane on December 14. To this production De Loutherbourg contributed at least two scenes. One of these was "entirely" new; the other was borrowed from an earlier production, *Sethona,* and, indeed, included some of the actual wings used in that earlier tragedy. The mixture of old and new designs resulted in a hodgepodge of Assyrian and Egyptian elements hardly flattering to the originality or genius of the designer.

In many ways, however, De Loutherbourg's designs for *Semiramis* were exactly what the play deserved. Indeed, some observers felt that the makeshift settings were actually a complement to the play. "This Play may crawl its nine Nights," notes the critic for the *St. James Chronicle,* "by the Assistance of Mrs. Yates as an Actress, Mr. De Loutherbourgh as a Painter, and the Men who roll the wretched Thunder Machine and Fire Rosin behind the Scenes."[44]

De Loutherbourg's only new design for the piece is described as follows by the reviewer for the *Whitehall Evening Post:*

The first scene, which exhibited the Peristyle of the Palace of Semirimas [*sic*] with several other superb edifices, bearing hanging gardens on their tops, terminated in a view of the tomb of Ninus, which, to our astonishment, was shaped pyramidically. We wish to know from whence Monsieur de Loutherbourgh derived his authority for thus forming a sepulchre of the King of Assyria. We have read indeed of the Pyramids of Egypt, but neither our reading, nor our conversation, has ever taught us to expect in Babylon a pyramidical stile or architecture. Perhaps one reason for the Managers adopting this form, was merely to be able to use the side wings and flat of Sethona for the nearer representation of the tomb of the Assyrian King—scenery, by no means in the *costume* of the place, where the plot of Semiramis is worked. In the first scene, a figure of one of the Egyptian Gods was also placed—*(we know not why)* —on the right hand of the stage. Exclusive of these (to us) apparent absurdities, the first scene was rich and magnificent, and exhibited a beautiful perspective. The other scenes were not new.[45]

There is considerable irony in this criticism. De Loutherbourg's remarkable accuracy in rendering familiar London sights, and the surface realism of his earlier exotic designs had helped to make the Drury Lane audience conscious of authenticity in historical as well as contemporary design. In *Semiramis,* De Loutherbourg was competing against himself, against the new rules of taste which he had inadvertently helped to formulate. Fortunately for the designer, a great many theatregoers were incapable of passing judgment on the historicity of his scenes. The "pyramids" of Assyria, for example, seemed truthful enough to the critic for the *London Chronicle,* who finds "the dresses and decorations . . . characteristic and superb."[46]

The five productions I have just described broke no new ground, and Sheridan's conservative policy proved temporarily profitable. By December, however, it began to pay decreasing dividends: "The playhouses [writes one critic] are now almost deserted by persons of fashion, taste, and letters, who seem disposed to see French Comedies and Tragedies in their first and original State, before they have been mutilated by Plagiarists and Translators."[47] It must have become apparent to Sheridan that if he wished to make further capital of the talents of his designer, then he must find a less hackneyed vehicle.

On January 4 that new vehicle appeared. To the surprise and delight of a great many playgoers, Sheridan had chosen *The Tempest* in the operatic version of Dryden. The same comedy was being performed concurrently at Covent Garden, and the radical decision to prepare new scenes for Shakespeare was presumably spurred by the threat of competition.

Without question the designs of De Loutherbourg were responsible for the overwhelming preference of the critics for the Drury Lane version. Shortly after seeing both productions, the reviewer for the *London Magazine* is moved to write: "[T]here cannot remain a single doubt that Drury-Lane has an apparent superiority, both in the tragic and comic walk over Covent Garden."[48]

Sheridan's radical decision to embellish *The Tempest* with new scenery may have been prompted partly by a sudden rash of newspaper complaints about the moribund state of spectacle in productions of the classic plays. Here, for example, is the critic of the *Morning Post,* writing about a Drury Lane revival of *Romeo and Juliet,* which appeared during the very week in which De Loutherbourg's elaborate scenery for *Selima and Azor* was first exhibited:

The scenery [of *Romeo and Juliet*] is ill adapted to the situation of the drama. We have long been disgusted with a greasy formal flat of fir trees and water because we have found it foisted into every piece whether tragic, comic, or pantomimic, for these seven years past, and the rock entrance of Friar Lawrence's cell resembled more the horrid den of Cerberus than the monastic residence of the catholic priest. . . . Is Mons. De Loutherbourg also grown fashionable enough to despise the tragedies of Shakespeare?⁴⁹

The new scenes for *The Tempest* temporarily silenced this kind of criticism, and the critics responded to the production with enthusiasm. As we might expect, the *Gazetteer* is the most emphatic in its praise:

Last Saturday night *The Tempest* was revived . . . with all the elegance and stage dignity which the united powers of the sister arts can produce. It may be said, that painting, music, and dancing, wait on the immortal genius of Shakespeare throughout the whole performance, like the Graces on Venus. The exquisite melodious composition of Mr. Linley, as well as the masterly pencil of Mr. Loutherbourg have too often been profaned; as for instance, in the *Christmas Tale,* and *Selima and Azor,* where they were made use of merely to deck the altar of folly: but in the *Tempest* they are properly employed to set off the wonders of the great Bard of nature. For this entertainment we are indebted to the judgment of the new manager, whose endeavors in promoting rational amusements deserve encouragement from the public. . . . The scenes and dresses are perfectly well concerted and produced a great effect.⁵⁰

A sour minority report is filed by the critic for the *Westminster Magazine,* who feels that the text of the play has been subordinated to the opportunity for spectacle:

As their [Sheridan and his partners] operations for the present season are to consist of expedients and shifts, we congratulate them on having thought of Shakespeare. But we did not know his works wanted *reviving* from the thrilling touch of *Sheridan,* the surprising talents of the musical Linley, or even the pencil of a Loutherbourgh. However, Shakespeare's works may serve our managers as a school, and when they have revived a few of his plays, they may possibly acquire a taste and knowledge enough for the most important part of their business.⁵¹

The principal complaint of this reviewer is that "the music and dancing . . . were rendered too consequential, they took up too much time, and made the whole tedious."⁵² A glance at the playbill tends to support this objection. Three dances are listed: the first, "a Dance of SPIRITS" in Act I; the second, "a FANTASTIC DANCE" by Mr. Grimaldi in Act III; and the third, "a Grand Ballet called, The DOUBLE FESTIVAL," borrowed "by particular Desire" from another play.[53] Apparently, the main purpose of these diversions was to provide De Loutherbourg with a chance to create some spectacular embellishments of the text.

How many of the scenes he designed is not known. Certainly, however, he created the storm in the first act, an imitation that was allowed to speak for itself without any of the words which Shakespeare wrote for the boatswain and his passengers and without any after-comment by Miranda. The reviewer for the *London Evening Post* applauds this revision: "The scenery at the opening is in general finely descriptive of this magic-wrought tempest, the billows 'mounting to the welkin's cheek', which contrasted with the sky by incessant lightenings' [*sic*] glare, forms one of the most picturesque and striking scenes we ever beheld."[54]

The reviewer for the *Morning Post,* however, is a purist. He strongly objects to the elimination of much of Shakespeare's dialogue "which gives [he feels] a far stronger representation of the horrors of shipwreck than all the distant sinkings of puppet vessel's [*sic*] that man's ingenuity can invent."[55] This casual observation contains the hint of an answer to the question we asked earlier about the neglect of spectacle in Shakespearean productions. If De Loutherbourg's innovations were, as I suggested, transforming the stage from a rhetorical to a pictorial art, such a transformation is surely of no great service to Shakespeare. A material illustration of the places so evocatively described in his dialogue will at best seem redundant, the painter's art setting limits to the vision of the spectator, showing him only one of the many possible worlds of the play.

So perhaps the managers were wise to give De Loutherbourg projects like *The Maid of the Oaks* and *Selima and Azor.* From those subliterary scenarios the Drury Lane artist fashioned a new poetry of the theatre not unlike Inigo Jones's masques. *A Christmas Tale* is incomplete when it lacks canvas and paint; *The Tempest,* conversely, can only be diminished by De Loutherbourg's kind of pictorial illustration.

After all, even the critic of the *Gazetteer,* hardly a sophisticated theorist of the drama, sensed that something was wrong: "The fireworks in the first scene might as well be spared, as the scent of gun-powder was a very disagreeable incense to the ladies."[56]

But even so, what about the aesthetic effect of De Loutherbourg's scenic innovations in general? Overkill in scenic effect may indeed drive a wedge between the values of the page and those of the stage in the reactions of many spectators. But the fresh imaginings, which De Loutherbourg materialized, made for an aesthetic experience when combined with many a text, which fascinated crowds upon crowds of theatregoers. Such experience, one must believe, varies from person to person and from time to time. It cannot have been the same for a Horace Walpole or a Mrs. Montagu as for a Hobson, the long-time stage-door keeper, or for Powney, the stationer, or for the proprietors of any of the 107 coffeehouse and tavern owners who did a continuing business with the theatres, and who attended a *Hamlet* as well as a *Selima and Azor,* enjoying the whole show sufficiently to return again and again. Increasing options for enjoyment became established in the "irrational entertainments" as well as in the rational ones, and the irrational portions contributed to making the whole evening's performance a delight.

NOTES

1. *Dramatic Genius* (London: Beckett and Hondt, 1772), p. 94.

2. *The Gray's Inn Journal,* Saturday, September 1, 1753.

3. Quoted by George C. D. Odell, *Shapespeare from Betterton to Irving* (New York: Scribner, 1920), I, 417-18.

4. *Gentleman's Magazine* (May 1789). A correspondent submitted the article as an item of curiosity, explaining that it had been written thirty years before and adding that the "censure may be now thought obsolete."

5. Tate Wilkinson, *Memoirs of His Own Life* (York: Printed for the Author, 1790), IV, 91-92.

6. See especially: "Hogarth's caricature of typical scenery about 1723" (Plate 32) and "Riot at a performance of Artaxerxes" (Plate 35) in Richard Southern, *Changeable Scenery: Its Origin and Development in the British Theatre* (London: Faber & Faber, 1952).

7. See David Erskine Baker, *Biographia Dramatica: or, A Companion to the Playhouse,* additions by Isaac Reed and Stephen Jones (London: Longman et al, 1812), II, 149.

8. *A Compleat Treatise on Perspective in Theory and Practice on the True Principles of Dr. Brook Taylor,* 2d ed. (London: Printed for the Author, 1779), Book III, Section 10, p. 316.

9. According to a biographical account authorized by De Loutherbourg himself in the *European Magazine* (March 1782). Harry A. Beard in "De Loutherbourg," *Enciclopedia dello Spettacolo,* (Roma: Unione Editoriale, 1968), IV, 427, lists the artist's place of birth as Basel not Strasbourg.

10. *European Magazine* (March 1782); see also, Samuel Redgrave, "Louther-bourg," *A Dictionary of Artists of the British School* (London: Longmans Green, 1874; rev. ed. London, 1878), pp. 122-123.

11. Denis Diderot, *Salons*, ed. Jean Seznec and Joan Adhémar (Oxford: Clarendon Press, 1957), I, 225-227.

12. *European Magazine* (March 1782).

13. E. Benezit, *Dictionnaire critique et documentaire des peintres, sculpteurs, dessinateurs & graveurs* (Paris: Roger et Chernoviz, 1911-1923), III, 152.

14. *European Magazine* (March 1782).

15. Ibid.

16. John Williams (Anthony Pasquin, pseud.), *An Authentic History of the Professors of Painting, Sculpture, & Architecture, Who Have Practised in Ireland . . . To Which Are Added, Memoirs of the Royal Academicians, Being an Attempt to Improve the Taste of the Realm* (London: H. D. Symonds, 1796), Part II, pp. 78-80.

17. A copy of the letter is contained in David Garrick, *Private Correspondence*, ed. James Boaden (London: S. Bentley, 1831-1832), II, 592.

18. Henry Angelo, *Reminiscences* (London: H. Colburn, 1828), I, 16.

19. De Loutherbourg's early retirement from theatrical matters is not difficult to explain, for the stage was only one of his many interests. Even during the years when he was most active at Drury Lane, he still found time to produce easel paintings, engravings, and caricatures. A study of his easel art is, of course, beyond the scope of this essay. Suffice it to say that his reputation was at its zenith in 1780 when he was made an associate of the Royal Academy. The next year (shortly before his break with Sheridan) he was elected a full member.

In 1783 he temporarily curtailed his artistic activities and joined with Cagliostro in what Williams describes as a "trial of experiments equally futile and unprofitable." The purpose of these experiments was apparently to find the philosopher's stone, a project that left De Loutherbourg "approaching fast to the threshold of common pity, cadaverous but not rich." For more than a year his paintings suffered. In 1784 he was finally persuaded to abandon alchemy, but this craze was soon replaced by another madness, even more dangerous than the first. Dreaming one night that he was blessed with a knowledge of the "Panacea, Catholicon, or remedy of all diseases," he proclaimed himself an adept at the art of healing, and narrowly escaped with his life when some of his patients failed to respond to his earnest prayers.

This last adventure apparently had the effect of restoring his sanity, and after 1790, he devoted his life exclusively to painting and study. His last important project was a series of aquatints of English scenery which were published in folio form in 1805.

In 1812, after almost forty years in England, he died at Hammersmith Terrace, having left behind him a distinguished record in nearly every branch of the arts of his adopted country. See W. H. Gerdts, "Phillip de Loutherbourg" *Antiques* (November 1955) no. 5, 80-81; John Williams, Part II, pp. 80-81; De Loutherbourg, *The Romantic and Picturesque Scenery of England and Wales, from Drawings made Expressly for this Undertaking, with Historical and*

Descriptive Accounts of the Several Places of which Views are Given (London: for R. Bowyer, 1805); and the brief obituary in the *European Magazine* (March 1812).

20. William Henry Pyne, *Wine and Walnuts* (London: Longman, Hurst, 1823), I, 278.

21. The celebrated designs, supposedly for *Richard III,* which were part of Henry Irving's collection, now almost certainly appear to be sketches for *Pizarro.* See, for example, Sybil Rosenfeld and Edward Croft-Murray, "A Checklist of Scene Painters Working in Great Britain and Ireland in the 18th Century (3)," *Theatre Notebook,* XIX, no. 3 (Spring 1965), 110.

22. October 21, 1776.

23. Entry for December 27, 1773. See *The London Stage, 1660–1800* (Carbondale: Southern Illinois University Press), Part 4 under date.

24. *The Letters of Horace Walpole,* ed. Mrs. Paget Toynbee (Oxford: Clarendon Press, 1903–1906), VIII, 398.

25. *A New Dramatic Entertainment Called A Christmas Tale, in Five Parts, Embellished with an Etching by De Loutherbourg* (London, 1774). Hereafter, this edition will be referred to as *A Christmas Tale.* It is interesting to note that De Loutherbourg's name appears on the title page of this edition, despite the fact that the author receives no credit. This clearly shows, I think, how closely the reputation of the designer was linked to the production.

26. Henry Angelo, *Reminiscences* (London: H. Colburn, 1828), II, 326–337.

27. For a detailed reconstruction of this production, see my article, "Topical Scenes for Pantomime," *Educational Theatre Journal* (December, 1965), XVII, No. 4.

28. November 8, 1776.

29. See "Topical Scenes for Pantomime."

30. November 12, 1776.

31. On several occasions, two of the elaborate productions were presented on the same bill. On November 9, for example (according to the playbill in the *Public Advertiser*), an observer might have witnessed both *The Fair Quaker* and *A Christmas Tale* for the price of one admission.

32. *Westminster Magazine* (October 1776).

33. October 1776.

34. *London Magazine* (November 1776).

35. See Willard Austin Kinne, *Revivals and Importations of French Comedies in England, 1749–1800* (New York: Columbia University Press, 1939), p. 145.

36. Nicoll, *Late Eighteenth Century Drama* (Cambridge: Cambridge University Press, 1952–1959), p. 379.

37. December 6–9, 1776.

38. December 1776.

39. Baker and others, III, 256.

40. December 7, 1776.

41. December 5–7, 1776.

42. George Collier, *Selima and Azor, a Persian Tale in Three Parts As Performed at the Theatre Royal in Drury-Lane* (London: J. Bell, 1776), III, v.

43. December 6, 1776.
44. December 14–17, 1776.
45. December 14–17, 1776.
46. December 14–17, 1776.
47. *Westminster Magazine* (February 1777). The observations of the critic refer to conditions existing around the first of the new year.
48. January 1777.
49. December 13, 1776.
50. January 6, 1777.
51. January 1777.
52. January 1777.
53. Playbill in the *Public Advertiser,* January 6, 1777.
54. January 6, 1777.
55. January 6, 1777.
56. January 6, 1777.

Part III

THEATRICAL MUSIC FOR SIMPLE ENJOYMENT AND AESTHETIC ENRICHMENT

ORCHESTRA AND SONG
Editor's Headnote

The eighteenth century, music minded from its start, fairly rang with song. Its opera flourished. It was the age of the oratorio. Choral and sacred music abounded. Composers and instrumentalists flocked to London from abroad. Catches and glees were sung in taverns and coffee houses, at festivals and in club rooms. Specialty singing and band music were features at Ranelagh and Vauxhall Gardens nightly, and the Great Rooms were often hired for performing vocalists. The sheet music trade flourished, and flourished well, as songs from the plays and entr'actes passed quickly from the theatres to the music publishing houses from the Strand up to Oxford Street. Attention at last is being paid to the theatre music of the time, since Roger Fiske's English Theatre Music in the Eighteenth Century *appeared in 1973. All competent actors in London had, of course, to be able to sing, and to dance, but some such as John Beard, England's foremost tenor, Samuel Champness and the Reinholds (bassos), and Susannah Maria Cibber, Sophia Baddelley, George Ann Bellamy, and Mrs. Barthelemon made the plays vibrate with their clear-voiced harmonies. The four following papers devote attention to the musical component of a night's "whole show." Those by Professor Knapp and Professor Lincoln are illustrated by piano, harpsichord, and vocal selections (on an accompanying cassette). Professor Stone suggests areas of cooperative work to be done by theatre historians and musicologists. Professor Phyllis T. Dircks discusses the genesis and success of the burletta "Orpheus" in Garrick's* A Peep Behind the Curtain. *His is an experimental and successful use of music for satire in a form pleasing to theatrical audiences in an age which bantered well-known classical stories. The seeming blandness of several texts always comes alive when the musical setting is recovered.*

6. The Prevalence of Theatrical Music in Garrick's Time

Geo. Winchester Stone, Jr.
Clark Library Professor, 1976–1977

In viewing the various components of a London evening's "whole show" in the eighteenth century, one comes inescapably to the large and fascinating study of theatrical music. Many modern scholars were reared to think *not* of the eighteenth century, but of Elizabethan England as singing England, musical England—a time when musical participation ran through all levels of society, from the Queen herself on her virginals to Duke Orsino and his lover's lute, to Bottom the weaver on his tongs and bones. But any who may have attended a Clark day of library lectures back in 1953 would have heard James Phillips and Bertrand Bronson set the record straight in their talks on "Literature and Music in Eighteenth-Century England."[1] Professor Bronson noted the range of musical activity, both instrumental and vocal, in opera, oratorio, burletta, specialty songs in the pleasure gardens, street ballads, hymnology in church and cathedral, and chamber music in the great houses. Dean Phillips treated the central argument of the day as to the priority (in vocal music) of words over notes among the aesthetic theorizers of the time.

Amid the wide range of possibilities to discuss, the scholars contributing to this volume focus on some specific music in Garrick's theatre in the midpart of the century.[2] Theatres in that period rang with music—three overtures opening each night's performance, entr'acte songs to change pace and atmosphere, background music for appropriate moods, and complete musical plays—aside that is from the run of oratorios and operas.

A myth has got around in modern times that those interested in music in the 1760s gravitated to Covent Garden theatre, to Ranelagh, or to Vauxhall, and eschewed Garrick's Drury Lane where comedy, tragedy, and farces supposedly ruled supreme. Charles

116

Dibdin, in his late reminiscences, even hinted that Garrick was tone-deaf, and basically uninterested in "sing-song." Gainsborough in a famous letter to the great manager (about stage lighting and scenic effects) included the comment "keep up your music by supplying the place of noise by more sound, more harmony, and more tune, and split that cursed fife and drum."[3] Result: what to some *now* seems a rich field for exploration "Garrick and theatrical music" has long been put down.

Roger Fiske has recently set the compass in a new direction, stating that Garrick "worked harder than Rich in the fourteen years they were rivals, and when Covent Garden under John Beard suddenly made English operas an artistic and financial success, Garrick stepped up Drury Lane's repertoire, and was forever searching for success on his own in this field. He also believed that quiet background music could heighten the emotion of such scenes as the one in *King Lear* in which the King and Cordelia are reunited. The background music he commissioned from Boyce for animating the statue of Hermione in *The Winter's Tale* is in the Bodleian. Shakespeare himself had asked for music in these scenes. Garrick was reviving a neglected tradition."[4]

How can one come at this music, to have a look at its quality and survey its prevalence? The bulk was once, indeed, large, and much of it still exists in printed form, scattered and forgotten though it be in British and American libraries. The musical scores of eight complete Drury Lane musical pieces were destroyed by German bomb hits on the British Museum, but fortunately duplicates appear in the holdings of the Royal College of Music.[5] Of the first-line index of 114 songs for which Garrick wrote the words, the music of 70 is readily available. Further search may turn up additional scores. *The British Museum Catalogue of Early Music* identifies holdings and their locations in England. The Library of Congress, the Folger, the Huntington, the Clark, and some additional private collections seem to hold others. And one must mention the efforts of Dr. Elizabeth Heisch who has published a selective bibliography of musical dramas and dramas with music from the seventeenth and eighteenth centuries to the number of nearly 500.[6]

Garrick *was* interested in songs in and for some eighteen of the forty-nine plays which he either wrote or considerably revised for production. He also maintained (at good salaries) an orchestra of twenty-one pieces, employed Dr. Thomas A. Arne and Charles Dibdin at various times as official composers for Drury Lane, but in the 1770s abandoned the practice of hiring a house composer, preferring to commission work from a wider number of musicians —some ten in particular: the Arnes (Thomas and his son Michael), Thomas Aylward, F. H. Barthelemon, William Boyce, Jonathan Battishill, Charles Burney, Charles Dibdin, James Oswald, William Shields, and Handel's pupil John Christopher Smith. But his ms "Theatre Account Books" show payments to a much larger group for his theatre music in general. His payroll and salary scale increased in size as the years of his management proceeded. The favorite composers whose pieces stocked the musical libraries of his and the other theatres (and some sorting needs to take place) were divided about equally between English and continental composers, with Handel, of course, towering above all others during the Lenten oratorio season. To the Englishmen just mentioned add William Bates, Henry Carey, Charles John Stanley and John Abraham Fisher. To Barthelemon and Handel from abroad add Carissimi, Giambatista Ciri, Balthazar Galuppi, Jomelli, LaMotte, John Adolph Hasse, Pergolesi, Piccini, and D. J. Pinguinet.[7]

Many fields for scholarly research embracing pairs of musicologists *and* literary historians now appear worth exploring in some detail.

First is the *theory and practice of musical composing for the stage.* Dean James E. Phillips opened up the subject in 1954, and Roger Fiske has carried it somewhat along the way. But consider several points. In 1763 Robert Maddison noted Handel's reply (possibly apocryphal) to a critic who complained that his music carried an effect contrary to the sense of the accompanying words. "The music is good. Damn the words!" Handel is supposed to have said. Maddison wanted oratorios to combine sense and sound to appeal to mind and ear congruently.[8] Four years later Joseph Reed, by Garrick's help, got Edward Toms to "compile the music" (as he phrased it) for his libretto of *Tom Jones,* turning the famous novel into an opera. "In the course of our conversation," wrote Reed, "Mr. Toms informed me (which I had no conception of) that it would be necessary to cast the characters before the songs were adapted to the music, as some airs would suit one performer better than they would suit another in the character."[9] Eight years later Thomas Linley passed the word to Garrick about *his* principle for composing music for plays: "The idea of reducing poetry to verse in order to make it fit musical expression is (especially in great and serious subjects) generally wrong: for it is the imagery and sentiments conveyed by the words that ought to inspire the musician, and not any particular kind of verse—the variety of rhythm and poetical feet are oftener found in poetical prose, or blank verse, than in verses which rhyme."[10]

Three possibilities are proposed here (among many others) for wedding music to theatrical script—damn the words, suit voice capability and personality of the singer to the composition first, or thirdly, take inspiration from the essential poetry of the dramatist rather than from the forced jingle of rhyme and meter. These points and the taste involved in adopting one or the other were much written about (and with great seriousness) by authors and composers of the period—such as Francesco Geminiani in a *Treatise on Good Taste in Music and Art* (1749), by James Harris in *Three Treatises* (1744), by Charles Avison in an *Essay on Musical Expression* (1753), and by Dr. John Brown in a long *Dissertation on the Rise, Union and Power of Poetry and Music* (1763).

A second field for research which one might see relates to the *effect of musical plays.* Examination here would involve comments in letters, diaries, journals, and reviews in the press focused on the musical parts of the "whole show" of a theatrical evening—a search for the particular, not for repeating general sweeping statements—the "tone was chaste," "the execution brilliant," and so on.

A third area might deal with *changes in musical techniques and effects.* Roger Fiske notes the year 1760 as marking a sort of watershed that left the baroque behind and moved on toward the galante. How and where, if it occurred, is this change reflected in theatrical music? Does Barthelemon's *Orpheus,* for example, move away from Handel's influence? And towards what? What examples illustrate a trend? And how aware of the shift were the audiences?

A fourth topic to explore would be the *quality of theatrical music,* and ways in which it advanced (or cheapened) the evening's enjoyment and aesthetic effect in the theatre—music taken, that is, along with the libretto, and with the general drive of the play with which it was integrated or combined. Garrick's 114 songs hardly compare when read with the songs of Blake, or Pope, or even with some of Shenstone. But to compare them with the verse of nondramatic poets is, of course, to compare apples and oranges. Charles Wesley's hymns are best compared with those of Watts or Sternhold, not with the odes (called hymns) of Milton, Donne, or Herrick. Wesley's words take on a quality administered to by the music (which it seems was of very special quality for him — though much altered in the nineteenth century) and the solemn occasion of religious services. Just so with songs in plays. The important thing to discover is the sound of the accompanying music. The Garrick songs with their music might well be compared with the songs of Ben Jonson, Shakespeare, and Gay along with the music specified for their plays.

A fifth field suggests itself in a *comparison* (for atmosphere and quality) of French, Italian, and German theatre music in the period — its theory, practice, and common denominators of taste observed. And so the possibilities go.

"Taste and fashion with us have always had wings," wrote Colley Cibber in his *Apology for My Life* in 1740, "have had wings to fly from one public spectacle to another." Public taste in the 1760s cried for more and more music on stage. We can now see that a new musical piece came out nearly every year during that decade and left audience after audience issuing into the night air humming tunes both new and familiar.[11] Taste in theatrical song was now and again simple, now and again requiring (and responding to) ornamentation. Gaetano Guadagni, Burney reminds us, had a small voice, but was master of great musical showmanship. All he desired was simple music with frequent pauses giving *him* ample opportunity to fill in and ornament the melody, unaccompanied by the orchestra. His modulations gave the quality of far off sounds, and suggested the dying notes of an aeolian harp.[12] This and the "shake" so popular in eighteenth-century vocal music might seem distant from modern taste, yet perhaps not so. One remembers Beverly Sills's interview (for TV, April 1975) in which she noted, "I ornament from dramatic need. When I feel the need for deepened or light expression I ornament the character vocally. I am seeing the character, after reading and studying the text." Such is, of course, creative interpretation at work. She instanced her change in the walk of Mignon from a shoeless country girl at the start of the performance to that of an extreme sophisticate at the end. And something like this she paralleled vocally. The following papers give some focus to wide-ranging musical activity in the theatres of the century.

They test each in its own way, the validity of the thesis that the music in the plays enhanced their value no end, widened the world of entertainment, and diffused a cultural phenomenon (the musical play) whose value *then* we have largely lost sight of *now*.

As the century moved along experimentation was widespread, and met all the desires among varied and growing audiences. Play plots and characters, we know, moved from preoccupation with the classics of Greece and Rome, to stories of the exotic orient, to situations centering on upper-, then middle-class people. Lovely ladies, pretty girls, handsome men in charming gardens, all involved with disguises, intrigues, jokes, yet mostly with happy endings constituted theatrical fare. Some plays were as frothy as Neil Simon's are today. Some carried seeds of satire and of social criticism, but even though comic the stories of most plays allowed dreams to come true — on stage, and vicariously for spectators, allowed manners to be shied at with a fine degree of sophistication, and yet to wring some hearts.

NOTES

1. *Music and Literature in England in the Seventeenth and Eighteenth Centuries:* Papers delivered by James E. Phillips and Bertrand Bronson at the Second Clark Seminar, 24 October 1953 (Los Angeles: W. A. Clark Library).

2. Professor J. Merrill Knapp, musicologist (Princeton); Professor Stoddard Lincoln, musicologist (Brooklyn College); Associate Professor Phyllis T. Dircks, English (Long Island University).

3. See *The Letters of Thomas Gainsborough,* ed. Mary Woodall [Bindford] (New York: Graphic Arts, 1963) ltr. 34, pp. 75–76.

4. *English Theatre Music in the Eighteenth Century* (London: Oxford University Press, 1973), p. 205.

5. *Cymon, The Election, The Maid of the Oaks, The Cunning Man, The Institution of the Garter, Ode to Shakespeare's Jubilee,* and *May Day.*

6. *RECTR (Restoration and Eighteenth-Century Theatre Research)* May 1972 and November 1972.

7. See *The London Stage, 1660–1800,* Part 4, Introduction and Appendix on Theatrical Music and on financial analysis, ed. G. W. Stone, Jr. (Carbondale: Southern Illinois University Press, 1962).

8. A sixty-three page pamphlet on oratorios at Covent Garden (London: Kearsley, 1763).

9. *The Private Correspondence of David Garrick,* ed. James Boaden (London: S. Bentley, 1831-1832) I, 261, ltr., dated 1767.

10. Linley develops at length the relationship between various poetical meters and musical measures. Boaden, Garrick's *Private Correspondence,* II, 99.

11. *The London Stage, 1660-1800,* Part 4, the years 1760-1770 passim.

12. Garrick had trained Guadagni as a careful actor-singer when he performed in the opera *The Fairies* in 1755. See Burney, Charles, *A General History of Music* (London: 1789; rev. ed. with critical and historical notes by Frank Mercer, New York: Dover, 1935), Book IV, 494-496.

7. English Theatrical Music in Garrick's Time: *The Enchanter* (1760) and *May Day* (1775)

J. Merrill Knapp

Professor of Music, Princeton University

The importance of music in Garrick's theatre is gradually becoming evident to modern scholars. I shall try to illustrate specifically by looking at two musical plays of which Garrick was author—plays that have probably not been examined in any detail since the eighteenth century. They are *The Enchanter; or Love and Magic*, a Christmas entertainment of 13 December 1760 with music by John Christopher Smith, Jr., pupil and close associate of Handel; and *May Day; or the Little Gipsy* of 28 October 1775 with music by Thomas A. Arne. Both of these works were popular, with twenty performances in two seasons for *The Enchanter*, and sixteen for *May Day* in a single season. They were written primarily to introduce two young singers to the Drury Lane audience—a boy, Master Leoni in the first, and Miss Harriet Abrams, aged seventeen, in the second.

Elizabeth Stein in her book *David Garrick Dramatist*[1] rather scorns both pieces as drama. She calls the first "a musical trifle which includes spectacle, music, dances and feats of magical display," and as to the second remarks "it has little to recommend it: the characters are types rather than individuals, and the humor is strained." The trouble with these judgments is that they consider the works almost wholly from a literary point of view and do not take into account the whole spectacle, particularly the music—a familiar problem with some literary critics who persist in lambasting opera librettos without really considering them as *words for music*.

Both works were afterpieces, playlets that came at the end of a long evening of overture, prologue, a three or five act drama (often Shakespeare; in this case Vanbrugh's *The Confederacy* for the first, and Nicholas Rowe's *The Fair Penitent* for the second), with further dancing and music. Afterpieces had to be light to capture the fancy of the working class, who came in at eight o'clock (at half-price) after their shops had closed. But there the similarity ends. *The Enchanter,* coming in Garrick's midcareer, is really a little opera (all sung), which appearing at Christmas time, was supposed to point a moral, although the substance of the plot indicates that Garrick did not take it too seriously. The *May Day* of 1775 came at the end of Garrick's career (he retired in 1776, as in effect did Thomas Arne the same year) and was an attempt to compete with Covent Garden's pantomime and dancing. Garrick called it a "musical farce," but it is really a play with incidental songs. The prose dialogue forms a basis for the central plot, with the songs heightening the characterization. Even though Garrick often called these entertainments "sing-song," they were musically several cuts above much previous ballad opera. After the popular musical, *Love in a Village* (1762) [Bickerstaff's pasticcio with about half the music by Arne], the music even of afterpieces had much greater weight. The songs had introductions and postludes for orchestra, and they often demanded full scoring for winds, brass, and strings, preceded by a solid overture. *The Beggar's Opera* (Gay and Pepusch) had set a course earlier and *The Maid of the Mill* (1765, S. Arnold and Bickerstaff) and *Love in the City* (1767, Dibdin and Bickerstaff) capitalized on the trend.

In *The Enchanter* Garrick knew he was attempting a little two-act opera in verse with its attendant difficulties about the text. He wrote in the *Advertisement* to the printed copy: "As the recitative commonly appears the most tedious part of a musical entertainment, the writer of the following little piece has avoided it as much as possible; and has endeavored to carry on what fable there is, chiefly by the songs."[2] This little proviso was a direct reflection of the English aristocracy's patronage of Italian opera since the early 1700s, where the recitative, not understood, was continually called a bore, starting with Addison's strictures in *The Spectator.*[3] As a result, emphasis, even with adapters of Italian opera librettos, had been placed upon the arias.

The cast was: Moroc—Samuel Champness; Kaliel—Master Leoni; Zoreb—Thomas Lowe; Zaida—Mrs. Vincent; Lyssa, a

Shepherdess—Miss Young. They were a mixture of professional singers attached to Drury Lane Theatre and actresses who could sing. Champness was a favorite basso who took part in almost all the Handel oratorios in the 1750s (particularly *Messiah* at the Foundling Hospital) and was known for his rendering of Hecate in *Macbeth* at Drury Lane. Thomas Lowe was a prominent tenor of the time, of whom Burney said "with the finest tenor voice I ever heard in my life [but] for want of diligence and cultivation, he could never be safely entrusted with anything better than a ballad, which he constantly learned by his ear."[4] The observation was probably exaggerated, but Lowe seems to have been deficient in expression, for he was more at home in Vauxhall and Marylebone Gardens than he was in the oratorios, although he sang in many of them as Handel's second tenor. The women of the piece were primarily actresses.

John Christopher Smith, Jr. (1712-1795, to distinguish him from his father) has been known primarily in musical history as the man who preserved most of Handel's manuscripts (probably the most complete of any great composer kept all in one place—in the British Museum). He received them from his father and gave them to King George III and Queen Charlotte because he was tutor to their children. He was also a composer of sacred and theatrical music. The full manuscript scores of four of his oratorios, three operas, and other incidental music have recently been found in the Hamburg State Library. He also wrote the music for Garrick's adaptations of *A Midsummer Night's Dream* (1755), performed as *The Fairies,* and *The Tempest* (1756).[5] His music is competent but derivative, particularly of his master, but some of his writing stands up as quite good. In *The Enchanter,* of which we have only the songs in the printed Walsh edition[6] with no recitative, dances, or choruses, he often broke away from the formal da capo aria and wrote short simple tunes, scored for a rather large orchestra of recorders, flutes, horns, trumpets, timpani, and strings. But the Handelian influence is not far away—Handel had died only the previous year. The beginning of the French overture (Grave and fugal Allegro) and the Dead March (shades of Handel's *Saul* then still being performed during Lent at Covent Garden) when Moroc shows Zaida Zoreb's body in the tomb, bear the unmistakable touch of Handel:

Selection 1

Overture to The Enchanter

Selection 2

Selection 3   Dead March

Two songs and a duet show the lighter side of the music and are really quite charming. No recitative occurs before "Intruder Sleep." The song is an A major arioso, labelled "Affetuoso" for four part strings and soprano. Smith neglects in it to do much with "the cankered rose" (last line) but his melody is graceful with a strong cadence in E major in the middle. Garrick leads up to the second song (the scene of which reads: "A tomb rises from the ground in which Zoreb lies. Kaliel is standing by him with his wand on his breast, a Dead March is heard in the background") by an accompanied recitative for Zaida, saying:

My Zoreb—dead—then sorrow is no more:
Now let the light'ning flash, the thunder roar! (Act II, Scene iii)

This display is followed by "Back to your source, weak foolish tears" — an Italianite rage aria (Presto in E flat) of rapid, rushing strings, a jagged vocal line that goes up two octaves on "eagle's wings" and even a cadenza, the whole properly evoking scorn and fury with Garrick's aerial metaphor to help. (If one were to become Handelian at this point, the first song recalls "I know that my Redeemer liveth," and the second "Why do the Nations.") The final duet for Lowe and Mrs. Vincent is a happy six/eight pastoral where each singer in turn sings the catchy melody and then join together in the customary thirds and sixths to reach a joyful conclusion. The preceding recitative reads (and one must remember there was music to this which gave a touch of class to the doggerel):

Zaida: O Zoreb — O my Lord — my bosom guest!
           Transport is mute! My eyes speak the rest.

Zoreb: And do I wake to bliss, as well as life!
           'Tis more than bliss — 'tis Zaida — 'tis my wife!

Kaliel: In Fate's mysterious web this knot was wove:
           Thus heaven rewards your constancy and love.
           [They join hands.]

The swift and simple plot shows the triumph of beauty, youth, and virtue over magic, lust, and arbitrary power. The beautiful Zaida is contracted to young Zoreb. The powerful magician Moroc, lusting for Zaida, imprisons Zoreb, and carries the maiden to his castle, hopefully to woo and win her. She resists his attempts. Unable to sleep she walks in his garden singing:

Selection 4   Songs

Intruder Sleep! In vain you try
To hush my breast, and close my eye;
   The morning dews refresh the flower,
   That unmolested blows;
But ineffectual falls the shower
Upon the canker'd rose.

Moroc, on fire for love but unpersuasive, directs his attendant spirit Kaliel to try to win Zaida with spectacles of magic and blandishments of sweet words. She remains true to Zoreb. Enraged Moroc declares Zoreb is dead. He will show her the body. A tomb, thereupon arises from the ground, with Zoreb lying therein (Dead march). She sings:

Selection 5

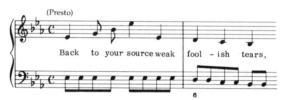

Back to your source weak foolish tears,
Away fond love, and woman's fears
A nobler passion warms:
The dove shall Soar with eagle's wing,
   From Earth I spring
And fly to Heav'n, and Zoreb's arms!

Thereupon she offers to stab herself. Moroc runs to prevent her, and drops his ebon wand. Kaliel retrieves it, and finds himself free and with power now over Moroc. Challenged by the magician, Kaliel waves the wand in the name of Virtue, strikes Moroc (who sinks into the ground) and awakens Zoreb to life. Zoreb and Zaida join hands, kneel before Kaliel and thank him for deliverance. They sing a duet as the curtain falls:

Selection 6

No power could divide us, no terror dismay;
No treasure could bribe us, no falsehood betray;
   No demons could tempt us, no pleasure could move;
   No magic could bind us, but the magic of love.

Zoreb: The spell round my heart was the image of you
        Then how could I fail to be constant and true!

Zaida: The spell round *my* heart was the image of you;
        Then how could *I* fail to be constant and true!

For *May Day* Garrick wrote in the preface:

The author of this musical farce begs leave to inform the reader, if there should be any, that it was merely intended to introduce the Little Gipsy to the public, whose youth and total inexperience of the stage made it necessary to give as little dialogue to her character as possible, her success depending wholly upon her singing. This reason added to another, which is that the piece was produced at an early part of the season, when better writers are not willing to come forth, is the best apology that the Author can make for its defects.[7]

Prompter William Hopkins in his *Diary* comments on the work:

This musical farce of one act was wrote by Mr. Garrick on purpose to introduce Miss Abrams, about seventeen years old. She is very small, a swarthy complexion, has a very sweet voice and a fine shake, but not quite power enough yet—both the piece and the young lady were received with great applause.[8]

It must be remembered that the fifteen years that separated the *Enchanter* from *May Day* saw the fundamental change in musical style, the passage from baroque to classical, even in England. In London the older Italian opera and Handelian practice had been pushed into the background in favor of *opera buffa* and the world of Mozart and Haydn.

Dr. Thomas Augustine Arne (1710-1778) falls between these two worlds and his music partakes of both. He was the one composer of originality and talent in mideighteenth century London who was native English. Although writing an enormous amount of stage music from 1733 to 1755, which included "Rule Britannia" in the *Masque of Alfred,* and those fine Shakespearian songs: "Blow, blow thou Winter wind," "Under the greenwood tree," "When daisies pied," to say nothing of a number of Italian operas and English oratorios, he never really fulfilled his early promise as the English composer who would vanquish the foreigners. Perhaps this disappointment was due to a defect of character. Samuel Johnson said of Arne: "Sir, the man's a fop, a rake, and there's an end on't." Fanny Burney, whose father Charles, had served an apprenticeship under Arne as a young man, put it more delicately but still unmistakably: "he took pride . . . in being publicly classed as a man of pleasure." Nonetheless, Garrick recognized Arne's talent and kept him on as a house composer at Drury Lane for fifteen years (1745-1760) and later had him write music on commission — a tribute to Garrick's diplomatic skill and Arne's musical ability. Their correspondence details a vivid account of musical activity at the theatre, including the sometimes stormy relations between the two men.

The cast of *May Day* was composed mostly of actors and actresses able to sing. Chief among them was Thomas Weston, the best comic in Garrick's company, who played Dozey, the town clerk. The funniest scene in the farce is one between Dozey and Furrow, the old farmer, where the latter is trying to get a marriage license. Arne took the music assignment quite seriously, at least in the overture, which is scored for flutes, oboes, and strings. It has an embryonic sonata form and shows quite clearly the stylistic difference between *May Day*[9] and *The Enchanter.*

The three illustrative songs appended herewith are very engaging. The first "Spread thy green mantle," is a lovely personification of Spring, with lots of pastoral echoes from the woodwinds in imitation of the voice, and a melting series of seventh chords that give distinctive flavor to the beginning, middle, and end of the song. The second "Young maids and young swains," introduces the operetta element (Gilbert and Sullivan if you like) in the form of a ballad with verses and refrain. In the first verse, notice the word painting on "above" and "below," and also on "whisper,"

Selection 7

Overture to May Day

which gets a pianissimo echo in the strings. Dolly, William's sister, dresses up as an old Gipsy and pretends to be the little Gipsy's mother in the dialogue which just precedes the song:

Dolly: What, did you run away from me, you little baggage? Have I not warn'd you from wand'ring in the fields by yourself these wicked times?

Gipsy: Pray, mother don't be angry: the morning was so fine, the birds so charming, and the lads and lasses so merry, I could not stay at home, and I knew you'd come limping after.

Dolly: Hussy, hussy! Have I not told you, that when the kid wanders from its dam, the fox will have a breakfast. . . . I don't much like the company you are in — who is that young rake there?

William: One that hates kid, mother, and is only giving your daughter a little good advice.

Dolly: Indeed the young fellows of this age are not so rampant as they were in my days. Well my lads and lasses, who among you longs to know their fortunes under the sun? [They all gather round her.]

The final song is a duet for the two lovers — a rhapsodic effusion that is very moving, almost hymn-like. Aside from the usual strings, two bassoons join the male voice, giving a striking color to the ensemble. William sings the first stanza, Gipsy the second, and then they join together on the first stanza again for the ending.

The plot of this Afterpiece involves William's tricking his father, Old Furrow, a rich farmer, into agreeing upon the young man's choice of a bride. Complication occurs because Furrow himself has fallen in love with a little Gipsy, who, unbeknownst to him, is his own son William's beloved in disguise. To the little farm community in which the Furrows live Squire Goodwill has left a legacy of £100 to the first couple married annually on May Day. Furrow seeks the Gipsy and the bounty for himself. She coming from outside the Parish, and hence disguised lest she bring the wrath of the local girls upon herself, declares she will not marry until he first makes his son happy. Furrow agrees before witnesses to do so, asking William what he chooses. William to the old man's horror and dismay chooses the Gipsy to be his bride. Furrow cannot break his word, but can rage. The villagers dance round the Maypole laughing him out of his incipient anger, closing with a grand chorus:

> When the Heart is unkind
> With the frost of the Mind
> Benevolence melts it like May.

At a gathering during the action William's beloved (in collusion with old Dolly, a member of the community) tests her ingratiating powers (Scene II), appearing from copse, singing of Spring, agreeing to tell fortunes, and singling out William. Her song "O Spread the green mantle," displayed the charming voice of Harriet Abrams, a seventeen-year-old Jewess whom Garrick was introducing to the stage:

> O spread thy green mantle, sweet May, o'er the ground.
>   Drive the blasts of bleak Winter away.
> Let the birds sweetly carol, thy flowrets around
>   And let us with all Nature be gay.
>
> Let spleen, spite and envy, those clouds of the wind
>   Be dispersed by the sunshine of joy;
> The pleasures of Eden had bless'd human kind
>   Had no fiend enter'd there to destroy.
>
> As May with her sunshine can warm the cold earth,
>   Let each Fair with the season improve,
> Be the Widows restor'd from their mourning to mirth,
>   And let hard-hearted Maids yield to love.

In Spring's choicest treasures the Village be dress'd,
  Festive joy let the season impart;
When rapture mounts high and o'erflows from each breast,
  'Tis May, the sweet May of the heart.

Selection 8

To enable the Gipsy to take William aside, Dolly appears and takes over what she announces as "real" fortune telling. The Villagers were magnetized by Mrs. Wrighten's sweet voice and bantering song:

Selection 9

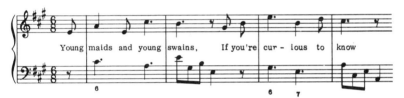

Young maids and young swains, if you're curious to know
What husbands you'll have, and what wives,
  From above I can know what you'll do here below,
  And what you have done all your lives.

        Don't blush and don't fear
        As I'm old I am wise
        And I read in your eyes —
        I must whisper the rest in your ears.

If you a false man, should betray a fond maid
I'll read what the stars have decreed;
  If you a fond maid, should be ever betray'd,
  You'll be sorry that page I should read.

        Don't blush . . .

If youth weds old age, tho' it wallow in gold
With sattins, and silks, and fine watch,
   Yet when for base gold, youth and beauty are sold,
   The Devil alone makes the match.

   Don't blush . . .

If an old man's so rash, to wed a young wife,
Or an old woman wed a young man;
   For such husband and wife I read danger and strife,
   For Nature detests such a plan.

   Don't blush . . .

Dolly then leads the villagers off as they join in the blushing chorus. William and his Gipsy come forward, singing a duet that not only tells their rapture but states their fears, and advances the plot:

Selection 10

Passion of the purest nature
   Glows within this faithful breast.
While I gaze on each lov'd feature,
   Love will let me know no rest.

Thus the ewe her lamb caressing
   Watches with a mother's fear,
While she eyes the little blessing
   Thinks the cruel wolf is near.

As the strains die away, Old Furrow's voice is heard off stage — "Where's the Gipsy?" *William:* "The wolf is near indeed!" Gipsy soon thereafter extracts the promise from Old Furrow to make his son happy.

Obviously this small selection of music provides only a taste of the whole. To get the proper effect, one would need the full orchestra in the theatre, with appropriate staging. Only then can one judge what the total spectacle was like and come to a fair appreciation of its dramatic value. This can be the task of both theatre historian and musicologist.

NOTES

1. Modern Language Association Revolving Fund Series No. VII (New York: M. L. A., 1938), pp. 119 and 154.

2. Text readily available in the Greg Reprint (Wemsted, 1969) of the *Dramatic Works of David Garrick Esq.* (London, 1768), vol. 2.

3. *Spectator* 29 (April 3, 1711).

4. Charles Burney, *A General History of Music,* rev. ed., with Critical and Historical notes by Frank Mercer, 2 vols. (New York: Dover, 1935), II, 1010.

5. See *The London Stage, 1660–1800* (Carbondale: Southern Illinois University Press, 1962), Part 4, for comment and performance records.

6. *The Enchanter,* a Musical Entertainment as it is performed at the Theatre Royal in Drury Lane, Composed by Mr. Smith (London, printed for J. Walsh, n.d.).

7. Printed for T. Becket (London, 1775).

8. *The London Stage, 1660–1800,* Part 4, III (1923).

9. The Score, *May Day, or the Little Gipsy,* with the Much Admired Overture and Dance tunes, Dispos'd for the Voice, Organ, Harpsichord, and Pianoforte . . . compos'd by Dr. Arne, was printed for Hodgson, Maiden Lane, Convent Garden (n.d.).

8. Garrick's Fail-Safe Musical Venture, *A Peep Behind the Curtain,* an English Burletta

Phyllis T. Dircks

Professor of English, Long Island University

Current scholarship is rapidly dispelling the view that David Garrick was not sensitive to the impact of music on his Drury Lane audiences during the twenty-nine years of his managerial tenure. Examination of the calendar of Garrick's plays demonstrates that Garrick had, from his earliest days as manager, an imaginative and intelligent view of music and a readiness to incorporate it into both the plays he produced and those he wrote whenever that music would heighten their theatrical value.

But despite his open-mindedness and theatrical cunning, sustained and varied success in writing wholly musical productions other than Christmas plays seemed to elude Garrick. His first immediate and enduring success in regular-season musical plays was *A Peep Behind the Curtain,* which he brought out on 23 October 1767 during the twenty-first year of his managerial tenure. In this play Garrick mounted a satiric dramatic framework, into which he set a play with music by François H. Barthelemon.

I wish to explore the background of the burletta form that Garrick used in *A Peep Behind the Curtain* and to examine Garrick's particular contribution in setting this form within a satiric play so as to make the burletta both the agent and object of the satire. Such an examination demonstrates Garrick's sophistication both as a practical theatre manager in limiting his financial risks and as a sensitive man of the theatre in perceiving audience tastes, and it, therefore, supports the view that Garrick's penetrating and comprehensive interest in music was an inevitable aspect of his overall theatrical acumen.

Garrick's burletta was similar to the burlettas that had been heard in London for almost twenty years and, significantly, had captivated Covent Garden audiences during the 1753-1754 season. In a display of business skill, John Rich had engaged a small opera company headed by Carmine Giordani to present four comic operas in Italian that year. According to Burney, serious opera had been "languishing in poverty and disgrace" since the last appearance of Monticelli in 1746, and considerable interest attended the expected arrival of Abate Francesco Vaneschi, who was to reintroduce serious opera at the King's Theatre in November.[1] But Rich's slate comprised the only Italian comic opera presented in that 1753-1754 season and, although only the first production, *Gli Amanti Gelosi* (17 December), was truly successful, the audience sustained sufficient interest in the form to allow for three additional productions: Giovanbattista Pergolesi's *Lo Studente a la Moda* (18 January); Leonardo Leo's *L'Amour Costante* (11 February); and Balthazar Galuppi's *La Cameriera Accorta* (4 March). In all they staged ten performances and won the enthusiasm of the playhouse audience, mostly on the strength of the high-spirited satirical and farcical acting of Giordani's daughter, Nicolina, who became so fully identified with the role of Spiletta in *Gli Amanti Gelosi* that she afterward was universally known by that name.[2]

Dr. Burney felt obliged to say that "the Music of this burletta, by Cocchi, was not of the first class," yet he, too, was charmed by Nicolina, and wrote of her being frequently encored two or three times in the same air, "which she was able to vary so much by her singing and acting, that it appeared at every repetition, a new song, and she another performer."[3] Horace Walpole, in writing to Horace Mann, was also enthusiastic about Nicolina Giordani: "There are no less than five operas every week, three of which are burlettas: a very bad company, except the Niccolina, who beats all the actors and actresses I ever saw for vivacity and variety." Walpole, in addition, notes how beneficial it was for the burlettas to be staged at the patent theatre, rather than at the King's Theatre: "These [burlettas] being at the playhouse, and at play prices, the people instead of resenting it, as was expected, are transported with them, call them their own operas, and I will not swear that they do not take them for English operas."[4]

The current popularity of the burletta form was exploited by

Garrick in preparing his musical play, *A Peep Behind the Curtain*. Sure that his Drury Lane audience would respond to the satire and broad comedy of the burletta, Garrick may still have been uncertain what the effect of the music would be. He decided, therefore, to write a burletta, and, then, by encasing it in a satirical play, to create a uniquely effective fail-safe device. The resultant play, *A Peep Behind the Curtain,* became a substantial theatrical success.

The public flocked to see the play, the only musical production newly brought out in Drury Lane that year, and it was acted twenty-three times during its first season. It remained a favorite piece for many years. *A Peep* may well have given Garrick particular satisfaction because it was his first venture in writing musical plays, other than Christmas pieces, and because it represented the climax of an almost twenty-year flirtation with the type of musical production that had come to be known as the burletta.

The term "burletta" originally came into the consciousness of the English theatregoing public through a production of Rinaldo da Capua's *La Comedia in Comedia* at the King's Opera House on 8 November 1748. Advertised as "a Burletta or Comic Opera . . . being the first of this species ever exhibited in England,"[5] *La Comedia* had been so well received that it launched a whole season of full-length comic operas. Prior to its appearance, the only Italian comic operas that Londoners had enjoyed were four intermezzi, performed as interval music between the acts of serious opera by the renowned Carlo Farinelli for the Nobility Opera Company during the 1736 season.

The receptive London audience of 1748 encouraged Lorenzo V. Ciampi's talented group of young comic singers to perform other comic operas in the same vein and they responded with performances of Pietro Auletta's *Orazio* and Signor Ciampi's own *Li Tre Cicisbei Ridicoli.* All of their plays were described as burlettas and all were characterized by low comedy, much physical movement, and lighthearted music in the brisk *style galant.* Burney complained that "this species of composition was now so new and the acting of Pertici and Laschi, so excellent, and so fully engaged the attention that critics had little leisure left for a severe examination of the Music."[6] Garrick, newly settled as manager of Drury Lane, undoubtedly watched the new troupe with interest; Walpole quotes him as describing Pertici, the leading comedian, as "the best comedian" he ever saw.[7]

Garrick, who was perhaps the shrewdest analyst of the tastes of the playhouse audience of his day, perceived the theatrical possibilities of the burletta during its early exposure in England. He knew that, from medieval times on, the English playhouse audience had relished music in the theatre, particularly in comedy. The songs of the shepherds in *The Second Shepherds' Play*; the abundant songs in the text of Udall's *Roister Doister*; the numerous songs, as well as the references to music and musical matters, in thirty-two of thirty-seven Shakespearean plays; and, finally, the activities of the leading Restoration composers, Purcell and Eccles, in composing theatrical music, all demonstrate the English enthusiasm for music in the playhouse. It was predictable, therefore, that the eighteenth-century English theatregoing audience would, in the same tradition, respond favorably to the new burlettas in which light music energized simple and amusing plots.

Serious Italian opera, however, the darling of the aristocrats since its initial English appearance, had never captured the enthusiasm of the devotees of the playhouse. Colley Cibber explained, "the Opera is not a Plant of our Native Growth, nor what our plainer appetites are fond of, and is of so delicate a Nature, that without excessive Charge, it cannot live long among us."[8] In addition to its exoticism, most middle-class English theatregoers found the complicated plot structure of Italian opera, sung in a foreign language, a barrier to the enjoyment of the music. Moreover, English composers and librettists seemed unable to adapt the weighty Italian style to native subjects and purposes.[9] Finally, the English audience, strongly supportive of its own fine tradition of spoken drama, highly developed in the time of Shakespeare and Jonson and strongly revived after the Restoration, did not respond favorably to the use of recitative to carry the dramatic burden of serious drama.[10]

The Italian burletta, in contrast, appealed to English audiences because it combined the strengths of its musical predecessors and contemporaries and, at the same time, simplified the musical-dramatic experience. It satisfied the same love for sophisticated original music as did previous opera; but, in place of the solemn dignified music of earlier opera, it used lively melodies. Like the ballad opera the Italian burletta presented low comedy or farce that could be appreciated by all, despite the fact that it was sung in Italian.

Examination of the plots of some of the most popular Italian burlettas illustrates their dependence upon standard comic situations and, by implication, their ready intelligibility to an audience not versed in the language of the performance. *La Comedia in Comedia* (1748) is constructed on the play-within-a-play device. The noble and beautiful young Lucinda loves and is loved by the humble Celindo, but each of her parents has selected another suitor for her. Lucinda and Celindo, therefore, under the guise of presenting a comedy for the entertainment of her father, court one another, while he watches in delight. Soon, word is received that Celindo is the only son of a Bolognese senator and the final chorus sings of the now-appropriate approaching nuptials. The comedy of *Il Maestro di Musica* (1753), however, arises from the interaction of familiar comic types: Lamberto, the egotistical, driving music master; Lauretta, the talented, independent and virtuous young student; and Colajanni, the lascivious older man. Each of the men pursues Lauretta, who manages to evade them gracefully. Pergolesi's *Lo Studente a la Moda* (1754), one of the burlettas Rich brought to Covent Garden, is energized by yet another standard comic element, the machinations of the wily servant, Giuletta. Her chicanery allows the lovers, Odoardo and Violante, to marry, despite the many objections of other characters.

In short the Italian burletta refined the plot to a single simple jest or humorous incident (Italian, *burla*) that was cleverly elaborated upon through visual and musical communication. This assured that the English audience would understand at least the main outlines of the Italian comedy. Moreover, the Italian burletta used the recitative to achieve obvious comic effects of exaggeration and ridicule, rather than for serious dramatic purposes, as the Italian *opera seria* had. Finally, as the burletta form developed, the performers frequently exploited elements of bawdy comedy and prided themselves on a characteristic gusto of burlesque performance.[11]

Kitty Clive captured the gusto of burletta performance in a light comedy, *The Rehearsal: or Bayes in Petticoats,* which she wrote for her own benefit night at Drury Lane on 15 March 1750. Garrick had played Hamlet that evening in the mainpiece. In the role of Mrs. Hazard, the author of a burletta that is about to go into rehearsal, Kitty Clive rendered in recitative one of her most effective lines: "Oh if that dear Garrick cou'd but sing." When she is asked what a burletta is, Mrs. Hazard, that is, Mrs. Clive, replies, to the delight of the audience: "I believe it is a kind of poor relation to an Opera."

Garrick kept a shrewd watch on that poor relation as he attempted to maintain a balance between elevating the level of dramatic production at Drury Lane and responding to the demands of public taste. Alert to the drawing power of musical productions at other theatres, Garrick found it increasingly difficult to fasten himself exclusively to tragedy and farce. During the decade of the 1750s, as he noted the growing popularity of the Italian burlettas and other musical pieces, he became increasingly receptive to musical entertainments. In 1759, in the wake of a run of successful burletta productions at Marylebone and at the Haymarket by Reinhold and Seratina, two popular burletta singers, Garrick engaged the two to sing *The Tutor*, a burletta translated into English from the Italian, with music by Johann Hasse. The burletta failed, having only one performance, and Garrick suffered a professional defeat.[12]

The concept of a truly English burletta was not a viable one until Kane O'Hara wrote a successful musical play, *Midas*, in 1764. In subtitling his play, "an English Burletta," O'Hara made it clear that he was extracting the musical essence of the Italian burletta. He then seasoned it with the flavor of the French post-Renaissance tradition of burlesque literature and thereby created a form quite distinct from the Italian burletta.

The age of burlesque literature had been initiated in France with the publication of Paul Scarron's *Le Virgile Travesti* (1648), a lengthy poem that mocked the gods, goddesses, and heroes of antiquity by reducing them to contemporary types and placing them in ludicrous situations. Burlesque of the classics soon went on stage in the plays of the *Comédie Italiènne* in Paris and appeared also in the *Théâtres de la Foire* at St. Germain and St. Laurent, where the burlesque tradition strengthened and was strengthened by the developing *comédie en vaudevilles*.[13]

In addition to incorporating the French burlesque spirit, O'Hara, in creating a specifically English burletta, had used the nuances and inflections of the English language, had employed recognizable English type characters, had reset a host of English and Irish ballads and airs, and had exploited a particularly British form of humor. O'Hara's 1764 English burletta production of *Midas* was a reworking of his original 1762 Dublin production, which had been brought out as a chauvinistic response to the Italian burlettas that were enjoying great success at Smock Alley and were luring patrons away from the Viceregent's favorite theatre at Crow Street. It is instructive to note that the quality of the language in the 1764 London production is markedly different from that in the original Dublin production; the language in the second production is directed specifically to the tastes of a relatively refined London audience. The idiom of the Irish *Midas* may be characterized as bold, concrete, and earthy, with a propitious use of slang, whereas the language of the London production is considerably more genteel. Even in making this relatively minor change in environment, from Dublin to London, O'Hara was aware of the need to attune his language to the ears of his playhouse audience. He had also rejected the crudities of language that had appeared in English translations of Italian burlettas, indicating his intention in the sprightly deprecation that appears in the Irish *Midas*: "Foh upon Cetras Italian!" (III.ii.19).

In characterization, also, O'Hara had employed an English conception. Midas, the rural English Justice of the Peace; Damaetas, his dull-witted clerk; Silenus, the kindly shepherd, and Pol, the brash and handsome bucolic depiction of Apollo, are closer to the humorous English pastoral tradition, which dated back to the Renaissance, and which was becoming increasingly popular, than to the characters of the Italian burletta, who were essentially derived from the *Commedia dell'Arte* tradition.[14] Addison had given a thoroughly English stamp of approval to the comic use of mythology, defending its use in mock-heroic poems as "not only excusable but graceful."[15]

Moreover, O'Hara's choice of music for *Midas* was also distinctively English. He included airs that had been used in popular plays and pantomimes, well-known tunes and contemporary songs that had become popular at the minor theatres and public gardens, and a number of original compositions, allowing the music itself to figure in the satire, as, for example, in setting two of Burney's pieces from his Queen Mab pantomime to mocking words in the Finale. Moreover, as W. J. Lawrence has noted,

O'Hara, in his frequent reliance on concerted music at the end of the acts in *Midas* and at key dramatic points in the play, helped bridge the gap between ballad opera and the late-century English comic opera.[16]

In addition to identifying the language, characterization, and music of *Midas* as essentially English, O'Hara had, significantly, retained the hallmarks of the original Italian burletta: the simplified plot, the focusing on the single jest or burla, Midas's faulty judgment in the singing contest between Pan and Apollo; the use of the rhymed recitative for comic purposes; and the generous use of brisk galant music. O'Hara had succeeded in grafting the virtues of the English manner onto the Italian form to create a successful English burletta. Indeed, *Midas* was destined to become one of the favorite afterpieces on the eighteenth-century English stage and was performed 226 times by the end of the century.

Some response by Garrick to the overwhelming popularity of *Midas* at Covent Garden was inevitable. His reaction was characteristically clever and shrewd. He conceived of a burletta which would itself be the butt of the joke. He commissioned François Barthelemon, a musician of some distinction, to compose a burletta fragment for him, and then inserted this burletta fragment, called *Orpheus,* into a rehearsal-type farce as the second act of *A Peep Behind the Curtain.* In this way, Garrick's audience heard and enjoyed popular burletta music, while they heartily laughed at the burletta situation.

For the mythological hero of his burletta, Garrick chose Orpheus, a figure well-known to both the operatic and the playhouse stages. The tale of Orpheus returning to Hades for his beloved Eurydice had been a favorite on the operatic stage since Monteverdi's 1607 production of *Orpheus* at Mantua. The legend, moreover, had been given new importance for music lovers through the revolutionary 1762 production of Gluck's *Orfeo ed Euridice* in Vienna. To the English theatre audience, Orpheus was familiar through productions of masques and pantomimes since the beginning of the century. Henry Fielding, for example, had burlesqued the story in two of his plays, *Eurydice* (1737) and *Eurydice Hiss'd* (1737). Anxious to exploit the comic possibilities of the situation in true burletta fashion,

Garrick absorbed the flavor of Fielding's *Eurydice*. Like Fielding, Garrick set his play within the rehearsal framework, which had long been a favorite device for topical comedy, in particular for comedy dealing with theatrical performance itself. Most important to the Drury Lane audience, however, was the fact that Garrick had achieved one of his greatest successes as an actor in playing Bayes in Buckingham's *Rehearsal* and was readily identified in the public mind with that role. One factor in Garrick's popularity in the part was his skill in using it as a vehicle for imitating the idiosyncrasies of his fellow actors.[17] Although Garrick himself did not play in *A Peep Behind the Curtain*, he imbued the play with the spirit of his earlier success, *The Rehearsal*, and incorporated in it the same devices. *A Peep* contains some sharp and amusing sallies against the veteran actor, Thomas King, against the popular Kitty Clive, and against himself. The play is peopled with a number of recognizable lesser characters from the world of Drury Lane: Saunders, the carpenter; Hopkins, the prompter; Johnson, the housekeeper; and the women sweepers, all of whom simulate the activities of the theatre during the early morning hours. Garrick echoed his earlier success, therefore, when he titled his new play: *A Peep Behind the Curtain, or The New Rehearsal*.

The character most interested in the rehearsal in Garrick's farce is Glib, author of a burletta, who has invited guests, Sir Toby Fuz and Lady Fuz, with their ingenuous daughter, Fanny Fuz, and Sir Macaroni Virtu, to attend a rehearsal of the first act of his new burletta, *Orpheus*. During the performance, Miss Fuz runs off with her lover, Wilson, according to their prearranged plan. Her mother's discovery of this fact causes the entire party to leave and brings all action to a halt as the author, Glib, tries to explain his intention in an Epilogue.

As the burletta *Orpheus*, which is the second act of the play, begins, Orpheus awakens from sleep with a compulsive urge to rescue Eurydice from Hades, but is discomfited by the angry screaming of his now-to-be-jilted mistress, Rhodope. His only control over her lies in his magical lyre, which he plays to put her to sleep. Orpheus and Rhodope render a drowsy duet in accompaniment to the lyre. As he leaves, Orpheus intones in recitative:

> Behold what's seldom seen in life,
> I leave my mistress for my wife.

In passing through the countryside on his way to the underworld, Orpheus meets an irascible old shepherd, curiously like the old shepherd of O'Hara's *Midas*. Soon, he, together with the other shepherds, and the sheep, cows, and goats, are dancing to the music of Orpheus' strings, and are led offstage by Orpheus in a grand chorus of singing and dancing. Thus ends the first act of the author's burletta.

Glib explains that Orpheus will, in the second act, enter into a wife-swapping episode with Pluto and the play will end with a resounding chorus of "Exchange is no robbery." Through Glib, Garrick emphasizes the contemporaneous aspect of the play as the author explains to the manager, Patent: "I make Orpheus see in my hell all sorts of people, of all degrees, and occupations — say, and of both sexes — that's not very unnatural, I believe — there shall be very good company too, I assure."

The success of *A Peep Behind the Curtain* and of the burletta, *Orpheus,* in particular, was a considerable triumph for Garrick. By this time, 1767, Garrick's experience with music on stage was abundant and varied. As a student of Shakespeare, he had attempted to restore music to the place it had held in the original Globe productions. As manager of Drury Lane, he had for some time recognized the effectiveness of music to heighten atmosphere, to deepen characterization, and to develop themes. As a playwright of substantial talent himself, he had interpolated songs in works such as *Lethe* and *Lilliput* to help convey his satiric statement. In Christmas plays, such as *The Enchanter* and *Cymon,* he had used music lavishly as part of the exotic, fanciful, spectacular fabric of the play. What is notable in *A Peep Behind the Curtain,* however, is that this was the first time that Garrick had used music in a substantive way to function as an agent of satire. Clearly, what Garrick had derived from his acquaintance with the burletta of the 1760s was the proper form to enable him to use music as a functional rather than a decorative element in his plays.

NOTES

1. Charles Burney, *A General History of Music* (rev. ed., New York: Dover, 1935; rpt. New York: Dover, 1957), II, 852.

2. Arthur Murphy wrote that Spiletta "has such a quick Expression of

Humour in her Countenance, such a Vivacity of Action, joined to such Variety, that she is allowed, in this fantastic Part of Acting, to be an excellent Performer." (*The Gray's Inn Journal*, No. 64 [5 January 1754], p. 66). Her acting was also praised in *The Tatler:* "Her Action is inimitable, and so well adapted to the Part she performs, that I am certain, had Demosthenes been present, he would have agreed with me in this, viz. That with the Assistance of Learning, she would form the most excellent and powerful Orator that ever appear'd in this World" (no. 1, 20 December 1753).

3. Burney, II, 852.

4. 28 January 1754.

5. *Daily Advertiser*, 8 November 1748.

6. Burney, II, 848.

7. Walpole, *Correspondence with Sir Horace Mann*, W. S. Lewis, et al. eds. (New Haven: Yale University Press, 1958–1971), IV, 357.

8. Colley Cibber, *An Apology for the Life of Colley Cibber*, ed. with an Introduction, by B. R. S. Fone (Ann Arbor: University of Michigan Press, 1968), p. 210.

9. The effort to adapt the Italian style peaked in 1732 and 1733, with the composition of seven wholly English operas: Carey's *Amelia*, music by Lampe (1732); Lediard's *Brittania*, music by Lampe (1732); Carey's *Teraminta*, music by Smith (1732); Gay's *Dione*, music by Lampe (1733); Addison's *Rosamond*, music by Arne (1733); Humphrey's *Ulysses*, music by Smith (1733); Fielding's *The Opera of Operas*, music by Arne (1733). The seven productions were received without enthusiasm, and attained only 42 performances within a fifteen-month period. In addition, English playwright Aaron Hill made the following appeal to Handel on 5 December 1732, attempting to enlist his aid: "My meaning is, that you would be resolute enough, to deliver us from our Italian bondage; and demonstrate, that English is soft enough for Opera, when compos'd by poets, who know to distinguish the sweetness of our tongue, from the strength of it, where the last is less necessary." Quoted in Otto E. Deutsch, *Handel: A Documentary Biography* (New York: Norton, 1954), p. 299. There is no record of Handel's having responded to this appeal. After the failures of this period, there were only sporadic attempts to write wholly English operas.

10. The recitative or sung dialogue of Italian opera was probably the single most irritating aspect of Italian opera to the average Englishman and remained the object of complaint and criticism for many years. For representative comments, see John Dennis, *An Essay on the Operas after the Italian Manner, which are about to be Establish'd on the English Stage: with some Reflections on the damage they may bring to the publick* (London: J. Nutt, 1706); and J. Lockman, *Rosalinda, a musical drama . . . To which is prefixed, An Enquiry into the Rise and Progress of Operas and Oratorios, with Some Reflections on Lyric Poetry and Music* (London: W. Strahan, 1740). Even George Hogarth, who is sympathetic to the problem, complains that "in listening to the dialogue of *Artaxerxes*, the actors all appear to be Italians, speaking broken English (*Memoirs of the Musical Drama* [London: R. Bentley, 1838]).

11. Dr. Paul Hifferman pointed out the necessity of exaggerated acting to the burletta: "Some over-nice Critics, forgetting, or not knowing the Meaning of the

Word Burletta, cry that her Manner is *outré*. Would she not be faulty were it otherwise? The thing chargeable to her is (perhaps) too great a Luxuriance of comic Tricks; which (an austere Censor wou'd say) border on unlaced Lasciviousness, and an extravagant Petulance of Action" (*The Tuner*, no. 1 [London: M. Cooper, 1754], p. 17).

12. The failure of *The Tutor* was a considerable disappointment for both Reinhold, who was known as a fine bass, and Seratina, who had been described as "in no way inferior to the famous Spiletta" (*Public Advertiser*, 12–13 June 1758), as well as for Garrick. There is little information on the performance, Cross having noted simply in his Diary, "Burletta damn'd." The burletta was not printed; see Larpent MS 165.

13. Authoritative histories of this period are: Maurice Albert, *Les Théâtres de la foire* (1660–1789), (Paris: Hachette, 1900); Francis J. Carmody, *Le Repertoire de l'opera-comique en vaudevilles de 1708 a 1764* (Berkeley: University of California Press, 1933); and Felix Gaiffe, *Le Drama en France au XVIII siecle* (Paris: A. Colin, 1910). Representative anthologies are: Evaristo Gherardi, *Le Théâtre italien de Gherardi*, 6 vols. (Paris: Cusson et Witte, 1700); and A. R. Le Sage and D'Ornaval, *Le Théâtre de la foire. ou L'Opera-comique*, 9 vols. (Paris: E. Ganeau, 1731–1737).

14. See Winifred Smith, *The Commedia dell' Arte* (New York: Columbia University Press, 1964); and Pièrre Louis Duchartre, *The Italian Comedy* (London: Harrap, 1929; rpt. New York: John Day, 1966).

15. *Spectator* #523.

16. "Early Irish Ballad Opera and Comic Opera," *The Musical Quarterly*, VIII (July 1922), 407.

17. Arthur Murphy, *The Life of David Garrick, Esq.* (London: J. Wright, 1801; rpt. New York, 1969), I, 53–56.

9. Barthelemon's Setting of Garrick's *Orpheus*

Stoddard Lincoln
Professor of Music, Brooklyn College

Before focusing on Barthelemon and his setting of Garrick's burletta, *Orpheus,* I want to stress the fact that eighteenth-century London was, musically, undoubtedly the most cosmopolitan capital of the world. Although this internationalism can be traced back to the Renaissance, for our purposes we must recognize and evaluate it from the end of the seventeenth century.

Charles II openly showed a preference for French music, especially dance music. This style was easily absorbed and Anglicized by a group of fine composers which culminated in the genius of Henry Purcell. During the last years of his life, the first Italian singers arrived and stunned London audiences with their music and manner of singing. This was inevitably followed by the advent of Italian opera, first in the form of pastiches made up from grab bags of Italian arias which were strung together by recitatives and delivered in bad English translations. Then came operas by single composers sung in Italian, and finally the arrival of Handel. This event, in turn, led to the importation of more Italian singers to perform his works and Italian composers to compete with him. Besides Italian singers and composers, first-rate Italian instrumentalists came to London to make a fortune off of one of the first societies that put music on a commercial basis. Although the Italian influence was certainly the strongest during the eighteenth century, we cannot readily ignore the Germanic influence, especially that of instrumental music.

Now, studies of English music have, until recently, mostly ignored the foreigners and dwelt heavily and almost exclusively on native English composers. This trend, of course, has produced a somewhat lopsided picture that tries to present a purely native

148

school of English music. There are those scholars, however, who put all the emphasis on the foreign influences and ignore the fact that there was a native English school, however modest. The truth lies somewhere between these two views: There was a native English school which coexisted with various foreign schools. But the various styles intermingled in many curious ways and at times produced a musical language that could have been only the product of such a cosmopolitan center as London. Thus a composer in England could and did write in many styles or mixtures thereof. The point is, however, that no composer wrote simply in his own style as a matter of personal choice; he wrote in the style appropriate to the genre in which he was working. If a composer wished to be faithful to the Italian style, he wrote *opera seria*. If he wished to write in an Italo-Germanic style, he wrote concerti grossi and sonatas. If he wished to write English melody tempered with Italian grace, he wrote incidental theatre songs. If he wished to be purely English, he turned to the ballad opera or to pantomime. If he wished to write a little something in each style, the burletta was his medium. Thus there was a place in the English musical landscape for every known style of music. Some composers specialized in one particular style, other composers moved easily from one style to another. The bothersome factor in studying the music of eighteenth-century England is this stylistic ambivalence. I believe that an understanding of the problem will only be reached by study of the various genres and their stylistic characters. It is also my fond hope that this present study of Barthelemon's music for Garrick's burletta will shed some light on this complex situation and eventually lead to a more complete study of the materials at hand than we have at the moment.

François Hippolyte Barthelemon is the perfect example of an international musician who came to London to make his fortune and who also contributed substantially to the well-being of English music. He is also the perfect example of a composer who is neglected by scholars in the country of his birth, France, because he worked mostly in England, and who is also neglected by the English because of his French birth.

Barthelemon's birth in Bordeaux, 27 July 1741, is well documented. As for the occupation of his father, we are given three choices: he was either a wig-maker, a French officer, or a cellist. It is agreed that his mother was Irish. Two choices are offered for the first years of his maturity: he was either an officer in the Irish

Brigade, or a French officer stationed in Paris. In any event, he received his musical training in Paris and was a violinist in the orchestra of the *Comédie Italiènne* in 1764. That same year, the Earl of Kelly, an English patron of music and an amateur composer, pointed out to Barthelemon the advantages of furthering his career in London rather than in Paris. Following his sound advice, Barthelemon came to London and made his debut as a violinist on the same program that presented the Mozart prodigies to that city. The following year he appeared in the famous Hickford's Room concert which again featured the Mozarts. Barthelemon arrived in good if not overwhelming company — for Mozart and his sister were then but gifted children. Certainly these events plus what was to follow demonstrate London's cosmopolitan makeup. Because of his gifts as a violinist, Barthelemon soon became the leader of the Covent Garden orchestra. In this milieu it was only natural that Barthelemon's first musical offering to London would be a serious Italian opera, *Pelopida*, which received its premiere in May of 1766. Later the same year he made an excellent marriage, at least from the viewpoint of an aspiring musician in London. His bride was Miss Mary (or Polly) Young, a niece of the famous singer Mrs. Thomas Arne.

Garrick, always on the lookout for good composers, was so impressed by this opera that he sought out the composer in order to see if he could set English. The story goes that Garrick, in order to test this important requirement, wrote out a lyric for him. As he did so, Barthelemon stood over his shoulder and set it as the words flowed from the master's pen. Garrick then handed the young Frenchman the verses saying, "there, sir, is my song." The young Frenchman immediately responded, "there, sir, is my music to it." Barthelemon had obviously learned English well from his mother.

Garrick introduced the song into *The Country Girl*.[1] Encored every night, it was an overwhelming success. Garrick, recognizing a good thing when he saw it, or rather heard it, immediately commissioned Barthelemon to set his burletta, *Orpheus,* to music.

Although we are primarily interested in Barthelemon at this early stage of his career, it is well to note that *Orpheus* was no single musical venture for him. Barthelemon continued composing for the theatre in both England and France and also continued his concert career throughout the Isles and on the Continent. Besides his dramatic music, he also produced an impressive amount of chamber music.

In order to understand English theater music, it is important to be familiar with the forces employed. Despite the fact that *Orpheus* was published in short score,[2] enough verbal indications appear in it to show what the orchestration was. The basic orchestra was, of course, string and continuo. As for woodwinds, the composer calls for two each of oboes, flutes, and bassoons. The brass section seems to have consisted of a pair of horns. There are no indications for trumpets or percussion. This, for its period, was a full complement, not a pared down orchestra designed to save money and space. London was not yet plagued by unions.

As for singers, Barthelemon had the best Drury Lane could offer. The part of Orpheus was sung by Joseph Vernon, a fine actor who, upon occasion, sang expressively if not with a somewhat rasping voice. In 1763 the tenor Lowe had left Drury Lane. Vernon, pushed into his place, found himself singing operatic roles. Thus when Barthelemon wrote for him, he was not only a fine actor, but also a fully seasoned tenor capable of negotiating any style of music set before him.

The part of Rhodope was conceived for Mrs. Arne (not the composer's wife, but rather Miss Elizabeth Wright who had just at the age of fifteen or sixteen married the composer's natural son, Michael). Her death, two years after the production of *Orpheus,* was a much lamented loss to the English musical stage.

James William Dodd, who played the old shepherd, was primarily a comic actor who could also turn out a song and gracefully move through a dance. He was in the tradition of his famous predecessor, Thomas Dogget.

Barthelemon, like any composer of his day, knew his singers' capabilities intimately. Vocally, the most taxing role he gave to Mrs. Arne. Her first aria requires a fine legato, and her final one is a vengeance aria filled with extended coloratura, and frightening leaps. It thinks nothing of shooting up to high B's (see example 5). Vernon's part, although the longest, is not as difficult as Mrs. Arne's, but it does include styles that range from ballad opera to high operatic style. Dodd's part is limited to the ballad opera style.

Close attention to the music of the burletta shows just what was expected of this young, budding composer. In his paper in this series Professor Knapp has explained that the Handelian style did not die with its creator but outlived him by many years.[3] At the same time, though, the newer *style galant* had found its way to England (we must remember that John Christian Bach and Carl Frederick Abel came to London only a few years before Barthelemon) and had taken firm root beside the already flourishing Baroque style of Handel. Barthelemon was essentially a proponent of the *style galant,* but one must recall that his background was unusually broad, ranging, as it did, from French opera to Italian opera. It also included much of the English taste because of his Covent Garden years. As the libretto of the burletta spoofs classical mythology, so the music pokes fun at every genre. It ranges in its musical language from the popular ballad type of music to the most high-flown flights of the *opera seria.* Barthelemon had the equipment to turn from one style to another effortlessly and this is exactly what appears in the first part of his setting of *Orpheus.*

Before one hears the music, it is well to note the various styles in the order in which they appear. First the overture: Although the English remained faithful to the Handelian concept of the French overture long after it had fallen out of fashion on the Continent, the Italian sinfonia had been heard in London. Barthelemon opts for this more novel form and begins the work with a bright, three movement sinfonia. The second movement, however, is in the style of a Scotch air. Scotch airs had been popular in London since the Restoration, and J. C. Bach was not above introducing them in his piano concertos.

The last movement is unusual because of its final cadence. The typical ending of a sinfonia is usually loud and brilliant. Barthelemon ends his so, but then he tacks on this curious little passage.

This ending is obviously designed to set the mood for what is to follow, that is, Orpheus sleeping. This matching of music to mood is very forward-looking in an age when the overture was ceremonial and rarely related itself to the action of the opera.

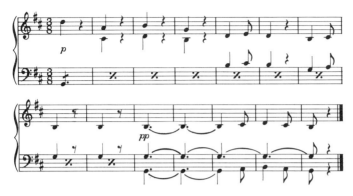

Orpheus's first utterances take the form of an accompanied recitative in which the orchestra vividly describes each word of the text. In *opera seria* accompanied recitative is reserved for moments of high passion in which the composer wished to express the meaning of the text more than the usual *recitativo secco* allowed him to do. It is ludicrous here because of the text and its references to thumping and scratching.

Rather than continuing with a serious aria, as one would expect after an accompanied recitative, Orpheus launches into a ballad opera style that requires perfect diction in order to get the words out so rapidly. It is the forerunner of the patter song.

The plot is now carried forward in *recitativo secco,* which musically is on a par with that heard in the *opera seria.* But the witty text with its saucy rhymes turns this high-flown style into farce. Rhodope's first air is serious and lyric. It could easily find a place in a French play intermingled with arriettas. Orpheus immediately picks up the first phrase of this air and turns it into a mockery. Now Rhodope turns to the sentimental weeping style of the ballad opera in order to seduce her lover back.

When Or - pheus you was kind and true, Of joy, of joy I had my fill

Having no luck with this, she lashes out into a full-fledged vengeance aria, which would have stopped the show with its pyrotechnics in an Italian opera at Covent Garden.

I would rat - - - - - - - - - - - - - - - - - - tle and there would give you bat - tle like the thun-der I would rat-tle, I would rat - - - - - - - - - - - - - - - - - tle, I would rat - - - - - - - - - tle.

Orpheus replies in an operatic style, but the text of the second section is so absurd that again the result is farce. The next number is a duet that is unusual because of its lack of an instrumental introduction and its through-composed form. If we did not know the words, we would think it is a forerunner of Mozart in *The Magic Flute,* but Orpheus's nonsense syllable imitation of a lute:

Rodope

My eyes be-gin to twin - kle, my tongue has lost its

Orpheus

tin - kle tin - kle tin - kle tin - kle

Continuo

twang.   My hands   din - gle,   my eyes   twin - kle,

tang tang tang tang   tang tang tang   tin - kle tin - kle

and Rhodope's grotesque manner of becoming paralyzed into sleep (complete with rests for yawns and unladylike snoring over-exaggerated Neapolitan harmonies) again reveals the musical means of achieving farce in the burletta.

Orpheus, now freed from his harlot, gives us a reprise of his first tune as he leaves for Hell to pick up his wife.

Our musical example must end here, but in the remainder of the work even more styles are introduced. There is a ballet for the beasts. Orpheus sings a beautiful love song about Eurydice. When the old shepherd enters, the style changes to that of *opera buffa* and then into folk song. The work ends with a contagious vaudeville, a genre imported from France some fifteen years before *Orpheus*.

The musical thrust of the burletta, then, is achieved by the juxtaposition of serious musical genres and the expectations they arouse and comic words that deflate such expectancies. At times the music is absolutely serious when taken without its text. At other times, however, certain mannerisms of the genre being aped are deliberately exaggerated. Musically the burletta is a sampler of styles; there is something in it to satisfy everyone's taste. No wonder it became so popular with London audiences. The plot of *A Peep Behind the Curtain*, of which the *Orpheus* is a central episode, has been discussed in detail by Professor Dircks.[4] The songs that follow, for which brief introductory bars of music have been given, spell out the story of *Orpheus*.

Orpheus: A Burletta

Orpheus: I come — I go — I must — I will [Half awake]
Bless me! Where am I? Here I'm still [Quite awakened]
Tho' dead she haunts me still, my wife!
In death my torment, as in life;
By day, by night whene'er she catches
Poor me asleep, she stamps and scratches;
No more she cries with harlot's revel,
But fetch me Orpheus from the Devil.

Tho' she scolded all day, and all night did the same,
Tho' she was too rampant, and I was too tame;
Tho' shriller her notes than the ear-piercing fife,
I must and I will go to hell for my wife.

As the sailor can't rest, if the winds are too still,
As the miller sleeps best by the clack of his mill,
So I was most happy in tumult and strife;
I must and I will go to hell for my wife.

Rhodope: Your wife, you driv'ler! Is it so!
Then I'll play hell before you go.

Orpheus: (aside) With fear and shame my cheeks are scarlet
I've prais'd my wife before my harlot.

Rhodope: Go, fetch your wife you simple man;
What, keep us both! Is that your plan?
And dar'st thou Orpheus, think of two?
When one's too much by one for you!

Orpheus: My mind is fix'd, in vain this strife
To hell I go to fetch my wife. [Going Rhodope holds him]

Rhodope: [in tears] Is this your affection, your vows and protection,
To bring back your wife to your house;
When she knows what I am, as a wolf the poor lamb,
As a cat she will mumble the mouse.

Orpheus: Pray cease your pathetic, and I'll be prophetic
Two ladies at once in my house:
Two cats they will be, and mumble poor me;
The poor married man is the mouse.

Rhodope: Yet hear me Orpheus, can you be
So vulgar as to part with me,
And fetch your wife? Am I forsaken?

O give me back what you have taken!
In vain I rave, my fate deplore
A ruin'd maid is maid no more;
Your love alone is reputation;
Give me but that, and this for reparation

When Orpheus you were kind and true
Of joy I had my fill:
Now Orpheus roves, and faithless proves
Alas! the bitter pill!
As from the bogs the wounded frogs
Call'd out, I call to thee;
O naughty boy, to you 'tis joy,
Alas 'tis death to me!

Orpheus: In vain are all your sobs and sighs,
In vain the rhet'rick of your eyes;
To wind and rain my heart is rock;
The more you cry — the more I'm block.

Rhodope: Since my best weapon, crying fails,
I'll try my tongue, and then my nails.

Mount if you will and reach the sky,
Quick as Lightning would I fly,
And there would give you battle;
Like the thunder I would rattle.
Seek if you will the shades below,
Thither, thither will I go,
Your faithless heart appall!
My rage no bounds shall know —
　　Revenge my bosom stings
　　And jealousy has wings,
To rise above 'em all!

Orpheus: [snatching up his lyre] This is *my* weapon, don't advance,
I'll make you sleep, or make you dance.

One med'cine cures the gout, another cures a cold
This can drive your passions out, nay even cure a scold
　　Have you gout or vapours?
I in sleep your senses steep,
Or make your legs cut capers.

Duetto: [accompanied by the lyre]

Rhodope: I cannot have my swing
Orpheus: Ting, ting, ting.

Rhodope: My tongue has lost its twang
Orpheus: Tang, tang, tang.

Rhodope: My eyes begin to twinkle
Orpheus: Tinkle, tinkle, tinkle.

Rhodope: My hands dingle dangle
Orpheus: Tangle, tangle, tangle.

Rhodope: My spirits sink
Orpheus: Tink, tink, tink.

Rhodope: Alas, my tongue,
Orpheus: Tang, tang, tong.

Rhodope: Now 'Tis all o'er, I can no more
But-go-to-sleep—and—sno-o-re [Sinks by degrees and falls asleep on couch]

Orpheus: 'Tis done, I'm free,
And now for thee, Eurydice.

Behold what's seldom seen in life,
I leave my mistress for my wife.
Who's there? [Calls a servant who peeps in]
Come in—say never peep;
The danger's o'er, she's fast asleep.
Do not too soon her fury rouse.
I go to hell to fetch my spouse.

Tho' she scolded all day and all night did the same,
Tho' she was too rampant, and I was too tame;
Tho' shriller her notes than the ear-piercing fife,
I must and I will go to hell for my wife [Exit singing]

We see from the pages of *The London Stage* that Barthelemon's brand of musical-genre satire—accomplished by shifts and turns of the familiarly serious to fit absurd situations explained by the libretto—is but one of many such delightful musical spoofs that enlivened London evening performances and drew crowds to the theatre for the musical refreshment they found there.

NOTES

1. "Tell me not of the Roses and Lillies . . ." composed and sung by Sparkish in Act III of the play.

2. François Hippolyte Barthelemon. *Orpheus an English Burletta* (London: Welcker, 1768).

3. Chapter 7 herein.

4. "Garrick's Fail-Safe Musical Venture; A Peep Behind the Curtain, an English Burletta," chapter 8, herein.

Part IV

PROMPTBOOKS, DANCE NOTATION, AND CRITICAL THEORY

THE ACTING COPY AND PROMPTER'S GUIDE
Editor's Headnote

Only in very modern times have the rich suggestive sources for play production—theatre promptbooks and marked-up acting copies—been much consulted by scholars and teachers in considering the printed texts of plays once popular. Professor Shattuck discusses the fascination involved in studying prompt copies, and the losses and gains for theatrical audiences in the cuts made, textual rearrangements, and new lines provided by actor managers who were keen on keeping alive old as well as current drama in the eighteenth century. Before the age of photography and the moving picture promptbooks provide a vade mecum for all teachers of drama.

10. Drama as Promptbook*

Charles H. Shattuck

Professor of English, University of Illinois

In a Foreword to a book of Kalman Burnim's, George Winchester Stone once wrote as follows:

A number of us who teach eighteenth-century drama have long tried to present the plays as plays—vibrant as they were in the first instance of their performance. Even in the classroom we have sought to look upon the plays not as books but as promptbooks, whose life lies not only in the text, but in its stage presentation.[1]

And something like this I have been asked to demonstrate: What did a play consist of, what did it mean, when it was put before an audience in the eighteenth century?

*The original talk was illustrated with some forty slides of pictorial material and pages from promptbooks.

Now for purpose of clarity, as well as convenience, I shall not deal altogether with plays *written* in the eighteenth century, but mainly with plays we all know by heart, those of the century's *favorite* playwright, as he is ours: Shakespeare. What did Shakespeare's plays (and one or two others) consist of when they were staged in the eighteenth century?

My task is not easy. The eighteenth century was a long time ago. We can perceive it only through many layers of darkened glass — the limited keeping of records at that time, the loss of records since that time, the inability of all of us but the most deeply committed students of eighteenth-century life to see with eighteenth-century eyes, to bypass two centuries of human experience and reconstitute ourselves citizens of that remote time.

Let me suggest the difficulty of knowing what a stage performance was *then,* by reference to the wealth of information we have about stage performances of recent vintage.

At Stratford-upon-Avon in 1959 Glen Byam Shaw produced *King Lear,* starring Charles Laughton. Here, in part, is a report by that most sensitive and intelligent of reviewers, Muriel St. Clare Byrne, of what Act IV Scene 6, the "mad scene," looked like and meant.

The scene, a simple "landscape with figures," peasant women and "sunburnt sicklemen with August weary," opens out in its full spaciousness, drenched in warm, rich color and late summer sun, beneath a wide-arching sky. Reapers and gleaners draw in their wagon, stacked with some sheaves of corn and a few bales of straw, leaving it downstage as they go off to the "high grown field" to gather in the last of the harvest. It is significant that everyone who discusses the production refers to Lear's encounter with Gloucester and Edgar not as "the mad scene" but as "the scene with the cart." . . . [Lear] now clambers almost immediately on to the cart; there is no lost, pathetic, restless wandering about the stage. He sits squarely but casually on a bale of straw, easy and relaxed, his own quiet emphasized by the blinded Gloucester and the outcast Edgar, who stand leaning against the cart on either side like heraldic supporters, as still as he.

And in many more sentences Miss Byrne spells out the realization that this mumbling, mad, but gentle old man, seated on his haycart, has come a long way from the tyrant of the opening scene, delivering his brutal judgment of Cordelia, seated then on his "great, square, black throne, towering aloft against the encircling Sarsen stones."[2]

A dozen other competent reporters would confirm the facts of the case, if not the wise interpretation which Miss Byrne develops for us. If in conjunction with these published descriptions we were to consult the promptbook of the 1959 production, we would find opposite page after page of the text of Act IV Scene 6 the exact positions and movements of the gleaners, the cart, the king, and all the company.[3] Somewhere too (I have not sought them out) are Angus McBean's photographs of this splendid scene.

All *this* evidence and much more, including the voice and physical presence of Charles Laughton, as registered in countless films and recordings, are preserved for us by the machinery of our technological age.

But to understand what a play was like on the stage in the eighteenth century, we must make do, comparatively speaking, with crumbs. There are acting editions, of course; some prompt-books marked in sufficient detail to merit study; *some* genuinely informative reviews and spectators' reports; *some* useful writings by the actors. Very few scenic designs have been preserved (though Sybil Rosenfeld has catalogued the works of some 179 of the century's scenic artists).[4] There are scores of portraits and cartoons of actors, and a number of paintings of famous *scenes* from plays: Hogarth's *Beggar's Opera* and his Garrick as Richard III waking from The Dream; William Hamilton's painting of Kemble as Richard in the same scene; Zoffany's Dagger Scene in *Macbeth* with Garrick and Mrs. Pritchard, and his Trial Scene in *The Merchant* with Macklin's Shylock. Yet in comparison with later ages the evidence is sparse. It is indeed remarkable how much our dedicated historians of the eighteenth century have been able to make of it.

A good place to begin (anticipating our period of little) is with the earliest known promptbook of *Hamlet*. Samuel Pepys first saw *Hamlet* in 1661, when Thomas Betterton "did the prince's part beyond imagination"; and Pepys notes already that it was *"done with scenes very well."* (By "scenes" he meant, of course, scenery painted on *flat wings and shutters* which slid onstage and off in grooves). We have no description of those "scenes," but we know very well what kind of theatre was built not long thereafter to display scenes. Christopher Wren's design for Drury Lane Theatre, shows three galleries facing the stage, and two levels of boxes; the stage, which was raked, consisted of two main sections — a twenty-foot deep forestage flanked by two entering doors at right and two at left, and behind the proscenium arch a twenty-foot rearstage with five sets of grooves for wings and shutters.[5] By 1674 the London Theatre was not only well equipped for production of plays "with scenes" but numerous foreign visitors remarked on the skill and beauty of English scenes and machines, comparing them favorably with the best in use on the continent.

No London promptbook of *Hamlet* survives from this period, but we do have the promptbook of the Smock Alley Theatre in Dublin, dating from about 1678; and as it is believed that the Smock Alley followed London theatre practice rather closely, we may regard this promptbook as fairly representing the play as London audiences saw it.

The Smock Alley book, based on pages of the Third Folio, is by modern standards a crudely scribbled document, but it is a remarkably informative one.[6] A glance at its first pages tells us, for one thing, that the play was backed by changeable scenery. Scene 1 is marked "Castle" (A castle exterior painted on a pair of shutters). Scene 2 is marked "Court." The word "Sceane" in the margin near the end of Scene 1 is a cue to be ready to thrust on the "Court" or palace room shutters. Four other scenes, or sets (all these are obviously stock pieces) are used throughout the play: Chamber, Bed Chamber, Towne, and Church.

Calls for actors to be "Redy" regularly appear a dozen or more lines in advance of their entrance, and the exact moment of entrance is marked by a horizontal line cross-hatched. The "Cock," by the way, is alerted more than twenty lines before his direction to "Croe."

Most interesting for our purposes here are the *cuts*. All references in the first scene to sitting—"Sit down a while," "Well, sit we down," and so forth, are eliminated, for the stage arrangements of the scene provided no objects to sit on. "Before my God," and all further references to Deity, are suppressed. The "sledded Polax" is omitted, presumably because nobody knew what it meant.

Larger cuts in the first scene include most of the lines detailing the past conflict with Norway and the present preparations for war. In the second scene and thereafter Voltimand and Cornelius are excluded from the *dramatis personae*. The poetical but dispensable account of the holiness of Christmas Eve, when "the bird of dawning singeth all night long," is cancelled.

It is not surprising, on the one hand, in the second scene that the king's speeches are much shortened, or on the other hand that the rapid-running passage in which Hamlet receives the news about his "father's spirit in Armes" is retained almost verbatim. What *is* surprising is that Hamlet's first soliloquy, "Oh that this too, too solid flesh would melt," which seems to us in every syllable the very essence of Hamlet, is slashed down to a mere half its size. Why?

In the third scene, Laertes's advice to Ophelia and her counterwarning to him are reduced to a minimum. Polonius's famous advice to Laertes is suppressed altogether, and Polonius's final scolding of Ophelia is reduced to a mere injunction that she have no more talk with Hamlet. In Act II, expectably, the entire Polonius-Reynaldo scene is cancelled.

Much of Hamlet's initial banter with his old friends Rosencrantz and Guildenstern ("Denmark's a prison," and so forth) is dropped, as is of course the theatrical shop talk about the child actors and a good many lines between Hamlet and the first player. But again, amazingly, Hamlet's second soliloquy — "Now I am alone" — is cut in half, the most passionate lines unspoken. We do not hear

> Yet I
> A dull and muddy-mettled Rascal, peake
> Like *John-o-Dreams*, unpregnant of my cause,
> And can say nothing.

nor do we hear

> Am I a coward?
> Who calls me Villain? breaks my pate across?
> Plucks off my Beard, and blowes it in my face?
> Tweaks me by the Nose, gives me the Lye ith' Throat
> As deep as to the Lungs? who does me this?
> Ha? why I should take it.

He does not call Claudius

> bloody, Bawdy villain,
> Remorseless, Treacherous, Lecherous, kindless villain

And so forth.

But just as we are ready to conclude that the principle behind the cutting was to eliminate everything that did not contribute directly to the forward movement of the plot, we come upon the meditative, sermon-like Third Soliloquy, "To be or not to be," and find that it is given *entire*. So, too, Hamlet's advice to The Players, which later generations would reduce or omit altogether, is given entire, and Hamlet's long address to Horatio—"Thou art e'en as just a man/ As e'er my Conversation cop'd withall"—loses not a syllable.

At the start of the Play Scene Hamlet's lines to Ophelia are relieved of their bawdry. In the Play itself, the problem of the Dumb Show, which has tortured critics' brains for centuries, is solved simply: the Dumb Show is omitted.

Hamlet's scene with his mother is given with very few cuts. Looking backward, we find that the Hamlet-Ophelia scene loses very few lines. Looking forward into the fourth act, we find that though there is much cutting of the King and others, Ophelia's lines are hardly touched. These facts suggest an effort to keep as much emphasis as possible on the actresses.

The fifth act is hardly reduced at all. The entire Clowns' Scene is played verbatim; the Funeral and the fight over the grave lose only a half line or two. Hamlet's long narrative of his adventure at sea, his dialogue with Osric, the duelling and the deaths are given with very few cuts—and, wonder of wonders, Fortinbras and the English Ambassadors arrive to share with Horatio the honors of the finale.

So what we have in this text is, apparently, an effort at all costs to speed the early sections of the play. By the fifth act the arranger has earned enough playing time to give the play its head and let it run freely. Throughout the play, Claudius yields so much of his part that he hardly qualifies as a "mighty opposite." The cuts inflicted upon Hamlet are perhaps intended to "ennoble" him: He speaks no impiety and no bawdry; in his early soliloquies he is emotionally restrained, does not give way to the wilder outbreaks of passion and revulsion that Shakespeare wrote for him; rather he extends himself in the humorous and playful, the serene, meditative, and solemnly earnest passages.

Throughout the eighteenth century *Hamlet* was performed in practically every season. The most brilliant executant of the title role was, of course, David Garrick, who "hamletized" for thirty-

five years, from 1742 to 1776.[7] For most of that time he played a
version differing in detail but not much in principle from the
version we have been examining. But in 1772, as the editor of
Bell's *Shakespeare* put it, he "too politely frenchified it."[8] Yielding to the opinions of Voltaire and other French critics, Garrick
"had sworn that I would not leave the stage till I had rescued that
noble play from all the rubbish of the fifth act."

So in 1772 he broke off Shakespeare's play at Ophelia's last exit
in Act IV and brought Hamlet thundering in on Laertes, the
King and Queen, with "This is I, Hamlet the Dane!" In some
thirty lines adapted mainly from the Grave Scene and the final
scene, Hamlet fights the King and kills him, then is himself killed
by Laertes. The Queen, who has run off in fright, is reported to
have gone mad. Horatio concludes the play with lines of Fortinbras. Laertes is left alive to take over the kingdom. In this oddly
truncated form, the play held the stage at Drury Lane, profitably
and often, for several years. Garrick and the Drury Lane management never allowed it to be printed, and apart from conjectural
reconstructions it was unknown until Professor Stone discovered it
among the Garrick books at the Folger and described it in the
PMLA in 1934.[9] Only then, by the way, was Garrick for the first
time given credit for the *positive* aspects of his version. He
restored over 600 lines which earlier actors had omitted. He
restored Voltimand, Cornelius and Reynaldo to the *dramatis
personae*. He gave the third scene in full, including Polonius'
advice to Laertes, gave the whole of the play-within-a-play, and
spoke the fourth soliloquy, "How all occasions do inform against
me," which was not printed in the Folios and so had not been
spoken on the stage since Shakespeare's time — if ever.

Garrick's principal successor as Hamlet was John Philip
Kemble, who made his Drury Lane debut in the role in 1783.[10]
Kemble, too, played Hamlet over a span of thirty-five years, and
he published his own acting edition. His version was essentially
that which Garrick used before the grand frenchification. But
Kemble studied Shakespeare's text with minute care, and managed to restore dozens of phrases which earlier actors had
modified to suit modern taste or intelligibility. He read "'Tis not
alone my inky cloak" instead of "my mourning suit;" "wild and
whirling words" not "windy words;" "'twas caviare to the
general" not "the multitude;" "the native hue of resolution" not

"the healthful face of resolution;" and "flights of angels" not "choirs of angels." Once when his friend John Taylor persuaded him to make some changes in the text, he said, "Now, Taylor, I have copied the part of Hamlet forty times, and you have obliged me to consider and copy it once more." I suspect Kemble's reputation for Shakespearean scholarship owed especially to his close study of *Hamlet*.

The rough-and-ready style of promptbook marking persisted far into the eighteenth century. But from 1780 or thereabouts there comes a handful of books in which the prompter writes a firm round hand and seems to care about order and intelligibility. An *As You Like It* book from Covent Garden well represents the improved style.[11]

At the head of the first scene we find a list of property manuscripts:

2 papers wrt. This means two written scrolls — the poems which Orlando would tack upon trees in the third act.

1 Lre wrote. This means the letter, written and folded, which Rosalind would receive from Phoebe in the fourth act.

1 B Paper. This means a blank paper, but I cannot discover where it was used in the play.

Next we find a circle, which is an eye-catching device to remind the prompter to be sure the correct wings and shutters were in place. Then the words "Carver's Gar., 4th Gr., Carpet C.T."

"Carver's Garden" was a stock set named after the man who painted it — Robert Carver (fl. 1754–1791), a distinguished scenic artist of the day. It was used here to represent Oliver's Orchard, and the shutters stood in the *fourth grooves*. A *carpet* was laid at *C.T.*, which I take to mean *Center Trap*.

At the head of the second scene is a circled (W) and the words "Stone Palace, 5 Gr. Gilt chair."

The W tells the prompter to blow his *whistle*. At this signal the "carpenters," as they were called, drew off the "Carver's Garden" units to reveal a *Palace Exterior* painted on a pair of shutters at the *fifth grooves*. The *Gilt Chair* was a throne of sorts from which Duke Frederick observed the wrestling, which took place at center stage on the aforementioned *Carpet*.

At the head of the third scene is a circled (W), a circle with a dot in it, and the words "Govern House, 2nd Gr."

At the prompter's whistle, the carpenters thrust onstage, at the *second grooves,* a pair of shutters known in the stock room as *The Governor's House*. It was an interior: the scene is that in which Rosalind receives notice of her banishment.

At the end of Act I, "Drop Landskip" means that an act drop came down, painted with a landscape scene. During the interval "Rosalind and Celia Dress"—that is, to change their court dresses for what they were to wear as Ganymede and Aliena. Then a circled (W) and "Forrest, 4 Gr."

When the act drop rose, the audience saw a *Forest* scene painted on shutters at the *fourth grooves.*

At Act II, Scene 2, is a circled (W) and "Gov House, 2 Gr."

At the prompter's whistle the carpenters thrust on the *Governor's House* shutters, again in the *second grooves*. It is the scene in which the Duke hears about the runaways.

At Act II, Scene 3, again at Oliver's House, is a circled (W) and "Wood, 1 Gr." Also we notice "Shut Pd." Orlando is to "knock at Pd" and "Enter Adam Pd."

At the whistle, the carpenters thrust on a Wood scene at the *first grooves*. The prompter made sure that the promptside (stage left) *Proscenium Door,* giving onto the forestage, was closed. Orlando knocked there and old Adam came out there.

At Act II, Scene 4, is a circle (though, oddly, no W in it) and "Open Cty, 3rd Gr, Bank on OP side." Now we are in Arden.

At the whistle, the carpenters drew off the Wood shutters, revealing what I take to mean a view of *Open Country* painted on shutters at the *third grooves*. An *earthen mound* is *Opposite Prompt*—that is, at stage right.

We need not pursue all the changes of Country and Forest scenes.
It should be noted that in the third act, when Orlando is to pin
his verses on various trees, the trees are provided.

The setting is at two levels: a *Cut Wood* (that is, a pair of shutters
consisting of cut-out trees and bushes) at the *fourth grooves*, through
which one sees a *Landscape* backing at the *fifth grooves*.

At the end of the play is a rather elaborate business of "A Dance
of Forresters. A Bench put on each side to sit down and when the
dance is finished all rise and make a circle while Rosalind speaks
the Epilogue."

One of Garrick's most popular *non*-Shakespearean plays was
Vanbrugh's *The Provok'd Wife*, in which he played the provok-
ing husband, Sir John Brute, whose name defines his nature.[12]
From 1744 to 1776 he played the role 105 times. This magnificent
comedy had the great good luck to be written in 1697, a year
before the publication of Jeremy Collier's *Short View of the
Immorality and Profaneness of the English Stage*. Thus, whereas
The Provok'd Wife is a serious presentation of problems of love
and marriage, by no means sentimentalized, at the same time it
sparkles with wit (*mildly* naughty now and then), is warmed with
humanity and full-bodied humor, and glows with the sensuosity
of a Rubens painting. One scene, in which Sir John, in a drunken
caper through the streets, disguises himself as a clergyman, gave
especial offense to blue-nosed moralists like Collier. But long
before the play came to Garrick's hands Vanbrugh replaced this
drab little joke with a far livelier one. Sir John appropriates a
cloak and wrapping gown of his *wife's* and, disguised as a woman,
is arrested, scandalizes the Judge by vulgar talk and drunkenness,
and delivers a salty satire on the behavior of Ladies of Quality.
For this much we may *thank* Jeremy Collier, that he compelled
Vanbrugh to improve what was already a masterpiece.

The fable is a simple one. In fact the richness and strength of
the play depends on this simplicity: by avoiding the tangle of plots
and counterplots which renders so many seventeenth-century
comedies forgettable, Vanbrugh was able to develop his themes
and scenes in unusual depth.

A beautiful and witty young woman has got herself married to a singularly repulsive husband: Sir John Brute is a rakehell, a bully, a drunkard, a lecher, a coward withal—gross, foul-mouthed, insulting, hateful. Lady Brute is pursued by a devoted lover, a young gallant named Constant, and she is more than half in love with him, but their case is hopeless. She will not commit adultery, and there is no escape from her disastrous union. It is a comedy with a sorry ending.

Meanwhile Constant's fellow-gallant, a brisk young wit named Heartfree, who has been involved in a flirtation with an affected belle, one Lady Fancyfull, falls genuinely in love with Lady Brute's charming niece Bellinda. It is a sort of Beatrice-Benedick affair: they resist each other as long as they can. But the crisis of the play drives them into commitment. Coming home late one night, tumble-down drunk, Sir John finds Lady Brute and Bellinda, and a table ready for a game of cards, and the two gallants hiding in a closet. Of course, Sir John suspects the worst of his wife, but they manage to convince him that the only love-game going is between Heartfree and Bellinda and that they are bound for matrimony. Sir John is only too glad to get rid of a quarrel and get rid of his niece.

The promptbook for *The Provok'd Wife,* made on the Dublin edition of 1743, is said to be the most fully marked Garrick promptbook which survives.[13] There are sixteen scenes in it covered by eight stock sets, and the sets and grooves are indicated so systematically that, as Kalman Burnim finds, it could serve as a basic document for our understanding of how scenic units were manipulated in the midcentury.

Thus Act I commenced with a "Chimney Chamber"—that is, a chamber with a fireplace—representing a room in Sir John's house, the shutters standing in the *second grooves.* At the prompter's whistle, these shutters were drawn off to reveal "Picture Chamber," which was a dressing room in Lady Fancyfull's house, set the *third grooves.* The "Picture Chamber" was drawn off to reveal an "Old Palace" set, representing St. James' Park, at the *fourth grooves.* For the final scene of the act, the Lady Fancyfull set, closed in at the *third grooves.*

Other sets that came into play in the following acts were "Palace" (the drawing room in Sir John's house, always at the *fourth grooves*), a Tavern Chamber, a Street, and a Wood (representing Spring Garden).

Although Professor Burnim has declared this play "ideally suited to Garrick's genius for comic and satiric interpretation of character" (p. 176), it seems to me that Garrick was quite wrong for the part, that he warped the character into something quite different from what Vanbrugh had written. Being small of stature, lively, and clear-voiced, he played Sir John as an old dandy, a debauched gentleman, a "joyous agreeable wicked dog." A critic of the time noted that he was not "morosely sullen": "In his manner, there is an Appearance of Acrimony, rather than downright Insensibility and Rudeness." Unquestionably Garrick's performance was technically brilliant, and it delighted audiences, but one needs only read any page of Sir John's rude and sullen dialogue to recognize that Garrick fitted the role to himself rather than himself to the role. Of the ponderous James Quin, his predecessor as Sir John, Churchill declared in *The Rosciad*:

> In Brute he shone unequalled; all agree
> Garrick's not half so great a Brute as he.[14]

With his huge figure and deep-toned voice, Quin was far better equipped for the role than Garrick.

Yet I suspect that if Garrick had kept true to Vanbrugh's intentions and exhibited the full coarseness of Sir John, the play would not have been acceptable to the rising sentimentalism of the age. Voices were raised in any case to denounce the play as "scandalously licentious," and only by lightening and jollifying the Brute could Garrick insulate the play against irresistible attacks on grounds of morality or taste.

He did not *cut* the part. As far as I can make out from the prompt book, he did not give up or modify one coarse syllable of Sir John's utterance. The text as a whole *is* reduced by some sixteen or seventeen pages, or about one-fifth of the total, but the cuts are made only upon what Garrick took to be supporting characters—four or five pages of Lady Fancyfull, a dozen or so pages from the dialogues of Lady Brute and Bellinda, Constant and Heartfree, Constant and Lady Brute. Some of the cut passages *are* perhaps overextended, and therefore in part dispensable, but none of them is particularly salacious. Garrick cut them rather than his own lines because he was intent on keeping the reins in his own hands, on making Sir John the be-all of the performances.

He chose not to notice that in Vanbrugh's consideration the provoked and abused wife, her niece, and their gallants are the central characters, and that Sir John, like a Malvolio or a Shylock, though dangerous, is only a satellite. At the exact middle of his play Vanbrugh set up a midnight conversation between Lady Brute and Bellinda—one of the most delightful dialogues in all of seventeenth-century comedy—and a sign, surely, of the central place of the ladies in the author's scheme of things.

Lady B. Sure it's late, Bellinda; I begin to be sleepy.

Bell. Yes, tis near twelve. Will you go to Bed?

Lady B. To bed, my Dear? And by that time I'm fallen into a sweet sleep (or perhaps a sweet Dream which is better and better) Sir John will come home, roaring drunk, and be overjoyed he finds me in a Condition to be disturb'd. . . . What Hogs Men turn, Belinda, when they grow weary of Women.

Bell. And what Owles they are whilst they are fond of 'em.

Lady B. But *that* we may forgive well enough, because they are so upon our Accounts.

Bell. We ought to do so indeed: But 'tis a hard matter. For when a man is really in Love, he looks so unsufferably silly, that tho' a Woman lik'd him well enough before, she has then much ado to endure the sight of him. And this I take to be the reason why Lovers are so generally ill used.

And they talk about men, and how silly men are, and how dull life would be without them, and how many pleasant vanities women would give up if there were no need to attract men to them. And while they confess their vanities, they turn to theatre and plays.

Lady B. Why then I confess that I love to sit in the forefront of a Box. For if one sits behind, there's two Acts gone perhaps, before one's found out. . . . I watch with Impatience for the next Jest in the Play, that I might laugh and shew my white Teeth. If the Poet has been dull, and the Jest be long a coming, I pretend to whisper one to my Friend, and from thence fall into a little short Discourse, in which I take Occasion to shew my Face in all Humours, Brisk, Placid, Serious, Melancholy, Languishing—

They both confess that they often practise facemaking before a glass, but Bellinda complains that

> my Glass and I cou'd never yet agree *what* Face I shou'd make, when they come blurt out, with a nasty Thing in a Play: For all the Men presently look upon the Women, that's certain; so laugh we must not, though our Stays burst for't. Because that's telling Truth, and owning we understand the Jest. And to look serious is so dull, when the whole House is a laughing.

Lady B. Besides, that looking serious, do's really betray our knowledge in the Matter, as much as laughing with the Company wou'd do. For if we did not understand the thing, we shou'd naturally do like the other People.

Bell. For my part I always take that Occasion to blow my Nose.

Lady B. You must blow your Nose half off then at some Plays.

Bell. Why don't some Reformer or other, beat the Poet for't?

Lady B. Because he is not so sure of our private approbation as of or publick Thanks.

And they talk of men again, Lady Brute of "poor Constant . . . if it be but to furnish Matter for Dreams," Bellinda of Heartfree, that "Son of Bacchus" for she is tempted to "rival his bottle" — and *should* she marry him? Surely she should not commit fornication. And they hit on a scheme to lure their men to an assignation in Spring-Garden. They must write them a billet without delay: "Let's go into *your* Chamber then," says Lady Brute, "and whilst you say your Prayers, I'll do it, Child."

Of this charming and necessary dialogue, *Garrick cancelled all but the plot lines at beginning and end.* Yet for the audiences, I suppose, the loss of this scene was more than compensated for by Garrick's Sir John disguised as a woman. Helling about the streets with drunken companions, he encounters a Tailor delivering dresses to his wife.

My Lady Brute! my Wife! The robes of my Wife — with Reverence, let me approach it! The dear Angel is always taking care of me in Danger, and has sent me this Armour to protect me in this Day of Battle. On they go. . . . Sancho, my Squire, help me on with my Armour.

Challenged by the Watch, he cries out that he is

Bonduca, Queen of the Welshmen, and with a Leek as long as my Pedigree. I will destroy your Roman Legion in an Instant. Britons, strike home!

When the Watch arrests him

Hands off, you Ruffians! my Honour's dearer to me than my Life! I hope you won't be uncivil!

He is hauled away squealing

O! my Honour! my Honour!

When the Constable reports to the Judge that a gentleman has been killed tonight, and perhaps this "Lady and her gang have done it, Sir John bellows,"

There may have been Murder for ought I know, and 'tis great Mercy there has not been a Rape too — for this Fellow [the Watch] would have ravish'd me.

The Watchman is scandalized at the accusation, and declares anyway that this "Lady" is probably a "Morphrodite." Sir John assures the Judge that he is indeed *Lady Brute*.

That happy Woman, Sir, am I! only a little in my Merriment tonight.

The Judge wonders whether her husband treats her well, gives her money enough, is true to her bed, but this line of questioning fizzles out. Finally at the Judge's request "she" rattles off her "method of Life" — the typical day of a Lady of Quality — her late rising, drinking of chocolate, being dressed by her maids, taking breakfast, attention to prayers *and* the playbills, taking tea, then a late dinner, annoying her husband, calling on friends, spending the evening at dice. When the Judge dismisses her she offers to buy him a bottle, and invites the Constable to go with her/him to pick up a Whore.

Professor Burnim has retrieved from the *London Chronicle* the following tribute to Garrick's female impersonation:

You would swear he had often attended the Toilet and there gleaned up the many various Airs of the Fair Sex: He is perfectly versed in the Exercise of the Fan, the Lips, the Adjustment of the Tucker, and even the minutest Conduct of the Finger.[15]

All this must have been purely delightful, even if it owed considerably more to Garrick than to Vanbrugh.

Garrick's most impressive tragic role was King Lear, which he initiated in 1742.[16] "The little dog made it a *chef d'oeuvre*," as Charles Macklin put it; and for thirty-five years London audiences were awash with tears over the old king's agonies whenever Garrick displayed them. Yet down to 1756 Garrick's vehicle was hardly Shakespeare's play, but Nahum Tate's 1681 rewriting of it—surely the rudest keel-hauling of Shakespeare by any of the seventeenth-century "improvers."[17]

Tate found the play, he says, "a Heap of Jewels, unstrung and unpolisht." He perceived at once how to string them: he would "run through the whole, A Love betwixt Edgar and Cordelia, that never chang'd word with each other in the Original." As a further contribution to plot integration, Tate would have lecherous Edmund lust after Cordelia as well as after the wicked sisters, and hire a pair of ruffians to waylay her during the Storm scene and hold her prisoner to await his pleasure. Then Tate would have Edgar standing by, naked but for Mad Tom's tattered rags, ready to attack the ruffians, rescue Cordelia, and once more declare his "aspiring Love" for her. This wins from Cordelia a remarkably *un*-Shakespearean invitation to

> Come to my arms, thou dearest, best of Men,
> And take the kindest Vows that e're were spoke
> By a protesting Maid.

His "hallowed rags," she says, his "abject Tassels" and "fantastick shreds" are dearer to her "than the richest Pomp of purple Monarchs." Cordelia is addicted to lady-like enthusiasms of this sort. For *male* characters in *un*gentle moods, Tate is ready with poetry of a contrasting kind. Thus, for instance, when Gloster is convinced of son Edgar's treachery, he proposes to

> bite the Traytor's heart, and fold
> His bleeding Entrals on my vengefull Arm.

Tate found that Shakespeare had not given Lear language enough with which to go mad at the end of Act II, so he contributed the following:

> Blood, Fire! hear — Leaprosies and bluest Plagues!
> Room, room, for Hell to belch her Horrors up
> And drench the *Circes* in a stream of Fire:
> Hark how the Infernals eccho to my Rage
> Their Whips and Snakes —

As for *polishing* this heap of jewels, Tate rewrote hundreds of Shakespeare's lines, relaxing their tension, flattening their metaphors into prosy banalities comfortable to his own dull ear and mind. His major act of "polishing," of course, was to eliminate Lear's Fool, on the principle that, like the gravediggers in *Hamlet,* he was unfit to travel in tragic company.

And last of all, Tate gave the play a happy ending, citing the authority of John Dryden that "'tis more difficult to save than to kill," that it requires far more art and judgment "to bring the Action to the last Extremity, and then by probable means to recover All." His final scene is in a Prison. Lear is sleeping on a truss of straw, his head on Cordelia's lap: she is soliloquizing. Enter Edmund's soldiers and Ruffians, sent here to murder them. Lear wakes out of a dream, snatches a sword, and slays the two Ruffians. At that moment Edgar and Albany arrive and disarm the soldiers. Kent arrives. Lear assumes that now he will be put to death by Albany, but Albany not only reassures him but explains that Edmund and the wicked daughters are dead and the kingship reverts to Lear. This unstoppers a notorious rant. "Is't possible?" cries Lear.

> Let the spheres stop their course, the sun make halt,
> The winds be hush'd, the seas and fountains rest,
> All nature pause, and listen to the change!
> . . . Old Lear shall be a King again.

And a moment later:

> Cordelia then shall be a queen, mark that,
> Cordelia shall be queen; winds catch the sound
> And bear it on your rosy wings to heaven,
> Cordelia is a queen.

Blind Gloster arrives. Lear blesses the union of Edgar and Cordelia, turns over the kingdom to them, and announces that he, Kent, and Gloster, having

> retir'd to some cool cell,
> Will gently pass our short reserves of Time
> In calm Reflections on our Fortunes past.

Incredible though it be, for over a hundred and forty years after 1681, theatre audience saw no other than Tate's unhappy happy ending.

Garrick acted the Tate version for fifteen years. In 1756, urged by friends, *in* the profession and out of it, he effected a very considerable restoration of the original.[18] He dared not restore the Fool, and he had to keep a few lines introducing the love affair between Edgar and Cordelia, because they played into the happy ending—and he *had* to keep the happy ending. His principle achievement was to scrub Tate's language out of Acts I, II, and most of III, and restore the language of the original.

When we remember that so formidable a character as Dr. Johnson could hardly endure to *read* the final scene as Shakespeare wrote it, we can partly understand why Garrick had to keep the happy ending. It functioned more or less as the *exodoi* of Greek tragedies are supposed to have functioned—to allay the pity and terror which the spectators suffered as they witnessed the agonies of the hero. Garrick's age was also the age of the Wesleys, of George Whitefield, and The Great Awakening. Sentimentalism and enthusiasm were then no mere literary terms—they were psychological diseases infecting the masses of the people. Charles Macklin tells of how Lear's reunion with Cordelia "drew tears of commiseration from the whole house." James Boswell records that Garrick's Lear drew from *him* "abundance of tears." In 1776 it took Sir Joshua Reynolds three days to regain tranquility and Hannah More four after what they suffered at Garrick's very last performance of Lear. The prompter William Hopkins reports the thunders of applause and cries of "Garrick forever" that attended every exit. And after one of the last performances Hopkins wrote, "Human nature cannot arrive at greater Excellence in Acting that Mr. G. was possess'd of this Night. All words must fall short of what he did & none but his spectators can have an Idea of how great he was—the Applause was unbounded."

When Garrick retired, *King Lear* practically disappeared from the Drury Lane repertory for a dozen years.[19] When Kemble reintroduced it in 1788, he played the Garrick revised version six times. But four years later he produced his own version, which was, alas, a wholesale return to Tate. He did omit a rant or two, one unlikely soliloquy of Gloster's just after his eyes were plucked, Tate's Grotto scene in which Regan makes love to Edmund. He restored the original language of Lear's curse of Goneril and a couple of passages of Edmund's, including the one in which he attempts to countermand the order for the death of Lear and Cordelia.

Kemble was not a particularly successful impersonator of Lear — see Charles Lamb's dismissal of him as an old man tottering about the stage with a walking stick.[20] But by publishing his version, he lent his massive authority (for by the end of the century he was regarded in the theatre as the high priest of all matters Shakespearean) to the continuation of the tatified text through his own generation and well into the next. And by this act — as well as by his treatment of *The Tempest* in which he reverted to the seventeenth-century operatized version, again bypassing all that Garrick had accomplished in the way of restoration[21] — he seriously damaged (for us, that is) the reputation for scholarship of which he was so proud.

Kemble did much better with *Coriolanus*. Purists would claim that he was no more faithful to Shakespeare with this play than with *Lear* or *The Tempest*. But it seems to me that he did not seriously damage the essence and tone of the original, and certainly he shaped a workable vehicle for his most fitting and famous characterization — "his peerless Coriolanus," as Macready called it. In Volumnia he found, and "improved," a role ideally suited to his great sister Sarah Siddons.

His *Coriolanus* consists of Shakespeare's first three acts much cut, plus two final acts in which he cunningly wove together matter from Shakespeare and matter from the 1749 *Coriolanus* of James Thomson.[22] The matter from Thomson achieved three ends: it strengthened the impact of Volumnia, it clarified the motivation of Aufidius, and it speeded the catastrophe. Shakespeare's Aufidius takes forever to talk himself into revolting against Coriolanus: Thomson provided Aufidius a "rough old friend" named Volusius who propels him into revolt by stinging

If these shows be not outward, which of you
But is four Volscians?—Follow Marcius! come!—

[Exeunt.

R. ¥. X. [A loud Flourish.—A Battle.—A Retreat sounded.] Scene IV.
R. U. E. Enter MARCIUS, COMINIUS, *Officers, and Soldiers.*

Com. If I should tell thee o'er this thy day's work,
Thou 't not believe thy deeds : but I'll report it,
Where senators shall mingle tears with smiles ;
Where the dull tribunes,
That, with the fusty plebeians, hate thine honours,
Shall say, against their hearts,—*We thank the gods,
Our Rome hath such a soldier!*

— *Mar.* Pray now, no more : my mother,
Who has a charter to extoll her blood,
When she does praise me, grieves me : I have done,
As you have done, that 's what I can ; induc'd
As you have been, that 's for my country.

Com. You shall not be.

The grave of your deserving ; Rome must know
The value of her own ;
Therefore, I beseech you,
(In sign of what you are, not to reward
What you have done,) before our army hear me.

— *Mar.* I have some wounds upon me, and they smart
To hear themselves remember'd.

Com. Should they not,
Well might they fester 'gainst ingratitude,
And tent themselves with death. Of all the horses,
(Whereof we 've ta'en good, and good store,) of all
The treasure, in this field achiev'd, and city,
We render you the tenth ; to be ta'en forth,
Before the common distribution, at
Your only choice.

— *Mar.* I thank you, general :
But cannot make my heart consent to take
A bribe, to pay my sword :-I do refuse it.-*[Officer gives the
    signal*

R. [A Flourish of Trumpets, &c.]
R. [wind instruments.

his pride, rousing his envy and wrath. Volumnia, in Shakespeare, has to talk endlessly to wear down her stubborn son's anger and thus save Rome from destruction. By Thomson's swifter tactic, she needs but one grand rant and sudden action to bring Coriolanus around. "Hear me, proud man!" she roars, and dares him to "Tread on the bleeding breast of her to whom thou ow'st thy life." At which she draws a dagger to stab herself—"to die, while Rome is free." Coriolanus cannot possibly resist this. At once he grants truce with Rome and raises the siege, and the play then moves swiftly into the quarrel with Aufidius and the assassination of the hero.

The staging of *Coriolanus*—first at Drury Lane, later at Covent Garden—was one of Kemble's proudest achievements, especially in the matter of *processions,* much loved by eighteenth-century audiences. In the second act, for instance, Rome produces an "Ovation" in honor of Coriolanus. The procession consisted of Four Divisions. They entered upstage, passed through an Arch, and went off into the night. In the First Division there were twenty entries, including SPQR, Silver Eagles, Chief Eagle, soldiers and officers, various Trophies, Golden Eagles, spears and shields, and so forth. In the Second Division, eight entries of Boys, Girls, Priests, Ladies, and Senators. In the Third Division, nineteen entries of SPQR, musicians, soldiers, prisoners, and trophies. In the Fourth Division, ten Musicians and a mass of Choristers singing "See the Conquering Hero Comes." The Musicians remained on the stage with Coriolanus, the Chief Eagle, and the women of Coriolanus's family until the scene ended.

By the end of the century popular taste in theatricals had become remarkably vulgarized, and the best new drama—that is to say, the most popular—was a kind of superior melodrama: domestic drama or heroic tragedy gone to seed. It consisted of farfetched situations in which absolute good collided violently with absolute evil, angers roared, hatreds screamed, and the love between lovers or friends or parents and children was expressed in language of syrupy sentimentality.

In the Kemble generation tears were shed not so much for the sufferings of King Lear, but for the remorse of a Mrs. Haller, who has abandoned her husband the Stranger, for the Stranger's five-act long siege of melancholy, and for the piteous joy of their final

CORIOLANUS. 48

And with the deepest malice of the war
Destroy what lies before them.

Mem. 'T is Aufidius:

Who, hearing of our Marcius' banishment,
Thrusts forth his horns again into the world;
Which were inshell'd, when Marcius stood for Rome,
And durst not once peep out.

R.   *Enter an Officer.*

Off. The nobles, in great earnestness, are going
All to the senate-house: some news is come,
That turns their countenances.

Sic. 'T is this slave:—

Go, whip him 'fore the people's eyes—his raising,
Nothing but his report.

Off. Yes, worthy sir,
The slave's report is seconded: and more,
More fearful, is deliver'd.

Sic. What more fearful?

Off. It is spoke freely out of many mouths,
(How probable, I do not know,) that Marcius,
Join'd with Aufidius, leads a power 'gainst Rome.

Sic. This is most likely!

Bru. Rais'd only, that the weaker sort may wish
Good Marcius home again.

Sic. The very trick on 't.

Mem. This is unlikely: ☓ R.
He and Aufidius can no more atone,
Than violentest contrariety.—
Let 's to the senate-house.

R. [*Exeunt.—Mem.*

SCENE IV.

A Plain, near Rome.

R. ✗ ✗ *Flourish of Drums and Trumpets.*

R.U.E. Enter Caius Marcus Coriolanus, Tullus Aufidius, Volsius, Officers, and Soldiers, & Banners.

— *Cor.* No more:—I merit not this lavish praise,
True, we have driven the Roman legions back,

reunion, their tender little ones clinging about their knees. The play called *The Stranger,* originally *Menschenhass und Reue,* was one of the highly seasoned dramas of the German Kotzebue which invaded the English theatre in the 1790s. The most spectacular of these was *Pizarro,* freely adapted by Richard Brinsley Sheridan from Kotzebue's *The Spaniards in Peru; or, The Death of Rolla*; and performed by John Kemble, his brother Charles, Sarah Siddons, Dora Jordan, and other prime actors of the day.[23]

It is depressing as it is incredible that the sometime master of the comedy of wit and manners should write such balderdash as *Pizarro* (and be proud of it too!) — but too many years of high living, and gassing in the House of Commons, had softened Sheridan's wits — or that the high priest of Shakespeare and his priestess sister should lend their authority to such stuff. But so it was in the year 1799 (and many years thereafter). All London — indeed, audiences everywhere — crowded to see *Pizarro,* hurried to read it too. More than 30,000 copies of the book were purchased during its first year in print. It exactly suited the popular taste of the time.

The plot is too elaborate to be fully described here. Thus, in brief: When the Spanish conquistador Pizarro attacked the Peruvians the first time, one of his officers, Don Alonzo de Molina, was so appalled by Pizarro's cruelty that he went over to the natives. He became great friends with the Peruvian hero Rolla, married an Indian maiden Cora (who was in fact betrothed to Rolla, who generously gave her to his friend). Their union produced a boy-child.

When Pizarro returns a year later for a second attack, it is his vindictive intention to capture Alonzo and execute him as a traitor. His soldiers do take Alonzo prisoner. Cora is distraught. Rolla, disguises as a monk, slips into the Spanish camp, gives the monk's robe to Alonzo so that he can escape, and himself remains as Pizarro's prisoner. When Spanish soldiers arrive with an infant they have kidnapped, Rolla recognizes it and calls out that it is Alonzo's child. He snatches the child, whips out a sword and slays several soldiers, climbs the rocks behind the camp, crosses a bridge over a chasm, and escapes. Struck by a Spanish bullet, however, he barely makes it to the Peruvian camp and deposits the child in Cora's lap, when he dies.

The remark they they they shall

PIZARRO *their answered 'em*

support; ————— is, Victory or death, our King, our King! our Country! and our God! ☞

Alu. Thou, Rolla, in the hour of peril, haft been wont to animate the spirit of their leaders, ere we proceed to consecrate the banners which thy valour knows so well to guard.

—— *Rol.* ———never was the hour of peril *nigh* when to inspire them words were so little needed. × *C.* My brave associates—partners of my toil, ~~my feelings~~ and my fame!—can Rolla's ~~words add~~ vigour to the virtuous energies which ~~inspire~~ your hearts? ——— No—you ~~have~~ judged as I have, *the* foulness of the crafty plea by which these ~~bold~~ invaders would delude you—Your ~~generous~~ spirit has compared *as mine has* the motives, which, in ~~a war like this~~, can *animate their* ~~minds~~ and ours.—THEY, ~~by~~ a ~~strange frenzy driven~~, fight for power, for plunder, and extended rule—WE, for our country, our altars, and our homes.—THEY follow an Adventurer whom they fear——and obey a power which they hate——WE serve a Monarch whom we love——a God whom we adore.——Where'er they move in anger, desolation tracks their progress!——Where'er they pause in amity, affliction mourns their friendship!——They boast, they come but to improve our state, enlarge our thoughts, ~~and~~ free us from the yoke of error!—— Yes——THEY will give enlightened freedom to our minds, who are themselves the slaves of ~~passion~~, avarice, and pride.——They offer us their ~~protection—Yes, such protection as vultures give to lambs—covering and devouring them!~~ ——They call on us to barter all of good we have inherited and proved, for the desperate chance of something better which they promise——Be our

3

The play is incredible, humanly impossible. The plot is a patchwork of stale motifs, the emotions are varieties of hysteria, the characters stereotypes. Or rather, they are megaphonic devices for projecting Sheridan's florid, banal, humorless, noisy oratory. But this is easier to demonstrate than to explain.

Here is the voice of *outraged virtue*. When the curtain rises we see Pizarro's mistress Elvira sleeping in his tent. One Valverde approaches, intending to seduce her. She wakes, rises, and looks at him with indignation. (This is Sarah Siddons speaking.)

Elv.   Audacious! Whence is thy privilege to interrupt the few moments of repose my harassed mind can snatch amid the tumults of this noisy camp? Shall I inform your master of this presumptuous treachery? shall I disclose thee to Pizarro? Hey!

Here is the voice of *militant feminism*. At a certain point Pizarro tells Elvira to retire from his tent, "because men are to meet here, and on manly business."

Elv.   O, men! men! ungrateful and perverse! O, woman! still affectionate though wrong'd! The Beings to whose eyes you turn for animation, hope, and rapture, through the days of mirth and revelry; and on whose bosoms in the hour of sore calamity you seek for rest and consolation; THEM, when the pompous follies of your mean ambition are the question, you treat as playthings or as slaves! — I shall not retire.

Piz.   Remain then — and, if thou canst, be silent.

Here is *mother-love*. Cora is seated on a bank playing with her child. Alonzo stands by gazing at them affectionately.

Cora   Now, confess, does he resemble thee, or not?

Al.   Indeed he is liker thee — thy rosy softness, thy smiling gentleness.

Cora   But his auburn hair, the color of his eyes, Alonzo — O! my lord's image, and my heart's adored! [Pressing the Child to her bosom.]

Al.   The little daring urchin robs me, I doubt, of some portion of thy love, my Cora. At least he shares caresses, which till his birth were only mine.

Cora   Oh no, Alonzo! a mother's love for her dear babe is not a stealth, or taken from the father's store; it is a new delight that turns with quicken'd gratitude to HIM, the author of her augmented bliss.

Al.   Could Cora think me serious?

Cora   I am sure he will speak soon: then will be the last of the three holydays allowed by Nature's sanction to the fond anxious mother's heart.

Al.   What are those three?

Cora   The ecstacy of his birth I pass; that in part is selfish: but when first the white blossoms of his teeth appear, breaking the crimson buds that did incase them; that is a day of joy: next, when from his father's arms he runs without support, and clings, laughing and delighted, to his mother's knee; that is the mother's heart's next holyday: and sweeter still the third, when'er his little stammering tongue shall utter the grateful sound of, Father, Mother! — O! that is the dearest joy of all!

Al.   Beloved Cora!

Cora   Oh! my Alonzo!

Here is an *oration before battle*. (And, here, by the way, is one of the reasons for the enormous appeal of the play in 1799 and after. By the Peruvians Sheridan meant the English; by the Spanish invaders he was pointing to the French under Napoleon, who were expected at any moment to cross the Channel and attack England.) The Peruvian king calls upon Rolla to inspire the troops:

Rol.   My brave associates—partners of my toil, my feelings and my fame!—can Rolla's words add vigour to the virtuous energies which inspire your hearts?—No—You have judged as I have, the foulness of the crafty plea by which these bold invaders would delude you—Your generous spirit has compared as mine has, the motives, which, in a war like this, can animate *their* minds, and OURS.—THEY, by a strange frenzy driven, fight for power, for plunder, and extended rule—WE, for our country, our altars, and our homes.—THEY follow an Adventurer whom they fear—and obey a power which they hate— We serve a Monarch whom we love—a God whom we adore.

72   PIZARRO :

Piz. Rolla! ~~still~~ art ~~thou~~ free to go---this boy
remains with me.

— *Rol.* Then was this sword Heaven's gift, not
thine! *(Seizes the Child)*---Who ~~moves one step~~ to
follow ~~me,~~ dies upon the spot.

                              [*Exit, with the Child.*

Piz. Pursue him inſtantly---but ſpare his life.
[*Exeunt Almagro, and ſoldiers.*] With what fury
he defends himſelf!---Ha!---he fells them to the
ground---and now——

                    Enter ALMAGRO.

Alm. Three of your brave ſoldiers are already
victims to your command to ſpare this madman's
life; and if he once gains the thicket——

Piz. Spare him no longer. [*Exit* Almagro.]
Their guns muſt reach him---he'll yet eſcape---
holloa to thoſe horſe---the Peruvian ſees them
---and now he turns among the rocks---then
is his retreat cut off. [*Piſtols twice.*

(Rolla croſſes the wooden bridge over the cataract,
purſued by ~~the~~ ſoldiers---~~they~~ fires at him---a
ſhot ſtrikes him---Pizarro exclaims——

Piz. Now! quick! quick! ſeize the child!---

(Rolla tears from the rock the tree which ſupports
the bridge, and retreats by the back ground,
bearing off the child.)

                Re-enter ALMAGRO, & Davila.

Alm. By Hell! he has eſcaped!---and with
the child unhurt.

Dav. No---he bears his death with him---
Believe me, I ſaw him ſtruck upon the ſide.

Piz. But the child is ſav'd---Alonzo's child!
Oh! the furies of diſappointed vengeance!

                                        Alm.

They boast they come but to improve our state, enlarge our thoughts, and free us from the yoke of error!—Yes—THEY will give enlightened freedom to *our* minds, who are themselves the slaves of passion, avarice, cruelty, and pride.—They offer us their protection—Yes, such protection as vultures to lambs —covering and devouring them!—

(The metaphor of the vultures and lambs Sheridan plagiarized from one of his own orations in Parliament.)

They call on us to barter all of good we have inherited and proved, for the desperate chance of something better which they promise.—Be our plain answer this: The throne WE honour is the PEOPLE'S CHOICE— the laws we reverence are our brave Fathers' legacy—the faith we follow teaches us to live in bonds of charity with all mankind, and die in hope of bliss beyond the grave. Tell your invaders this, and tell them too, we seek no change; and, least of all, such change as they would bring us.

Enough: *Quod erat demonstradum.*

I am sorry to finish on the road downhill, but that's the finish of the century. The great event in the theatre of 1799 was Sheridan's *Pizarro,* and there you have it. Even though that thought be a melancholy one for created drama, the fact remains that stage historians and students interested in the vitality which the older plays continued to exhibit must have access to prompt books and acting copies. For in them is revealed the sequential variations which brought together the three basic elements of drama as an art—a text, actors, and the temper of the changing audience.

NOTES

1. Kalman Burnim, *David Garrick, Director* (Pittsburgh: University of Pittsburgh Press, 1961), p. vii.

2. M. St. Clare Byrne, "*King Lear* at Stratford-upon-Avon, 1959," *Shakespeare Quarterly,* XI (Spring 1960) 199.

3. The stage manager's promptbook is preserved at the Shakespeare Centre in Stratford.

4. Sybil Rosenfeld and Edward Croft-Murray, "A Checklist of Scene Painters Working in Great Britain and Ireland in the 18th Century," *Theatre Notebook,* XIX (Autumn 1964 to Summer 1965), 6-20, 49-64, 102-113, 133-145; XX (Autumn 1965 to Winter 1965/66), 36-44, 69-72.

5. Reproduced in Allardyce Nicoll, *The Development of the Theatre.* 3d ed. (New York: Harcourt Brace, 1946), p. 164.

6. G. Blakemore Evans, ed., *Shakespearean Prompt-books of the Seventeenth Century*, vol. IV; *Smock Alley Hamlet* (Charlottesville: University Press of Virginia, 1966).

7. For extended discussion of Garrick's *Hamlet*, see Burnim, pp. 152-173.

8. *Bell's Edition of Shakespeare's Plays*, III (London: J. Bell, 1774), *Hamlet*, 71.

9. G. Winchester Stone, "Garrick's Long Lost Alteration of *Hamlet*," *PMLA*, XLIX (September 1934), 890-921.

10. Charles H. Shattuck, ed., *John Philip Kemble Promptbooks*, 11 vols. (Charlottesville: University Press of Virginia, 1974). Kemble's *Hamlet* is in vol. 2.

11. This *As You Like It* book is preserved in the Theatre Collection of the New York Public Library.

12. For extended discussion of Garrick's *Provok'd Wife*, see Burnim, pp. 174-188.

13. This promptbook is preserved in the Folger Shakespeare Library.

14. Charles Churchill, *The Rosciad* (London: Printed for the Author, 1761), 11: 651-652.

15. *London Chronicle*, March 3-5, 1757.

16. For extended discussion of Garrick's *King Lear*, see Burnim, pp. 141-151.

17. For Tate's *Lear*, see Christopher Spencer, ed., *Five Restoration Adaptations of Shakespeare* (Urbana: University of Illinois Press, 1965), pp. 201-274.

18. G. Winchester Stone, "Garrick's Production of *King Lear:* A Study in the Temper of the Eighteenth-Century Mind," *Studies in Philology*, XLV (January 1948), 89-103.

19. John Henderson played three performances of Garrick's version at Drury Lane in 1779 and during the next five years played the Tate version at Covent Garden. For Kemble's *King Lear*, see *John Philip Kemble Promptbooks*, vol. 5.

20. Charles Lamb, "On the Tragedies of Shakespeare . . ." *The Works of Charles Lamb*, ed. Thomas Hutchinson, 2 vols. (London and New York: Oxford University Press, 1924), I, 136.

21. *John Philip Kemble Promptbooks*, vol. 8.

22. Ibid., vol. 2.

23. For both *The Stranger* and *Pizarro*, see ibid., vol. 11.

THEATRICAL DANCE
Editor's Headnote

In the Garrick period alone more than 600 titles occur for stage dances, performed by more than 1,000 dancers on the payrolls of the theatres, under the leadership of ballet masters and ballerinas which the theatres of Paris, Rome, Vienna, and the German courts could provide. Dances of figures, dances for atmosphere, dances narrating classical stories and commenting on the local scene, national dances, dances of trades (and bantering satire upon them) abounded. The London Stage *(Southern Illinois University Press, 1960–67) records all performances, and in the Introduction to each part discusses the kinds and progress of theatrical dancing in the period. Emmett L. Avery, "Dancing and Pantomime on the English Stage," SP XXXI (1934) gives a modern treatment of the forms. Contemporary writings of John Weaver (discussed by Professor Wynne), Kellom Tomlinson,* The Art of Dancing Explained *(1744), from which Professor Wynne made some slides, and Giovanni Andrea Gallini's* Treatise on the Art of Dancing *(1772) are eminently worth consulting, as is Deryck Lynham's* The Chevalier Noverre, Father of Modern Ballet *(London, 1950). An important film on the eighteenth-century theatrical dance, produced by Professor Wynne and Professor Allegra F. Snyder, Chairman of the Dance Department, UCLA, and sponsored by the National Endowment for the Arts, brings many aspects of the dance of that period alive. Kellom Tomlinson lists 171 subscribers to his "Art of Dancing" comprised of nobles, their ladies and daughters, twenty dancing masters, a number of medical doctors, many ladies from the counties, actors and theatrical dancers, engravers, masters of music, booksellers, lawyers, and unspecified ladies and gentlemen.*

Two problems are faced by Professor Wynne in her presentation: one, the seriousness of approach to the dance adopted by idealistic dancers and dance theorists from the Renaissance through the eighteenth century (along with their notations for performing), and two, a suggestion as to how the dances of the early eighteenth century can now be revived, not only with authenticity (the matter of lesser importance) but with imaginative conviction. In the performance at the Clark Library she and dancer Ron Taylor demonstrated convincingly by live performance, by slides, and by a film, the possibility of turning what she terms "recipes" (the signs and instructions of early dance manuals and notations) into "style" (the beautiful balance and proportion of concentrated energy revealed in gracious movement). Her thoughts on the history and the difficulty of fulfilling the desire to breathe life into page notation are the subject of her paper. The art of dancing in the eighteenth century received close attention in many levels of society. The Walpoles, Cavendishes, Somersets, Lady

Denbighs, Viscounts, and Countesses, as well as their host of middle-class companions, all reared under some tutelage from the dozens of thriving dancing masters in London, had a basis for critical evaluation of dance performance in the theatres. They watched the hundreds of dances eagerly. The very bulk and variety of dance in the repertory indicates its reigning popularity as a component of the "whole show" of an evening.

11. Reviving the Gesture Sign: Bringing the Dance Back Alive

Shirley Wynne
University of California, Santa Cruz

John Weaver, a reasonable, honorable and courageous dance master and scholar writing in 1717 regretted that he had "too much inclined to the modern dancing."[1] He had just produced his revival of an ancient pantomime "The Loves of Mars and Venus" on the London stage. Reading this passage recently, having just revived a divertissement including song, orchestra and dance, first performed at Les Sceaux in 1715, I understood his statement in a new sense, and wondered why it had not occurred to me before. Clearly my experience in the trials and discoveries of revivalism had come to a point where I understood, as if I had been there, Weaver's passion for the past and his frustrations in recreating it.

Dancers and choreographers face a dilemma unique in the field of arts and letters. Imagine knowing that Shakespeare existed, that his work was of highest value in its day yet no text survived, or Mozart living on his reputation alone with no scores remaining for us to study, practice, and still be touched by. A dancer faces his/her history with some such sense of loss and dissatisfaction. Such feelings are tinged with shame because in Western culture that which goes unrecorded has little value, and it has long been thought that no significant literature on dance exists. When existing records are dismissed, tossed out, remain uncatalogued and unexamined, the frustration deepens. Only within the last twenty years (with one or two important exceptions) have dance notation scores been studied seriously with the aim to transpose their abstract information into live performance.

The object of this essay is to consider the process of reviving ancient scores, to describe the delicate business of transforming abstract signs and the disordered information of our history into living performance; to raise questions about authenticity and the limits of stylistic range; and to analyze the elements that determine this range. When all living tradition has vanished, and life has changed utterly, how does a revivalist come to decisions that will give the abstract formalities of the past meaning for performers and audience today? My discussion in its historical development will center on the lonely work of John Weaver, not a popular artist in his day, but one who, because of his academic interest and deep concern for social and artistic standards, left invaluable records for those of us on the same mission today.

Interest in reviving performance practices has long been a motivating source in Western theatre practice. Again and again dance artists have looked to ancient Greece for inspiration and to regenerate their respect for their art by reclaiming the ideals of the best of that culture. Records begin to appear from the fifteenth century confirming this revivalism in the "art" of dance. Those so engaged turned to the dance of the ancient past because of abundant literary records, the breadth of expression described in the literature, and the high value dance held among the arts. Those recreators (the last being Isadora Duncan) believed they were creating authentic reproductions both of the spirit and form of classical Greek dance. Though each revival was the setting of a new style inspired by ancient Greece, each was believed to be a return to "natural" expression. Greek theatre at its most vital and productive period was linked to religious ritual. Though this connection has long been open to scholarly debate, I believe there can be no argument that because of some deep relationship between art and ritual, dance was esteemed then as a performing art for the expression of the widest range of human passion.

In the centuries following the decline of Greek civilization dance was condemned as a social recreative form and proscribed in performance. Not only was the body denied its expressive power in public performance but it was constrained, tightened, and repressed by social proprieties, as if to contain by force the sources of depravity seething within. The Greek model, however, offered the dancer, who survived in spite of suppression, an almost divine release. The human body recovered its dignity. It stood at ease, vertical, balanced, a vessel for the worthiest human expression. In the fifteenth century along with returning recognition of beauty in the physical presence, some dancing masters saw the need for literary expositions. Documents began to appear describing the wondrous new dance that was believed to be the revival of the venerable older form. The new art was not thought to be merged with ritual, but it recaptured its powers to teach, to exemplify, and to be a model for social ideals. The "art" dance was to be practiced faithfully as it served to represent perfection in social behavior. The dancer in society became an example of the ideals in movement attitudes of the time: order, balance, memory, musicality, and judgment. The term "judgment" may be defined as aesthetic taste in reference to movement behavior. Subtle and subjective, "taste" is among the most evasive of conventions in art. The courtier in the ballroom might enjoy and even "express" himself (to use a modern much misunderstood term) but was obliged first of all to reflect the social attitude of restraint. This fine line of taste is the crux of reconstruction today: The dancer must perform expressively yet with propriety. Our notions of proper restraint (and they do still exist) are very different from those of the fifteenth century. Then the courtier-dancer was to appear artless and uninvolved while showing as artful mastery of the technique and ornaments of the dance. The beauty of the dance was precisely identified with the manner of virtue in society. Beauty and virtue were one. The connection between aesthetics and morality in body communication may be an aspect of Western dance shared by other cultures. In Western tradition beauty and virtue were to be combined in the mastery and cool control of feats of extraordinary virtuosity and daring. This attitude has remained in Western movement systems and can be seen in today's ballet dancers who perform breathtaking passages yet appear totally unconcerned, unruffled, chaste, and superhuman. Failing to perform a difficult movement sequence well remains both highly comic and a breach of etiquette or good taste.

Style, then, in any art has to do with limits and restraints, not willful nor free expression. In studying historical documents one learns what behavior was *preferred,* what was *tolerated,* and what was *forbidden* at any given place or time. The third category is always rich because of the need in society to right abuses and correct behavior deemed detrimental to social order. These expressions of wrongdoing give an indication of the fine shades of propriety. The researcher explores and evaluates the importance of these boundaries; the recreator of a dance performance must make public subtle choices of good taste in accordance with what he/she decides are convincing of the correct practices of an earlier time.

In the late seventeenth and early eighteenth centuries numerous works appeared on the history of pantomime and dance, John Weaver's among them. Thoughtful comparisons were made between the ancient and modern forms. The closer the resemblance to its ancient model the better dance became, and in the eighteenth-century historian's mind much improvement had been made from the crude revivals of the fifteenth to the innovations of the eighteenth century. Dancers still today tend to cling to a naive idea that their art has advanced and improved through the course of its history. In one sense it has, for the value of the body as an expressive instrument, its respectability among the arts, has begun to match its rank and stature in ancient Greece, as well as in almost any other non-Western culture in the world.

In writing so, I become John Weaver's colleague and supporting friend. He was striving for expressiveness and respectability in 1712 and deplored the "low ebb to which dancing is now fallen." He continues in his letter to the *Spectator*[2] "the Art is esteem'd only as an amusing Trifle. . . . It is therefore, in my opinion, high time that someone should come to its assistance, and relieve it from many gross and growing Errors that have crept into it, and overcast its real Beauties." His passion to revive the dignity, beauty, and significance of the ancient Greek dance is akin to my own desire to revive the eighteenth-century ballet, a high point of stylistic richness and excellence in the history of Western dance. In spite of the most stringent social regulations, it has left music and graphic images expressive of playful, sensuous, ardent, and tender physicality, the *danse gracieuse*. The *danse noble*, after the Greek fashion, embodied the perfection of ideal physical attitudes and energies of restraint and represented in movement signs the heroic and divine aspects of mankind as they were believed to be. John Weaver, too, saw the need to record dance. Following the earliest notation system in the fifteenth century, scholars continued to invent new ways to record dance movement in a fashion more explicit than word description. In 1700 the most impressive system to date appeared. Its function was to record the details of a dance style greatly valued in its day, to preserve for posterity, to perpetuate a tradition through future time and to make available to a wider public what had been approved as excellent and beautiful in the centers for opera and ballet, Paris and Versailles. Soame Jenyns believed that the dance of that day, preserved in abstract signs, was eternal and universal. In 1729 he wrote:

> Long was the Dancing Art unfix'd and free;
> Hence lost in Error and Uncertainty:
> No Precepts did it mind, or Rules obey,
> But ev'ry Master taught a diff'rent Way;
> Hence e're each new-born Dance was fully try'd
> The lovely Product, ev'n in blooming, dy'd:
> Thro' various Hands in wild Confusion toss'd,
> Its Steps were alter'd, and its Beauties lost:
> Till Fuillet at length, Great Name! arose.
> And did the Dance in Characters compose:
> Each lovely Grace by certain Marks he taught,
> And ev'ry Step in lasting Volumes wrote.
> Hence o'er the World this pleasing Art shall spread.
> And ev'ry Dance in ev'ry Clime be read;
> By distant Masters shall each Step be seen,
> Tho' Mountains rise, and Oceans roar between.
> Hence with her Sister-Arts shall Dancing claim
> An equal Right to Universal Fame,
> And Isaac's Rigadoon shall last as long
> As Raphael's Painting, or as Virgil's Song.[3]

Joseph Addison remarked on the novelty of reading a dance[4] in an anecdote describing disturbances in an upper floor of a London rooming house. Upon investigation the crashing and pounding noises above were found to be caused by a gentleman sight-reading a dance from a score held in his hand. The dancer, upon being questioned, explained that he had just received the dance by post from Paris, and that "there is nothing so common as to communicate a dance by letter."

Raoul Auger Feuillet, the "Great Name" to whom Jenyns refers, wrote and published *Choregraphie*, a system of dance writing which is said to have been invented by Pierre Beauchamps, maître de ballet to the king at the end of the century. For the next 30 years many scores of ballets and ballroom dances numbering over 350 separate works were published and recorded in manuscript. Translations of Feuillet's text were made in English (in 1706 two appeared, one by John Weaver), German, Spanish, and Italian during this period. New improved versions of the systems were published later in the century, and reprints of old favorites among the dances appeared into the 1780s. Diderot included a sample of the characters in his *Encyclopedia*; however, the vigor of the style had reached its peak before 1750. The system could not or did not shift and expand to incorporate the stylistic upheaval of the late eighteenth century; yet some elements of the step tradition continued alongside and were absorbed into the more timely interest in mime-dramas or full-length ballets of Salvatore Vigano, Jean Georges Noverre, Gasparo Angiolini and Franz Anton Christoph Hilferding. In 1830, after the maelstrom of revolution at the end of the century, a new system appeared, devised by an otherwise little-known dance master, Theleur. The symbols were entirely new, retaining none of the conventions of the Feuillet system. Transposing the signs of movement, however, demonstrates the continuity of ballet tradition: the steps are changed, yet are clearly derived from earlier practices. Thereafter more systems appeared. Today several are so fully developed that it is now possible to copyright a ballet.

Feuillet's manual, and many hundreds of dance scores utilizing his method, provide the modern revivalist with the kind of information necessary to recreate dance: foot positions, step direction, shape, elevation or level, floor plan, and, absolutely essential, correlation to music. Known Greek sources, to this date, have not provided this kind of requisite information.

Because energy in performance, coming from some kind of conviction or belief, stirs an audience, I turn again to John Weaver as a source of inspiration for early eighteenth-century

English values. He clearly instructs the reader on the proprieties of manners, on a powerful yet discreet performance of dance, on exemplary behavior in the theatre and the ballroom. His attitudes on aesthetics and etiquette are essential to the process of reconstructing the good judgment I spoke of earlier, the approved constraints which define the contours of a movement style.

In his *An Essay Towards an History of Dancing*[5] Weaver recorded his views of history as well as his observations and instructions on the contemporary dance in London and Paris. He noted therein the difference between ballroom and stage dancing. The first he called "common," the second "serious":

Serious Dancing differs from the Common-Dancing usually taught in schools, as History painting differs from Limning. For as the Common-Dancing has a peculiar Softness, which would hardly be perceivable on the stage; so Stage-Dancing would have a rough and ridiculous Air in a Room, when on the Stage it would appear soft, tender, and delightful. And altho' the Steps of both are generally the same, yet they differ in the performance.

The fundamental steps were indeed the same, yet those for the stage were of far greater complexity, requiring far more skill than those typical of ballroom dancing. Demeanor in dancing practiced in society also had parallels with that appropriate for the stage. Weaver described this attitude as an "artful carelessness, as if it were a natural motion, without a too curious and painful practising." He admitted that "To Dance too exquisitely is, I must own, too laborious a Vanity."[6]

Yet, on stage, discretion was to be balanced with sufficient vigor to arouse an audience. If an actor was "lazy or unskillful . . . every one falls into Discourse with his next Neighbor; but when an Actor that has Life, Motion and Energy comes on, everyone is then attentive, and the Pit observes him with a Profound and respectful Silence."[7] Weaver praised the good taste of the English dancing master Josias Priest who composed the dances for Henry Purcell's *Dido and Aeneas* and compared French dancing to that of the English master: The French he acknowledged, danced well but committed gross errors "in having a confus'd Chaos of Steps, which they indifferently apply'd, without any Design, to all Characters; they car'd not by what ridiculous, awkward, out of the way Action, they gain'd Applause; and judg'd of their mean Performance by the mistaken Taste of the Audience."[8]

The term "motion" had particular significance for Weaver. Motion was "the Soul of Dancing," and an audience would be stirred to reflect upon seeing energy in motion, because of "so great a Sympathy between Motion and the Mind of Man."[9] "Motion" then could be thought of as the energy in performance which revealed the performer's humanity in relation to his world. I liken this to *belief,* for so long as performance structures or conventions are believed to have power and truth the performer has the possibility of reaching his fellows. (I do not equate belief in the form here with the performer's being personally moved by the form.) In addition to motion, two other principles, equally broad in significance, combined to form an ideal in dancing. The energies of motion were to be "contain'd in some Figure," which represented the "Operations of Nature, in which Order is perpetually observ'd, and Confusion avoided. . . . Necessity and Reason therefore join'd together."[10]

Motion and Figure were to join another principle to complete the harmonious perfection of the whole. "There is a sort of Harmony in Numbers, or Measures," wrote Weaver, "which gives the greatest delectation and Force to Musick."[11] "Motion" was to be regulated by "Measure." Motion, figure, and measure were not, then, mere instructions for the mechanics of dancing, but held the profound meaning of man's relation to the physical and spiritual universe. They signified a conception of the world which was kept in order by deliberate and conscious acts of man. Dance was deeply symbolic of the ordering of time (measure), space (figure), and energy (motion), those components that form all dance styles, and beauty was seen in the proper proportioning and balance of each performance. Propriety came to mean far more than social grace. Propriety was a public message of good taste, which demonstrated an artist's faith to represent order and beauty in life. The dance of the period (in the ideal sense that Weaver defines) seems deeply spiritual, more akin to ritual dances in a non-Western culture than to those of our own tradition. One can see how the confused chaos of the French dancers was a great breach of faith to someone of Weaver's standards. These beliefs seem archaic and foreign to us now, living as we do in a severely secular world, but his attitudes were entirely in accord with Western tradition from the early Renaissance to the end of the eighteenth century.

Guglielmo Ebreo in 1463 spoke of dance as a science of "great excellence and supreme value." The virtue of dance was in the "outward demonstration of the inward stirring of the spirit, which demonstration must accord with the measured and perfect consonances of this harmony."[12] Thomas Elyot in *The Book of the Governour* (1531)[13] assigns each weight change, in the steps of the basse dance, an aspect of prudence. A double step, for example, which is made up of three steps or weight changes, signified "thre braunches of prudence; election, experience, and modestie. By them the saide vertue of prudence is made complete, and is in her perfection." A man and all that he signified, dancing with a woman of complementary aspects, formed a perfect balance of opposites. Here again by performing a dance, the dancers personified the reordering of life's disparate elements. The performance was a repetitive, redundant act of confirmation of man's obligation to the forces of nature, as well as the joys received by participating in them with just discretion.

Weaver's theories on the art of dance in the theatre represent the fusion of the principles of the French *ballet d'ècole* and the *ballet d'action,* or the skill of technique, and the skill of expression. Order, unity, and control were practiced in the vertical, still, central torso of the dancer. The fine articulation of the feet and legs and the positioning of the arms in precise opposition to the legs, were manifestations of balance and harmony. Further, the dance figure was invariably symmetrical, and the steps in unison or mirrored opposites. These principles of technique were paired with the skill of "representing all manner of Passions."[14] The fine dancer had to show "Strength and Softness reconcil'd" so that he could express both "robustness" and "Delicacy."[15] His excellence lay in "Imitation of the Manners and Passions, and not from Agility, fine Steps and Risings, which only now seem to distinguish a Dancer."[16]

The spectator was instructed to be conscious of two forces: the symmetry of the movements and the "several Passions, Manners, or Actions; as of Love, Anger, and the like."[17] Passions or actions had their origin in what Weaver called "natural" practices:

Ancients probably observed, in the Motions of Mankind . . . the natural
Effect of particular Causes; whence they might compose the different
Actions of their Primitive Dances, as when Men are struck with Joy, they
leap; especially the ruder Sort, only inform'd by simple Nature, and
being strangers to the Modes and Customs of Urbanity. . . . Thus, when
Grief assaulted them, they cast down their Heads; Anger and Admiration lifted up their Hands; in like manner several Motions of the Body
arose from other different Passions of the Mind, especially the most
violent.[18]

The dancer who effectively fused the two techniques of symmetrical and balanced attitudes with the representation of the passions,
needed to train the torso, arms, and face in addition to the legs
and feet.[19] In his *Lectures upon Dance*[20] Weaver describes the
gestures of the face, which he calls the "Image of the Soul: Anger
and Scorn are seated on the Brow: the Eyes express the Sentiments of the Heart; and every Passion of the Mind is discover'd in
the countenance."

For him the ideal dancer-mime

must not be too tall, nor too low, but of a moderate Size; not too fat and
bulky, nor too lean like a Skeleton. . . . Our Pantomime ought to be of
an active, pliant, and yet a compacted Body; able to turn with Quick-
ness, and to stop if Occasion require with Strength. . . . [He] must be
every Thing exactly, and do all Things with Order, Decency, and
Measure like himself, without any Imperfection.[21]

The training of Weaver's performers was to conform to classical
ideals. The dancer was, in accord with Lucian's requirements, to
"express, and imitate all things, nay even his very own Thoughts,
by the Motions and Gesticulations of his Body."[22] He must in addition have an extensive knowledge of "the whole Attic Fable," all
that is to be found in classical writings, "and be ready to produce
them into Action on Occasion."[23]

A master in dramatic dancing had to have a sound learning in
rhetoric and elegance. Expressiveness in speech was to be paralled
in the movements of the dance:

an Elegance of Action consists, in adapting the Gesture to the Passions
and Affections; and the Dancer, as well as the Orator, allures the Eye
and invades the Mind of the Spectator; for there is a Force, and Energy
in Action, which strangely affects; and when Words will scarce move,
Action will excite, and put all the Powers of the Soul in ferment.[24]

Nature ordered that rude passions be given specific gestural signs. Gestures or the signs for deep feelings which without set conventions would be disordered, violent, and intolerable to observe, were synonymous with decency, "for nature assigned each motion of the mind its proper gesticulation and countenance, as well as tone, whereby it is significantly and decently expressed."[25]

Even with these explicit, albeit severe requirements, the matter of good judgment or decency in taste remains most important yet indefinable. Weaver does not assist in clarifying this subtlety, for he advises the reader to discover the correct manner for himself by looking in a mirror to "distinguish the Proper from the Improper."[26] We know that every motion must be regular rather than irregular, graceful rather than ungainly and awkward.[27] Yet this advice is as frustrating to the revivalist now as the note on the music score is to the level of speed. The word "grave" on a score from the period meant slow in relation to other terms, but when there were no established speeds with which to set up relationships, how fast was fast, how slow, slow? What shade of manner was the correct look?

Weaver was unable to direct his modern dancers to perform according to his design, even though he acknowledged their willingness to attempt something "so entirely novel and foreign to their present Manner of Dancing."[28] Weaver's pantomime was first produced at Drury Lane, then "borrowed" by John Rich for a performance at Lincoln's Inn Fields. Rich's popularized version succeeded whereas Weaver's failed.

An interesting question arises on this point as to the realities of performance practice in those days. Weaver writes of the ideal from his own point of view. Other evidence supports the assumption that there were those who agreed with him fully. Yet public taste typically preferred a less severe and obscure theatre. Popular taste rarely accepts innovation and on some levels never finds interest in literary theatre. It can be argued that Weaver, although delving into history, was nonetheless a spokesman for a small, elite avant-garde. His ideals were expressed in similar fashion again in 1750 by Louis de Cahusac[29] and, beginning in 1760, by Jean Georges Noverre,[30] who even at that later time was thought to be a revolutionary. That there was a wide range of taste as well as a wide variety of theatre activities merely provides the revivalist with more possibilities for interpretation of scores and the setting of the theatre context.

In analyzing dance style one contends with two large areas of movement: (1) what is done, or what I call movement recipes; and (2) how it is done, or the degrees and shades of energies. The latter elements are what make one care about the dance; the former what interests the mind and the eye. There can be, of course, no arbitrary separation of these factors, for every posture and movement transition carries significant information about a person's attitude toward his/her physical and social world.

Movement recipes are the easiest aspect to learn in an unfamiliar movement style, such as, for example, a highly refined, finely articulated Balinese dance. Though direction, facing, speed, level, body part, and so forth may present fundamental differences in approach to time and space, these "ingredients" are still within our grasp compared to indefinable and imprecise shifts of energies. After gaining some mastery over the recipe of a style, one would still be worlds away from truly dancing the dance of a different culture from one's own. The reluctance, even inability, of the body to change its deep-set behavioral modes prevents one from moving easily from one style to another. The fact is obvious on a personal level: I do not move the same way as my fellow in the dance studio. In our society these differences are valued and the object of our modern training programs is to refine and clarify the differences of individuality. What is generally not acknowledged in our search for innovation is our stylistic sameness, or the elements held in common and shared by a larger cultural group. The similarities in movement configurations come from activities in daily life, not from any conscious choice, or single creative genius; they are a combination of ancient movement attitudes, those of the immediate moment, and individual habit and initiative. All three are difficult to observe and define precisely. Old habitual patterns persist among today's young adults. Whites of European descent are just beginning to incorporate the rich undulating torso of non-Western peoples (principally some African cultures) into their habitual movement mode even though this influence has been present in our culture since the early part of this century when African art and life began to be valued. Still the Western torso particularly resists giving up its strict verticality and unity. For since the fifteenth century, as mentioned, uprightness and central unity have been valued as both beautiful and virtuous. Though we may not *think* this now, we still *move* it.

New patterns manifesting the immediate environment can be seen in another example. The movement of Martha Graham and her contemporaries, which evolved in the late 1920s and 1930s, had the marks of its day: sharp, hard-edged accented, stressful, excessive tension, stop-action. In the current scene young people look less angular, softer in contour, less stoppable than before. They prefer soft, ongoing transitions, a vague and undefined sense of time, and the sense of their own weight, easily giving into gravity. Today's mode calls up a very different image from that of the light, vertical, delicate ballerina. One could search out the elements influencing this change, but conscious choice or contrivance must be ruled out as contributing factors. Influences are coming from all aspects of today's life and are merging with the generations of behavior imbedded in our bodies. On this level of behavior, style finds its most subtle differences, those elements that make it difficult for me, a Westerner of European descent, trained and living in one kind of world of time, space, energy and weight, to dance with full integrity a Balinese, Hopi, or Ghanian dance.

Those of us of European descent can, however, dance an eighteenth-century French or English dance with a far greater chance of believability. A tradition of movement attitudes can both be felt within our bodies and recognized visually. Movement postures and rhythms, use of energy and body parts are components of kinetic as well as visual and aural memory. Though we never took part in a ball in the eighteenth century, generations of movement behavior locked in our body tissue maintain the restraints, possibilities, and preferences of our ancestors.

Weaver's proper judgment comes from this kind of amalgam. Even though time creates a vastly different world, we of this heritage can hope to come close to sensing correct behavior then and reliving it in a convincing manner. What Weaver saw in his revival struck him as unbelievable. It could not have moved the audience greatly else his pantomime would have been more successful. His dancers were unable to perform what was wanted in spite of their willingness. Their bodies could not be tuned to the energies of another style convincingly enough to perform the actions and passions of another mankind unfamiliar to them. Perhaps Weaver did not inspire his dancers to recollect their own tradition or what they could physically experience in 1717 as within their own living memory. Perhaps his imagination failed him. In any case he must not have been able to create a lively performance in spite of the excellence of his motives.

Movement instructions or recipes, alone, are lifeless relics, like fragments of words from a forgotten language. One can follow them precisely, given the right code, and perform the skeleton of actions, sometimes longer sequences; yet the total gesture is empty of meaning and expression. No one can be touched by unknown formulas. Neither the audience nor the performer is satisfied. A symbol in itself tends to inhibit life, as Diderot himself observed. A graphic sign for a gesture represents movement that has become officially standardized and sanctioned. No early dance notator invented a sign for a movement until that movement had become a well-established pattern. Further, the symbol, like notes in music notation, represents uniformity and regularity, not the great variety of possibility in expression which is actually available in all human performance. Notation is essential, then, for reconstruction and preservation of performance and is merely a skeleton framework with which to begin.

In the texts of plays, in music scores, operas, divertissements, in the notations for dancing, human expressivity must somehow be reinvested into performance. Authenticity alone does not move an audience, though it may spark heated arguments among academicians. Arlene Croce noted, "Authenticity is so far from the point of enjoyment in dancing that it wouldn't much matter even if it were possible to be a hundred percent accurate — right down to the leather in people's shoes, the wood under their feet, and the quality of their muscle tone."[31] Julian Mitchell, referring to his work on Jennie Churchill[31] places the task of creative aliveness on the intuition:

But all this material, all this research . . . didn't tell me what Jennie was really like. A historical dramatist has eventually to reach beyond his research and trust to his intuition, knowing that historians will sneer at the drama, and that dramatists scoff at the history. The characters, though, can come alive — if you're lucky.

Even though eighteenth-century France is within our world of memory, it was still a radically different world — one in which we can take positions, give arguments, be disgusted and righteous about. In some ways it is too close to view as strangers: we are involved politically and morally (as well as kinetically, visually and aurally) with our historical past. Yet in order to recapture the intrinsic flavor of a time with belief rather than prior assumption tinged with derision, one must approach the milieu as a respectful outsider, pretending to know nothing. One must research with utmost care, persistently gathering details, and then free oneself from these endless instructions, strictures, and fragments of information to wander imaginatively back into another life. Facts and arbitrary rules hardly inspire feelings for people. One must find a way to believe in the artists then; to care about them as colleagues and friends; to be touched by their music, their dance and their sentiments; to sympathize with their struggles to survive, their pleasures, disappointments, their saddening anonymity. (The great ballerina, Marie Sallé, comes to mind. After a chaste life devoted to her art, she died alone and with no public notice.) One must dare to imagine beyond the facts and conjure up visions of intimacy which lie beneath the public announcements and general theoretical assumptions; for it is from the smallest detail of daily life that human expressivity comes and not the official insignia of gesture.

On first appearance, history seems to offer a safe harbor to the artist. What was once approved has survived in official records and critical judgments of those events. The artist-historian is often thought to represent a retreat from the uncertainties of creating "new" forms, those that have as yet no standards for approval. The past in our fantasy always looks better than the chaotic present. But that fantasy soon vanishes when it is faced with live performers and a live audience. The revivalist faces the same responsibilities as the experimental innovator: communicating the concerns of people.

To conclude, the aim of this essay is to clarify the problems of transforming the page of a theatrical source, particularly the abstract symbol of a dance movement, into live performance. Is it better to stay close to historical data or to be totally free in invention? The answer, predictably, lies somewhere in between. Of vital importance is the convincing look from the performers of conviction, and belief which comes from their being somehow involved with human concerns, energies and sentiments which move us to recognize something of our tradition. The recipes for eighteenth-century ballet are eminently capable of representing "the manners and passions of mankind." If we presume to undertake the task of reviving this form of theatre, we must, above all, make that language speak again with ever renewed energy — ever keeping in mind one's obligation to good taste!

NOTES

1. John Weaver, *The Loves of Mars and Venus* (London: Mears & Browne, 1717), Preface, xiii.

2. No. 334. 24 March 1712.

3. Soame Jenyns, *The Art of Dancing, a Poem* (London: W. P. & J. Roberts, 1729), Canto II, pp. 25-26.

4. *Tatler*, no. 88, 31 October 1709.

5. John Weaver, *An Essay Towards an History of Dancing* (London: J. Tonson, 1712), p. 162.

6. Ibid., p. 65.

7. Ibid., pp. 86-87.

8. Ibid., p. 167.

9. Ibid., pp. 86-87.

10. Ibid., pp. 87-88.

11. Ibid., p. 89.

12. Quoted by Mable Dolmetsch, *Dances of Spain and Italy* (London: Routledge & Paul, 1954), p. 10.

13. Thomas Elyot, *The Book of The Governour* (London, 1531), Chap. XXV.

14. Weaver, *History*, p. 166.

15. Ibid., pp. 143-144.

16. Ibid., p. 147.

17. Ibid., pp. 160-161.

18. Ibid., pp. 90-91.

19. Ibid.

20. John Weaver, *Anatomical and Mechanical Lectures on Dancing* (London: J. Brotherton, 1721), p. 5.

21. Weaver, *History*, pp. 144-145.

22. Ibid., pp. 123-124.

23. Ibid., pp. 131-133.

24. Weaver, *Lectures*, p. 144.

25. Weaver, *Loves of Mars*, xiii.

26. Weaver, *History*, p. 64.

27. Weaver, *Lectures*, viii-ix.

28. Weaver, *Loves of Mars*, x.

29. Louis de Cahusac, *La Danse Ancienne et Moderne* (La Haye: J. Neulme, 1754).

30. Jean-Georges Noverre, *Lettres sur la Danse et sur les Ballets* (Stuttgart et Lyon: A. Delaroche, 1760).

31. *The New Yorker* (May 16, 1977), "Dancing," p. 80.

32. *The New York Times*, 26 October 1975. "My Search for The Elusive Jennie Churchill," Section 2, p. 27.

CRITICAL NORMS
Editor's Headnote

For Professor Beckerman drama and theatre are dynamic rather than static affairs. He leads us away from the older approach in criticism of discussing four or five horizontal limits as separate entities—plot, character, setting, theme, dialogue—toward the simultaneous interplay of these. He points the value of reading a play text as a sequence of scene units, each embodying a structure or scheme of activity which the actor realizes by projecting himself at a fellow actor or at the audience. "The scheme of activity," he writes, "as it lies implicitly and provocatively among the words of the text, is of course only potential. It exists as an array of options rather than a defined blueprint of performance." Attention to it provides an understanding of both the performing demands made on the actor by the script, and the performing options available to him. Only then does one gain clear insight into the dramaturgic properties of the work. "The goal is not merely to 'see' a performance in the mind's eye, but to 'feel' it coursing through the body."

Aristotle reminds us that we know a thing by what we can say about a thing. It is fitting to close this series of papers with Professor Beckerman's suggestions for a different approach, and a different terminology with which to criticize both a play and its performance. He has tested the validity of his approach by convincing reference to the plays of George Lillo—whose George Barnwell; or The London Merchant *was one of the most popular of the newly created eighteenth-century tragedies.*

12. Schemes of Show: A Search for Critical Norms

Bernard Beckerman

Professor of English, Columbia University

Titling a book *The Stage and the Page* is deceptively simple. At first glance the partners in this title seem to bear equal weight, to demand equal respect, to exert equal strength. But do they? Do we all accept the straightforward equation? In critical literature

209

generally the stage and the page are not always considered so evenly balanced. One widespread, all too common formulation sees the page — that is, the text of the written play — as the soul of an art whose body is the stage. Indeed, this duality may be more deeply embedded in our thinking than we are prepared to concede. It is reflected in the very distinction we draw between drama and theatre. For many drama is the literary work, the poem, the enduring art, and because enduring more valuable art; theatre is the means by which the drama is transmitted.

My outlook is somewhat different. In my view, stage and page, theatre and drama, are not differentiated as body and soul, but as general and specific kinds of presentation. Theatre is the art of all kinds of presentation by living performers; drama the art of *fictional* presentation, also by living performers. Thus drama is a subdivision of theatre, just as dance and acrobatics are further subdivisions of the same medium. Actors and dramatists of the eighteenth century would, I think, have readily understood this formulation. Whatever preoccupation they may have had with lifting the tone of drama, in practice they put on the stage all sorts of shows, dramatic and nondramatic alike. This is apparent when we look at a customary program for a London playhouse. To take but one example at random. On March 11, 1740 Covent Garden offered a performance of *Henry V* interspersed at different times by three dances and followed by a performance of *The Mock Doctor*.[1] Not only do we find comedy following history but one kind of theatre mixed with another.

Seen then as a subdivision of theatre, drama is always a medium of presentation. Even when the drama is supposedly representational, it is representational through the art of presentation. The stuff of that art is human activity; not merely words, not merely gestures but the combination of both as acts of wonder and even truth. These are acts composed of a skillfully rendered surface of sound and movement vigorously sustained by the expenditure of human energy. As a rough analogy I would say that the human energy of presentation is like the energy that drives a plane. Unless it is strong enough to maintain a critical speed, the plane cannot rise. Without a minimum of concentrated vitality, the theatrical act cannot take place.

The theatrical act, though, more than word plus gesture is composed of both. Rarely, however, does drama give speech and gesture equal emphasis. In the western world, drama has tended to make greater use of spoken language through which to create acts of presentation; in the Far East, the opposite has been the case. As a result, it is generally easier to record the dramatic act of the west, so much so that the record has often been confused with the thing itself, the presentation.

As we know, the page cannot capture the full and continuous exchange of expression created by the actors. It cannot convey the inflection of the voice or the timing of a piece of business. It does, however, record the lines spoken and, in some small measure, the movements made. It may even indicate the supposed manner of delivery, as when a dramatist adds a stage direction, "with deep feeling." But the page also catches, embedded between the lines and reflected in the sequential arrangement, a trace of the actor's energy that enlivened the presentation. Because drama is conceived as presentation the dramatist does two contradictory things: (1) he leaves room between and within the lines for the actor to assert himself; and (2) he provides hints of transitions and gestures to guide that assertion. By studying both what is omitted and what is included, one can perceive the energy pattern of the actual or potential performance. Prompt books, costumes, engravings, diaries, and other artifacts of stage production will to some degree illuminate this pattern, but the principal key to the performance resides in the dynamic shape that emerges from the page.

We can speak of that dynamic shape in two ways: as it manifests itself in the script as a whole and as it assumes varied forms in separate scenes. Historically and habitually, we are accustomed to discuss theatre in the first of the two ways, namely in terms of a play's continuity—such as plot—or its effects—such as character and theme.[2] By an impulse that we have come to regard as natural, we seek to connect the varying impressions of a reading or a performance into a coherent vision of the writer. This binding process—illuminating as it may be—is also essentially reductive. We conflate the intricate and complicated interactions between a work and an audience into an easily comprehensible "idea." At times and for certain purposes, this reduction is useful—when for example we wish to compare gross features of one play to another. But turning a living play into a recital of its plot and characters or a critique of its theme does not aid us in understanding performance since in the course of performance we do not experience a play as strands of plot and character. Instead, we interact with a succession of discrete total presentational units — what we usually call scenes or scene units. The scene may be part of a tightly meshed plot sequence or it may be a rather autonomous, loosely connected production "number" or "turn."[3] Whatever the relationship of these parts to the totality, we only become aware of the totality through perception of and reaction to the subunits. Thus, in order to deal with performance we must separate out analysis of the scene from that of continuity. This distinction, rarely made, is absolutely essential if we are to study performance. It is especially applicable to eighteenth-century theatre with its unrestrained habit of offering a mixed evening to make up what Professor Stone calls the "whole show." Clearly, the taste of the period was not prejudiced against scenes or "turns" which only had tangential links to other events in the program.

So far I have used the words "number" or "scene" to indicate the subdivision of a whole play. It is convenient to do so, for everyone roughly knows what is meant. What one has to study, however, is the organic scene unit; that can neither be defined roughly nor determined mechanically. Such a unit is not merely the portion of a play that comes between entrances of characters though it may coincidentally be that too. Instead, it is a coherent segment of theatrical activity. When that activity is a dance interpolated between the acts of a play, as in the program at Covent Garden already cited, it is simple enough for us to distinguish the separate unit. When, however, the unit is stitched into the fabric of a play, we find it harder to separate the successive subordinate sections without consciously and persistently analyzing the structure of a piece.

In the course of separating and analyzing a unit, we become aware of its underlying shape or, more properly, scheme. But why "scheme?" Does not the word suggest something formulaic while the appeal of a play is its unclassifiable individuality? By using the term "scheme," I wish to emphasize the commonality of performing units. The "proviso scene" in Restoration comedy is an instance of one kind of scheme. Other kinds, less widely recognized, also abound in the theatre. And a virtue of anatomizing typical schemes is that one thereby becomes sensitized to those instances where a dramatist has transcended a commonplace pattern. By knowing the root dynamic of a scene unit, one can better appreciate how the exceptional scene has been realized and what its performing qualities are.

Let me cite one example: the seduction scene in Act I from *George Barnwell: or The London Merchant* by way of illustration. As a schematic type, the seduction scene is a subdivision of the general type of persuasion scene. Such a scene has four components: first, a persuader; second, someone to be persuaded; third, a mode of persuasion; and lastly, a mode of resistance to persuasion. The tacit assumption of such a type is that the person persuaded has freedom to act. In the segment I am citing the persuader is the seducer Millwood. The eighteen-year-old Barnwell is, if I may use the term, the seducee. There is a third person in this scene, Millwood's maid Lucy, who is there to second the seducer and comment on the seduction. As a type, the persuasion segment depends for its interest on the kind of impediment—that is, the kind of resistance—that the persuader encounters. To overcome the resistance, the persuader almost invariably employs one among a limited number of modes of persuasions. He makes the future attractive or repulsive, recalls the past, or arouses latent inclinations. So recurrent are these modes of persuasion that one can speak of the schema of persuasion in the same sense that E. H. Gombrich writes of visual schema.[4]

What distinguishes seduction from other kinds of persuasion is the sensual quality of the mode of persuasion. In *Julius Caesar* (I.ii), for instance, Cassius on the surface appears to be persuading Brutus to oppose Caesar, but the substance of his argument, with its semirational foundation and athletic comparisons, verges on seduction. Because this sensual mode of persuasion holds for seduction scenes in general, one can speak of this pattern as the primary dynamic of a unit. The task of the two performers in the unit is to create the illusion that the consequences are in doubt, and that some sort of internal, intangible process is coursing through the seducee.

When one examines the Barnwell scene as a variant of the persuasion type, one appreciates all the more readily what distinguishes this particular version of the seduction scheme. First, the calculated and adroit nature of the seducer is openly announced before Barnwell enters the scene, thus creating a frame of expectation. Second, the utter innocence of the seducee is established, thus making for strong contrast between seducer and seducee.

Third, the mode of seduction depends on arousing latent desires in Barnwell. Millwood does not paint a tempting future, nor is there a past to recall. Instead—seemingly inadvertently—she places her hand on that of the young apprentice; she talks of love; she weeps—in brief, she does not so much woo him as she exerts a presence. The resistance George offers is not opposed directly to Millwood's advances, but emerges as assertions of his very being.

Lillo gives the general scheme of seduction particular shape by arranging the action in three subsegments. First appears a unit of greeting, then a unit of discussion about love, and finally a unit in which Millwood persuades Barnwell to remain for dinner. Each unit ends in an aside by Barnwell that reveals the penetrating effect Millwood is having on him. The aside serves as the crux of each segment. During the first aside, Barnwell, reacting to Millwood's act of "Laying her hand on his, as by accident," says: "Her disorder is so great, she don't perceive she has laid her hand on mine. —Heavens! how she trembles! —What can this mean!" (I, p. 113). The second crux comes after talk of love, in another aside: "How strange, and yet how kind her words and actions are; and the effect they have on me is as strange. —I feel desires I never knew before. I must be gone while I have power to go" (I, p. 115). When Millwood weeps at his impending departure, the action moves to the third and final crux of the seduction scene when Barnwell says to himself, "Oh, heav'ns! she loves me, worthless as I am. Her looks, her words, her flowing tears confess it. And can I leave her then?" In asking this question, Barnwell comes to the crux of all the cruxes in the scene. His effort to depart comes into keenest conflict with his desire to stay with Millwood. And it is here that he makes his decision to remain. To the self-query, "And can I leave her then?" he answers, "Oh never, never" (I, p. 116). In progressive steps then the asides reveal the sensual effect that Millwood is having on Barnwell as well as the naïveté of his reactions.

The pattern I have described is the individualized scheme of show for that particular segment of seduction. To recapitulate: A scheme consists of several levels of structural abstraction—a primary level of abstraction that is common to all activity of a particular type, in this case, of persuasion. At this level we can say that A exerts pressure to persuade B through standard modes of persuasion; a secondary, less generalized level of abstraction

incorporates the primary level yet individualizes it through articu-
lating substeps in the persuasive process. It is this potential
scheme that is given a third level of abstraction in actual performance. The actors do not merely flesh out the text; they
connect with the immanent energy that courses through the
scheme. The compelling attraction of Millwood, conveyed
through mock innocence, silken tones, apparently inadvertent
contact, provides the impelling energy that disturbs and excites
Barnwell. But it is the actress's own energy that creates the illusion of the character's energy, both in its primal, almost hidden
flow, and in its secondary, more manifest appearance. For the
actor playing Barnwell, there are the resisting passages where he
must create the illusion of a young man attempting to maintain
his equilibrium contrasted with the private asides during which
he reveals the effect Millwood is having upon him. In this brief
sequence, then, one experiences quite a number of planes of
contrast: between what one comes to know of Millwood and how
she acts, between Barnwell's external behavior and the accumu-
lated inner tension revealed in the asides, and even between the
sexual energies that emanate from the two actors themselves.[5]

In differentiating the varying degrees of abstraction, I am
trying to suggest both the structural simplicity of a scene unit and
yet how extremely complex its effects can be. Since all the planes
of contrast in a unit stimulate and can stimulate differing kinds of
imaginative response, the potential range and depth of sensation
are indeed stunning. In this essay, obviously, I cannot hope to
treat them all. Therefore, out of all the possible planes of contrast
that make a scene an atom of imaginative power, I should like to
choose one that is, in my opinion, of special importance both for
the eighteenth century and for modern students of drama. It is
the contrast between the forward thrust of action and the sensation of stasis.

In recent years sensitivity to the declining interest in history
with its temporal emphasis has increased and a mounting absorp-
tion in anthropology with its comparative emphasis has largely
taken its place. Linguists and structuralists following the lead of
Ferdinand de Saussure have codified the duality as the diachronic
and synchronic way of ordering experience. In speaking of linguistics, Saussure noted that "Everything that relates to its static
side . . . is synchronic; everything that has to do with evolution is

diachronic."[6] It is sufficient here to note that the increasing emphasis on the study of synchrony—evident in semiotics especially—is in accord with a deepening interest in myth and emblem, that is, in discrete units that timelessly embody diverse elementary forces.

In theatre, of course, one expects the diachronic phase of experience to prevail. The passing of time is fundamental. In performance one is continually aware of something about to occur. The very nature of suspense depends on audience awareness of time passing, of things that have happened or are about to happen. And yet the theatre is tantalized by the absence of motion. As much as drama is the art of the virtual future, in Suzanne Langer's words,[7] it is an art of imminence arrested. Performers seek to surpass themselves just as do other artists. The painter—at least in the past—sought to surpass his medium by conveying three dimensionality in defiance of the two dimensions so obviously asserted by the canvas. In a parallel manner performers—actor and dramatist alike—attempt at certain times to stop time, to fix a living moment in living flesh. Sometimes, as with Maurice Maeterlinck, they make a creed of their effort. More usually, however, the illusion of timelessness is introduced into the prevailing pattern of onrushing action.

The illusion may be produced pictorially as is readily seen in performances of nineteenth-century melodrama. When *Uncle Tom's Cabin* caps its message with the tableau of a Little Eva "robed in white . . . discovered on the back of a milk-white dove . . . her hands . . . extended in benediction over St. Clare [her father] and Uncle Tom,"[8] goodness is eternized in a never changing emblem. Pictorialization, however, is only one of the means for stopping the clock and idealizing a dramatic situation. In order to explore other means, I would like to turn back to the work of George Lillo. He is a particularly apt figure to consider, both for the way he handles the problem of time and for what he reveals about the eighteenth-century theatre. In his introduction of new subject matter, he looks forward to the bourgeois drama; in his adaptation of older tragic forms he carries on a well-worn tradition. His work appears at a time when, after a long period of producing little but revivals of old plays, the London stage offered, according to Professor A. H. Scouten, "an infusion of novel types of drama and a remarkable increase in the total number of new plays."⁹ Although Lillo's first play in 1730, *Silvia, or The Country Burial,* was written in imitation of *The Beggar's Opera,* his second play *George Barnwell; or The London Merchant,* coming out a year later, was itself to be imitated. In it he created one of the more popular works of his day and one of the most influential. By the time he died in 1739, Lillo managed to write in addition three tragedies, two Elizabethan adaptations, and a masque. Although his later plays did not gain the audience his first domestic tragedy did, nevertheless, they were respectably received and, in some instances, extravagantly admired. For my purpose Lillo is instructive. He was a conscious artist who knew the drama of the past. He was original without being idiosyncratic. He took his writing seriously to the very end, as certain excellent passages in his unfinished adaptation of *Arden of Feversham* reveal. Finally, both audiences and critics testify to the power of his scene making, even those in his lesser tragedies.¹⁰

Two major motifs recur in Lillo's work. Here I speak not of moral themes that pervade the plays and which, in large measure, give the plays their sentimental tone. Instead, I refer to the fundamental dramaturgic situations that mark them. As I have said, there are two. First, Lillo dramatizes the yielding of an otherwise highly moral figure to pressures upon him to commit murder. Out of frenzied desire for Millwood, George Barnwell agrees to kill his rich uncle. Driven by despair and poverty, Old Wilmot in *Fatal Curiosity* slays a stranger who is actually his returning son in disguise.

The second motif—more widely used by Lillo—is the trial and fortitude of the moral figure in the face of positive or negative provocations. This situation is developed partially and romantically in *Silvia,* but receives full treatment in *The Christian Hero, Elmerick,* and in Lillo's version of Shakespeare's *Pericles* called by him *Marina.* Even in his other two tragedies, *George Barnwell* and *Fatal Curiosity,* he introduces important secondary characters, such as Maria and Charlot respectively, who exemplify the patient endurance of a moral hero.

In all these plays the main lines of narrative are rather simple. By and large Lillo does not attempt to trace a complicated intrigue. The course of Barnwell's fall has few turns, but follows the straight line from temptation through petty crime to ghastly crime and so on to apprehension, penitence, and death. This same directness of event characterizes *Fatal Curiosity* and *The Christian Hero*. Slightly more complicated, but not significantly so, is *Elmerick,* and in his adaptation of *Pericles* Lillo demonstrates a drastic simplifying hand. In short, Lillo utilizes the plot more as a frame for the scenes of the play than as a basis for arousing suspense or promoting surprise. As a result, our attention is thrown on the substance of the scene and hence on the shape of it.

As in the seduction scene quoted from *The London Merchant,* Lillo is able to build suspense and anticipation in an action when he wants to do so. That forward thrust of interest, which audiences so regularly expect in the drama, is often skillfully managed by him. At the same time, one detects another element, one that can be easily read as posturing. Indeed, it is a form of posturing, and therefore open to attack as bad dramaturgy. But I believe that it would be a mistake to dismiss such posturing as merely a sign of faulty workmanship. Lillo had a sort of credo about his work, though not a very original one. His dedication to *The London Merchant* puts it in conventional terms: "The end of tragedy [is] the exciting of the passions, in order to the correcting such of them as are criminal, either in their nature, or through their excess." The converse would be that the end of tragedy is to calm the passions in order to exemplify such of them as are noble. This form of the credo would apply to *The Christian Hero* and *Elmerick.* Yet whether correcting passions or exemplifying nobility, Lillo sought to construct powerful models for the audience. How he did this or attempted to do this can best be seen if one examines some of his key scene structures. By such examination, I think, one gains not only a fuller appreciation of Lillo himself but also a more precise anatomy of one aspect of eighteenth century dramatic form.

That Lillo could write scenes of conventional development is apparent in the first seduction scene of *The London Merchant.* He carries it further in a second seduction scene of the second act where he shows us Barnwell struggling to free himself from Millwood's power only to be dragged back again by a mixture of passion and generosity. Again, during the last scene of the play, in an ironic twist, Lillo presents another persuasion scene, but this time with Barnwell trying to persuade Millwood to repent. In the resistance she offers, she conveys hints of the diabolic cast of her nature, and at last the utter nihilism of her being. Her final words are:

> Incompassed with horror whither must I go?
> I wou'd not live — nor die — That I cou'd
> cease to be! — or ne'er had been! [I, p. 188]

Lillo utilizes the persuasion scheme here for a double purpose: to stress the power of faith and to reveal the inaccessibility of salvation to the truly damned. By urging repentance, Barnwell is strengthened and Millwood obliged to display her irredeemability.

The persuasion scheme, by its very form, is suited to stress the implacability of time which serves to initiate and terminate Barnwell and Millwood's relationship. It does not serve so well, however, to dramatize the eternal state of a man's soul, whether good or evil. That is why at other moments in the play Lillo avoids schemes of action which stress the passage of time and tries to find a scheme that would give a timeless impression. This can be seen clearly in the third act when Barnwell murders his uncle, as well as in the fifth act when Barnwell repents in prison.

The murder falls into four subdivisions or segments: first, a speech by Barnwell as he goes to encounter his uncle in the "close walk" where the latter takes his customary stroll; then the uncle expresses forebodings of death; third, Barnwell stabs his uncle; and last, he laments this act over the body of the slain man. The third segment, the lines leading to the murder and the murder itself, occupies little time, hardly one-eighth of the entire action. In contrast, the other segments are elaborated. In the first, Barnwell, while going to waylay his uncle, anticipates the murder with pain and anguish. The primary scheme, one would expect, should be inner conflict. Yet the most significant feature of the speech is its narrative quality. In the first scene of Act II Lillo showed that he could write an effective inner-struggle speech (I, p. 128); here in Act III, Scene iii he apparently wishes to make the scene more descriptive — one might even feel by his writing that he is alienating the action, in a Brechtian sense. Change the pronouns of the speech from the first to third person, as I have done, and one might have a novel:

A dismal gloom obscures the face of day; either the sun has slipt behind a cloud, or journeys down the west of heaven, with more than common speed, to avoid the sight of what *he is* doom'd to act. Since *he set* forth on this accurs'd design, where'er *he treads, he thinks* the solid earth trembles beneath *his* feet. [p. 150][11]

The uncle's speech, in his turn, is philosophical, and conventional in its fearful anticipation.

The murder, as I said, occurs hurriedly and the action is brief. The climactic moment of the passage, in effect the fourth segment, consists of Barnwell's lamentation over his uncle's body. Grief stricken, Barnwell "Swoons away upon his Uncle's dead body" (I, p. 153). When he comes to, he grieves that he still lives, then cries out:

Let heaven, from its high throne, in justice or in mercy, now look down on that dear murder'd saint, and me the murderer.

To emphasize this contrast — indeed, to fix it as a visual illustration of sin and innocence — Lillo continues the speech in a cautionary tone. Bear in mind the stage picture of murderer and murdered, most likely with Barnwell on his knees upstage of the body of the uncle. In that position he goes on to compare himself to Cain and Nero, he suffering by comparison from having slain a man who acted not only as brother and mother to him but also as father and friend. Finally, to cement the image strongly in the conscience of his viewers, Lillo shifts from prose to verse couplets in order to generalize Barnwell's guilt.

By laws and means well known we stand and fall;
And one eternal rule remains for all. (I, p. 154)

Here the act ends.

This scheme has a later counterpart when the repentant Barnwell and his dearest friend Trueman embrace each other in prison. Ironically, Barnwell's ecstatic joy at having found peace serves to mingle with Trueman's sorrow at Barnwell's imminent execution. Through their embrace Lillo pictures not only deep reconciliation but an image of the sweet agony of evil purged and united with goodness. Here and in Barnwell's later chaste embrace of Maria, the stage image embodies the best that can be expected for the failed moral figure. Thus, the time-bound tale of fall and redemption is vivified by timeless images of guilt and forgiveness.

In the scenes where the moral hero successfully preserves his or her integrity, however, Lillo has both a more tricky problem as well as need to seek a different solution. Why Lillo turned to Shakespeare's *Pericles* can only be supposed. The fact that he cut away virtually all scenes except those concerned with Marina suggests that he saw an opportunity to depict innocence assaulted, for him an attractive subject. With Shakespeare's scenes for comparison, the reader can see what Lillo did in revising the earlier play. The scenes that come closest to the originals are the two brothel scenes. Where for Shakespeare these scenes are the climaxes of the fourth act, for Lillo they are the heart of the play. He retains much of the Shakespearean dialogue, and makes little or no attempt to sanitize the situation. In the first brothel scene he does expand the exchanges between the Bawd and Bolt (there is no Pander in Lillo's version) and elaborates the bargaining over the sale of Marina to the Bawd by the pirates. His greatest change in the first brothel scene, however, is the addition of a segment between Bolt and Marina. On being left alone with her, while the Bawd is completing the sale off stage, Bolt attempts to rape Marina. Schematically, the scene falls into the category of physical assault. The trick in such a scene is for the one attacked to maintain a defense. Where both parties are armed we have a duel scene, à la Tybalt and Mercutio in *Romeo and Juliet*. But where the attacker is strong and the victim is weak, some other form of resistance must be maintained. In the resistance a dramatist chooses to utilize, he reveals not only his skill as a stage craftsman but also his deep convictions about what is central in human behavior. In this instance Marina is first dazed, but at the moment of crux, when Bolt is about to move from expressing his intention to executing his design, Marina's response is aloof and scornful. As he grasps her, she cries out: "Why do you rudely lay your hands upon me? I am not to be touch'd." Imagine the actress playing Marina. Can she cringe and say in a frightened way, "I am not to be touch'd." Obviously not. She must draw herself up with assured absoluteness, and speak like a holy thing. To my ear "I am not to be touch'd" has an inflection of the sacred, so that when Bolt responds with mocking hilarity, he appears to be blasphemous. Marina then responds by trying to break away from him and finally appeals to higher forces: "You powers that favor chastity, defend me." Here the segment ends as the Bawd returns and prevents the rape.

This last call to higher powers, though not unknown to Shakespeare, is especially important in Lillo's work. Here, the cry has the effect of reinforcing resistance through asserting the sacredness of Marina's person. This hint is further strengthened by Lillo's change at the end of the first brothel scene where, instead of closing on the Bawd's call to Marina, "Pray you, will you go with us?" he concludes by transposing Shakespeare's couplet from a penultimate speech to the end of the scene. Beset by both Bolt and the Bawd, Marina vows in Lillo's slightly altered version:

> If fires be hot, steel sharp, and waters deep,
> Unstain'd I still my virgin fame will keep [II, p. 81][12]

This tendency to iconize the moral figure—hinted at in *Marina*—is most fully elaborated in Lillo's two historical plays, *The Christian Hero* and *Elmerick*. Though these two plays deal with quite different kinds of events, they do share certain common structural features. The Christian Hero is Scanderbeg or John Kastrioti, the Albanian national hero. Known as Iskander Bey, he was raised as a hostage in the Turkish court, revolted from it, and returned to Albania to lead his people against Murad II or, as he is known in Lillo's play, Amurath. The play depicts Amurath's attempt to defeat Scanderbeg by forcing him either to renounce Christianity and return to Turkish allegiance or to see his beloved fiancee Althea put to death.

Elmerick, or Justice Triumphant concerns the court of Hungary under Andrew II. Determined to go on a crusade to Jerusalem, the king leaves Elmerick as regent to rule his country and care for his wife, Queen Matilda. The Queen offers her love to Elmerick, is rejected, and therefore helps her brother Conrade to ravish Elmerick's wife. As "justice triumphant," Elmerick has the Queen put to death and, facing the king who returns hastily, he justifies his acts.

Each of these plays contains a key scene in which the hero is sorely tried by the circumstances of the play. In *The Christian Hero* it is a scene in which Amurath sends Althea under guard to see Scanderbeg before the hero decides whether he will choose his faith or his beloved. In this manner, Amurath hopes to persuade — or seduce might be the better word — Scanderbeg to capitulate. In *Elmerick* the regent is wooed by Queen Matilda and must defend his honor. In both instances the moral hero, characterized hitherto by unswerving integrity, unblemished honesty, and chivalric courtesy, must withstand the call of love or the blandishments of inflamed desire.

Schematically, the framing action is not unlike. Though the scene between Scanderbeg and Althea does not involve overt persuasion, the outer frame of the scene is persuasive and Althea's very presence exerts a seductive pressure on Scanderbeg. In *Elmerick* the seductive appeal is more overtly expressed. Matilda attempts first to inform Elmerick of her feelings for him, then she seeks to arouse his passion. He offers resistance, first by not understanding and then by not wanting to understand what she means. He next conjures up a vision of what would happen were he to yield to her. The crux occurs when Elmerick faces her challenge that he give her love or scorn. As in *Marina* and as is not uncommon with Lillo, Elmerick addresses "Almighty powers" for strength, and then answers the Queen by avowing

> the ample power I hold,
> Each thought, each toil, my life, devoted all
> To gratitude and justice [II, p. 169].

At this point Elmerick is confirmed in his staunchness and through his invocation of spiritual powers welds the image of the moral hero to the overarching forces of the universe. Coming as it does, at a moment of crux, the image has static force. Indeed, one may say that it has the force of an emblem, an emblem of moral fortitude triumphant.

Such a scheme naturally demands a kind of acting capable of emphasizing the statuesque. The actor must convey the ideal rather than the idiosyncratic. It is no surprise then to learn that the famous actor James Quin played Elmerick in the original production in 1740.[13] Indeed, Allardyce Nicoll observes that "Lillo's *Elmerick* was so well fitted for Quin that we must suppose the play was written for that actor."[14] Quin's style of grandeur my indeed have enhanced the awesomeness of the moment when

Elmerick makes his solemn declaration and may have contributed to the goal of creating an enduring image. In 1740 Garrick had not yet challenged Quin who still dominated the serious drama. If Lillo did in fact write the play for Quin, then it further indicates to what degree Lillo's taste was formed by traditional example.

The scene between Scanderbeg and Althea takes a somewhat different form though it in part produces a similar effect. The frame, as I indicated, is seductive albeit Althea is an unwilling seductress. At the prospect of losing Scanderbeg she has to fight her grief lest she weaken his resolve. In facing Althea Scanderbeg is full of woe. He is stunned by her calmness. His reaction begins to arouse her own grief, thus promoting the seduction of despair. In the midst of her sorrow she stops and with great control, asks herself: "Shall I indulge my grief?" The text suggests a pause as she continues the struggle. Then she says, "The storm is o'er, and I am calm again" (I, p. 264). He admires how she has learned "the art/ To stop the tide of grief in its full flow." She answers: "do I not behold thee,/ Still constant as the sun" (I, p. 265). They virtually sing a paean to their steadfastness and when Althea iterates more directly whether he would choose to lose his faith, he replies:

> That were to purchase ev'n thee too dear:
> That were a misery beyond thy loss:
> That were, my princess, to deserve to lose thee. [I, p. 265]

Perhaps here, of all instances, Lillo came most closely to creating an icon of the moral hero at his most poignant. The scheme of using Althea as the figure to be loved or lost sets off an all too human anguish that must be overcome, not by giving way to passion as we find in the romantic tragedy of a Shakespeare or a Lee, but by conquering grief, by remaining "constant as the sun." When this happens, the characters achieve a steadiness of temper that is, Lillo suggests, timeless. They are unshakable and appear as human emblems rather than fallible beings. In dramaturgic terms Lillo achieves this emblematic effect by setting up a field of onrushing action and then deliberately decelerating it until he creates an impression of stasis.

Neither *The Christian Hero* nor *Elmerick* can be said to be enduring plays. No one would be tempted to revive them today.

No doubt Lillo's limited talents must partly account for the partial effectiveness of his historical plays in his own day. Yet I suspect the causes are also more profound. Tragic writing in the first half of the eighteenth century was weighed down by the combination of Shakespearean and neoclassical example. To impose upon those models an idealized hero, as Lillo tried to do, could only aggravate the artificial qualities of the genre. But if Lillo, the "best Tragic Poet of his Age" in the words of Henry Fielding (*The Champion,* February 26, 1740), could fail, what hope was there that another might succeed? Moreover, in seeking to emblemize that hero, Lillo had the additional task of stressing a moral position to which his audience may have given lip service rather than deep conviction. As *The Prompter* for February 18, 1735 observed about *The Christian Hero*: "the Pulpit seems the properest Theatre for such Representations."[15] No wonder Lillo's depiction of failed morality in *The London Merchant* and *Fatal Curiosity* proved more attractive than his moral portraits.

But our interest in Lillo's key scenes is not limited to the question of the success of one play or the failure of another. Quite the contrary! His attempt to create dramatic emblems offers an illuminating case history of a general fact of theatrical dialectics. The theatrical medium presents man's direct encounter with time. No literary comment mediates that encounter. Often man is shown ravaged by time. Occasionally, he is shown triumphing over time, though usually "off stage," by living happily-ever-after. Lillo, however, sought to present that triumph directly by celebrating the individual's assertion of moral worth, and in this respect Lillo wrestled with a problem that is of recurrent concern for the theatre.

Lillo's impulse to create emblematic moments, only occasionally imitated in the eighteenth century, did find ample expression in nineteenth-century drama and melodrama. The stage tableau provided a scenic device through which a moral issue could receive full emphasis, and in which it could be crystallized. It is fashionable to deprecate the tableau because it encouraged posturing and melodramatic oversimplification. Yet the impulse that gave rise to tableaux remains, and indeed seems to be growing stronger. It is particularly evident in the work of individuals and groups that see the theatre as a form of communal expression, individuals as diverse as Sean O'Casey and Peter Brook and groups as diverse as the Open Theatre and the Royal Shakespeare Company. The experiments of a writer like Sean O'Casey, for example, parallel those of Lillo. Like Lillo, O'Casey had early success in more conventional forms, and like him he tried to construct in such a character as Ayamonn in *Red Roses for Me* his own kind of moral hero. Unlike Lillo O'Casey sought to bolster the hero's vision with symbolic images of the future, something Lillo left to the audience's imagination. Nevertheless, in essence, both writers had the same goal: to celebrate virtue; and the same dramaturgic problem: to make time stand still, long enough at least to impress an image of virtue on the minds of the audience.

This encounter with time goes to the heart of the dramatic medium. In the theatre the actor by projecting his energy in a highly concentrated way enables the audience to experience the passage of one discrete moment into another. Reading a novel or poem is quite another matter. The reader has the option of scanning the page at his own rate, of stopping to muse over impressions, and, if he wishes, reread the text. Theatre takes control out of the hands of the reader and puts it in the hands of the actor. The actor creates an illusion of a time speeded up or, more often, of a time slowed down, in the one case promoting thrills, the other an awareness of fine shades of thought and feeling. The rate of acceleration or deceleration, however, does vary by culture. The Noh theatre, for instance, depends on a tempo so highly retarded that one can hardly appreciate the Noh style without previous training. In Lillo's case the attempt to decelerate time to the point of stoppage was aimed at creating an ecstatic moment where actors and audience could mutually share the headiness of moral perfection.

With this in mind reexamine the relation between page and stage. Reading allows the reader considerable autonomy. Playgoing requires surrender. The reader of plays is thus in the position of utilizing one medium to experience another. To do so demands an effort of imagination and, in particular, a sensitivity to encounters with time. As I urged initially and as I would like to reiterate, a play text needs to be read as a sequence of scene units. Each unit embodies a structure or a scheme of activity which the actor realizes by projecting himself at another actor or at the audience. Through the expenditure of immense psychic energy, he imparts a palpable shape to events, a shape that can be discerned and so appreciated as unfolding in a new order of time.

The scheme of activity, as it lies implicitly and provocatively among the words of the text, is, of course, only potential. It exists as an array of options rather than a rigidly defined blueprint of performance. By attending to it, the reader accomplishes two things. First, he gains an understanding of both the performing demands made on the actor by the script and the performing options available to him. Only then does one gain clear insight into the dramaturgic properties of a work. The goal is not merely to "see" a performance in the mind's eye but to "feel" it coursing through our body. However important sight and sound are to the stage, the kinesthetic dimension is no less vital. Indeed, the kinesthetic dimension provides the center that unifies visual and auditory impressions of a performance. Second, on such a foundation of response, one can build an understanding of the meta-dramatic elements of a scene. Sensing the potential life-shape of a scene, the reader can go on to distinguish the conventional from the individual dramaturgic characteristics of the author's work. Key scenes in particular reveal, not merely in the subject matter but mainly in the way the subject is structured, what the essential thought and experience is that a dramatist seeks to induce. The scheme of show is, after all, the imprint of the artist's mind.

In this essay I can only suggest how a mode of analysis might work and indicate what some of the results might be. For example, I have only dealt with one kind of contrast in a scene: that between temporality and stasis. It is evident, I am sure, that any thorough analysis of a scene would be voluminous. That is why I stress the idea of a scene unit's scheme, for ultimately by identifying the different schemes and charting their shapes one can begin to compare them and so provide a census of dramatic performance. Such a census would be extremely valuable for eighteenth-century studies. The extensive repertory of plays and the ample documentation of performances that the publication of *The London Stage, 1660–1800* has provided us make this period an ideal field for comprehensive dramatic analysis.

NOTES

All quotations from George Lillo's plays are taken from the edition of *The Works of Mr. George Lillo,* printed for Thomas Davies in London, 1785.

1. *The London Stage 1660–1800* (Carbondale: Southern Illinois University Press), part 3: 1729–1747, p. 824.

2. For further discussion of these points, see my *Dynamics of Drama* (New York: Alfred Knopf, 1972), pp. 35 ff., and "Dramatic Analysis and Literary Interpretation," *New Literary History,* II (1971), 391–406.

3. The vocabulary for designating discrete units, though not extensive, does contain some variants. Stanislavsky training in the United States adopted the term "beat," Emrys Jones in *Scenic Form of Shakespeare* (1971) uses "scenic unit"; I myself favor "segment."

4. E. H. Gombrich, *Art and Illusion* (Princeton: Princeton University Press, 1960), pp. 87 ff.

5. At the time he played Barnwell, Theophilus Cibber was 27 years old. Popular in foppish parts, he was known for his sprightly manner, a quality that may have tempered the sentimentality of the Lillo role. For his biography, see Philip H. Highfill, Jr., Kalman A. Burnim, and Edward A. Langhans, *A Biographical Dictionary of Actors, Actresses, etc.,* v. 3 (Carbondale: Southern Illinois University Press, 1975).

6. Ferdinand de Saussure, *A Course in General Linguistics* (New York: Philosophical Library, 1966), p. 81.

7. Suzanne Langer, *Feeling and Form* (New York: Scribner, 1953), p. 307.

8. George L. Aiken, *Uncle Tom's Cabin; or Lite among the Lowly* (New York: S. French, 1860), Act VI finale.

9. Arthur H. Scouten, Introduction to *The London Stage 1729–1747* (Carbondale: Southern Illinois University Press, 1968), p. cxxxviii.

10. William H. McBurney, Introduction to George Lillo, *Fatal Curiosity* (Lincoln: University of Nebraska Press, 1966), p. xxv.

11. Italics mark changes of pronoun.

12. The Shakespearean original is:

> If fires be hot, knives sharp, or waters deep
> Untied I still my virgin knot will keep [IV, ii. 159–160].

13. *The London Stage 1729–1747,* pp. 821–822.

14. Allardyce Nicoll, *A History of English Drama* (Cambridge: Cambridge University Press, 1952–1959), v. 2, p. 41.

15. *The London Stage 1729–1747,* p. 450.

Epilogue

One always wonders in pursuing a thesis such as the one adopted in these seminars whether one is imposing on an earlier period a sense of enjoyment in a mix, a complexity, a whole show with all of its component parts, that was really alien to the Burkes, the Dr. Johnsons, the Horace Walpoles, the Mrs. Montagus, the coffee house and tavern proprietors, the butchers, and bakers, and candlestick makers who actually went to the theatre in, say, the 1760s.

It is comforting, therefore, to touch base with a sentiment on the subject by Garrick who was right in the thick of performance, of playwriting, and of audience reaction. Apt documentation occurs in the rewrite he made (and performed) of poet-laureate William Whitehead's proposed Prologue for his successful comedy *The School for Lovers* (10 February 1762). Whitehead printed in the first published edition of his play the "Prologue, as it was intended to have been spoken" and "The Prologue as it is spoken by Mr. Garrick." Whitehead's drones on for twenty-eight lines, thanking the audience for having applauded his earlier tragedies, commenting on the delicate balance he hopes to have achieved in this comedy, which

> with strokes refin'd,
> Would catch the coyest features of the mind;
> Would play politely with your hopes and fears,
> And sometimes smiles provoke, and sometimes tears.

and hoping for modest acceptance of the play—modest, because he humbly notes that he is transgressing no standard rules of comic writing:

> Your giant wits, like those of old, may climb
> Olympus high, and step o'er space and time;
> May stride with seven-league boots, from shore to shore,
> And, nobly by transgressing, charm you more.
> Alas, our author dares not laugh at schools,

Plain sense confines his humbler Muse to rules.
Form'd on the classic scale his structures rise.
He shifts no scenes to dazzle and surprize.
In one poor garden's solitary grove,
Like the primeval pair, his lovers rove.
And in due time will each transaction pass,
— Unless some hasty critic shakes the glass.

Garrick seems to have thought this effort rather academic and unlively to whet the audience's appetite for what the curtain was about to rise on. So he streamlined by one-third the first twenty-three lines of Whitehead's effort, and then broke in on a lively contradictory tack, and with what (one supposes) his mixed audience wanted to hear, and surely what he believed to be the true ambience of theatric interest at the time, all with a characteristic lightness of touch:

He shifts no scenes — but here I stopp'd him short —
Not change your scenes? said I, — I'm sorry for't
My constant friends above, around, below,
Have English tastes, and love both change and show:
Without such aids, even Shakespeare would be flat —
Our crowded Pantomimes are proofs of that.

What eager transport stares from every eye,
When pullies rattle, and our Genii fly!
When tin cascades like falling waters gleam:
Or through the canvas — bursts the real stream!
While thirsty Islington laments in vain
Half her new river roll'd to Drury Lane.

Lord, Sir, said I, for gallery, boxes, pit,
I'll back my Harlequin against your wit —
Yet still the author, anxious for his play,
Shook his wise head — What will the critics say?
As usual, Sir — abuse you all they can! —
And what the ladies? — He's a charming man!
A charming piece! One scarce knows what it means,
But that's no matter — where there's such sweet scenes!

Still he persists — and let him — entre nous
I know your tastes, and will indulge 'em too,
Change you shall have; so set your hearts at ease;
Write as *he* will, we'll act it as *you* please.

Bibliography

Addison, Joseph. *The Spectator.* London, 1711–.

Aiken, George L. *Uncle Tom's Cabin; or Life Among the Lowly.* New York, 1860; 1959, French's *Standard Drama,* no. 218.

Albert, Maurice. *Les théâtres de la foire, 1660–1789.* Paris, 1900.

Allen, Ralph G. "Topical Scenes for Pantomime," *Educational Theatre Journal* (December 1965).

Angelo, Henry. *Reminiscences.* London, 1828.

Auburn, Mark. "The Pleasures of Sheridan's *The Rivals:* A Critical Study in the Light of Stage History," *Modern Philology,* 72 (1975).

Barthelemon, François Hippolyte. *Orpheus, an English Burletta.* London, 1767.

Beard, Harry A. "De Loutherbourg" in *Enciclopedia dello Spettacolo.* Rome, 1968.

Beckerman, Bernard. "Dramatic Analysis and Literary Interpretation," *New Literary History,* II (1971).

————. *Dynamics of Drama.* New York, 1972.

Bell, John. *Bell's Edition of Shakespeare's Plays.* 8 vols. London, 1774.

Benezit, Emmanuel. *Dictionnaire critique et documentaire des peintres, sculpteurs, dessinateurs & graveurs.* 10 vols. Paris, 1976.

Bernbaum, Ernest. *The Drama of Sensibility.* Boston, 1915; rpt. Gloucester: Peter Smith, 1958.

Bevis, Richard W. "The Comic Tradition on the London Stage, 1737–1777." Ph.D. Dissertation, University of California, 1965.

Biographia Dramatica; or a Companion to the Playhoyse. David Erskine Baker, Isaac Reed, and Stephen Jones. 2 vols. in 4 pts. London, 1812.

Biographical Dictionary of Actors, Actresses, &c., A. Philip H. Highfill, Jr., Kalman A. Burnim, and Edward A. Langhans. Carbondale, Ill., 1973.

Boaden, James, ed. *The Private Correspondence of David Garrick with the Most Celebrated Persons of his Time.* 2 vols. London, 1831.

Boswell, James. *Life of Johnson,* 6 vols. Ed. G. B. Hill. Rev. L. F. Powell. Oxford: Clarendon Press, 1934–1950.

Burney, Charles. *A General History of Music from the Earliest Ages to the Present Period, 1789.* in 4 books. London, 1776–1789; New York, 1957.

Burnim, Kalman A. *David Garrick Director*. Pittsburgh, 1961.

————. "La Scena per Angolo—Magic by the Bibienas," *Theatre Survey* (1961).

Byrne, Muriel St. Clare. "King Lear at Stratford-upon-Avon, 1959," *Shakespeare Quarterly*, XI (Spring 1960).

Cahusac, Louis de. *Danse Ancienne et Moderne*. La Haye, 1754.

Carmody, Francis J. *Le Repertoire d'opera-comique en vaudevilles de 1708 a 1754*. Berkeley, 1933.

Churchill, Charles. *The Rosciad*. London, 1761.

Cibber, Colley. *Apology for the Life of Colley Cibber*. Ed. B. R. S. Fone. Ann Arbor, 1968.

Collier, George. *Selim and Azor: A Persian Tale in Three Parts as Performed at the Theatre Royal in Drury Lane*. London, 1776.

Conolly, Leonard W. *The Censorship of English Drama, 1737–1824*. San Marino, 1976.

Cooke, William. *Elements of Dramatic Criticism*. London, 1775.

Croce, Arlene. "Dancing," *The New Yorker*, May 16, 1977.

Davies, Thomas. *Memoirs of the Life of David Garrick*. 2 vols. London, 1780.

De Loutherbourg, P. J. *The Romantic and Picturesque Scenery of England and Wales, from Drawings Made Expressly for this Undertaking, with Historical and Descriptive Accounts of the Several Places of which Views are Given*. London, 1805.

Dennis, John. *An Essay on the Operas after the Italian Manner, which are about to be Establish'd on the English Stage; With some Reflections on the Damage they may bring to the Publick*. London, 1706.

Deutsch, Otto E. *Handel: a Documentary Biography*. New York, 1954.

Diderot, Denis. "On Dramatic Poetry," appendix to *Le Père de famille*. Paris, 1758.

————. in *Salons*. Ed. Jean Seznec and Joan Adhemar. Oxford, 1957.

Dobrée, Bonamy. *Restoration Comedy*. Oxford, 1924.

Dolmetsch, Mable. *Dances of Spain and Italy*. London, 1954.

Donohue, Joseph W., Jr. *Dramatic Character in the English Romantic Age*. Princeton, 1970.

————. *Theatre in the Age of Kean*. Oxford.

Doran, John. *London in the Jacobite Times*, 2 vols. London, 1877.

Downer, Alan S. "Nature to Advantage Dress'd," *PMLA* (1943); In *Restoration Drama: Modern Essays in Criticism*. Ed. John Loftis. New York, 1966.

Draper, John W. "The Theory of the Comic in Eighteenth-Century England," *Journal of English and Germanic Philology*, 37 (1938).

Dryden: *The Works of John Dryden, XVII*. Ed. Samuel H. Monk and S. E. Wallace Maurer. Berkeley and Los Angeles, 1971.

Duchartre, Pierre Louis. *The Italian Comedy*. London, 1929; New York, 1966.

Elyot, Thomas. *The Book of the Governour*. London, 1531.

Enciclopedia dello Spettaccolo. Rome, 1968.

European Magazine, The. London, 1782.

Evans, Gwynne B. *Shakespearean Prompt Books of the Seventeenth Century*. Vol. IV. Charlottesville, 1966.

Feuillet, Raoul Auger. *Choréographie, ou l'art d'ecrire la danse*. Paris, 1700.

Fiske, Roger. *English Theatre Music in the Eighteenth Century*. London, 1973.

Foote, Samuel. *The Roman and English Comedy Consider'd and Compar'd. With Remarks on The Suspicious Husband*. London, 1747.

Forrester, Felicitée. *Ballet in England*. London, 1968.

Gaiffe, Felix. *Le Drame en France au XVIII siècle*. Paris, 1910.

Gainsborough, Thomas. *The Letters of Thomas Gainsborough*. Ed. Mary Woodall. New York, 1963.

Garrick, D. *A New Dramatic Entertainment called A Christmas Tale. In Five Parts, Embellished with an Etching by de Loutherbourg*. London, 1774.

————. *The Letters of David Garrick*. Ed. D. M. Little and G. M. Kahrl. 3 vols. Cambridge, 1963.

Gazetteer and London Daily Advertiser, The. London, 1741-1796.

Gentleman's Magazine, The. Ed. E. Cave. London, 1731-.

Gerdts, W. H. "Philip de Loutherbourg," *Antiques* (November 1955).

Gherardi, Evaristo. *Le Théâtre Italiènne de Gherardi*, 6 vols. Paris, 1700.

Goldgar, Bertrand A. *Walpole and the Wits: The Relation of Politics to Literature, 1722-1742*. Lincoln, 1976.

Gombrich, E. H. *Art and Illusion*. Princeton, 1960.

Grant, Douglas. *James Thomson: Poet of the "Seasons."* London, 1951.

Granville-Barker, Harley. *On Dramatic Method*. London, 1931; New York, 1956.

Gray, Charles Harold. *Theatrical Criticism in London to 1795*. New York, 1931; New York, 1971.

Heisch, Elizabeth. "A Selected List of Musical Dramas and Dramas with Music, from the Seventeenth and Eighteenth Centuries," *Restoration and 18th-Century Theatre Research*. Chicago, May and November, 1972.

Hiffernan, Paul. *The Tuner*. No. 1. London, 1754.

————. *Dramatic Genius*. London, 1772.

Hogarth, George. *Memoirs of the Musical Drama*. London, 1838.

Hooker, E. Niles. "Humour in the Age of Pope," *Huntington Library Quarterly,* 11 (1948).

Hughes, Leo. *A Century of English Farce.* Princeton, 1956.

———. *The Drama's Patrons.* Austin, 1971.

Hume, Robert D. "Goldsmith and Sheridan and the Supposed Revolution of 'Laughing' against 'Sentimental' Comedy," *Studies in Change and Revolution: Aspects of English Intellectual History, 1640–1800.* Ed. Paul J. Korshin. Menston, 1972.

———. "Some Problems in the Theory of Comedy," *Journal of Aesthetics and Art Criticism,* 31 (1972).

———. *The Development of English Drama in the Late Seventeenth Century.* Oxford, 1976.

———. "Marital Discord in English Comedy from Dryden to Fielding," *Modern Philology,* 74 (1977).

Hutcheson, Francis. *Reflections upon Laughter.* Glasgow, 1750.

Inchbald, Elizabeth, ed. *The British Theatre.* London, 1808.

Jackson, William. *Thirty Letters.* 3d ed. London, 1795.

Jeffares, A. Norman, ed. *Restoration Comedy.* 4 vols. London, 1974.

Jenyns, Soame. *The Art of Dancing: a Poem in 3 Cantos.* London, 1729.

Johnson, Samuel. "Thomson." In *The Lives of the English Poets.* Ed. G. B. Hill. Oxford, 1905.

Jones, Emrys. *Scenic Form of Shakespeare.* Oxford, 1971.

Kemble: *John Philip Kemble Prompt Books.* Ed. Charles H. Shattuck, 11 vols. Charlottesville, 1974.

Kenny, Shirley Strum. "Richard Steele and the 'Pattern of Genteel Comedy," *Modern Philology,* 70 (1972).

———. "Humane Comedy," *Modern Philology,* 75 (1977).

Kinne, Willard Austin. *Revivals and Importations of French Comedies in England, 1749–1800.* New York, 1939.

Kramnick, Isaac. *Bolingbroke and His Circle: the Politics of Nostalgia in the Age of Walpole.* Cambridge, 1968.

Lamb, Charles. "On the Tragedies of Shakespeare." In *The Works of Charles Lamb.* Ed. Thomas Hutchinson. 2 vols. Oxford, 1934.

Langer, Suzanne. *Feeling and Form.* New York, 1953.

Larpent, John. Collection of MS Plays (1737–1824). Huntington Library, San Marino.

Lawrence, W. J. "Early Irish Ballad Opera and Comic Opera," in *The Musical Quarterly,* VIII (July 1922).

Leacroft, Richard. *The Development of the English Theatre.* London, 1973.

Le Sage, A. R. and D'Orneval. *Le Théâtre de la foire, ou l'opéra-comique.* Paris, 1737.

Lloyd's Evening Post and British Chronicle. London, 1759.

Lockman, J. *Rosalinda, a Musical Drama, to which is Prefix'd An Enquiry into the Rise and Progress of Operas, and Oratorios, with Reflections on Lyric Poetry and Music.* London, 1740.

Loftis, John. *Comedy and Society from Congreve to Fielding.* Stanford, 1959.

————. "Review" of Sherbo's *English Sentimental Comedy, Modern Language Notes,* 74 (1959).

London Chronicle, or Universal Evening Post, The. London, 1757.

London Evening Post, The. London, 1747.

London Magazine, The, or Gentleman's Monthly Intelligencer. London, 1732-1785.

London Stage, 1660-1800, The. Carbondale, 1961-1968.

McBurney, William H. "Introduction" to his edition of Lillo's *Fatal Curiosity.* Lincoln, 1966.

McKechnie, Samuel. *Popular Entertainments Through the Ages.* London, 1936.

McKillop, Alan D. ed. *James Thomson: Letters and Documents.* Lawrence, 1958.

MacMillan, Dougald. "The Rise of Social Comedy in the Eighteenth Century," *Philological Quarterly,* 41 (1962).

Maddison, Robert. *An Examination of the Oratories Performed this Season at Covent Garden.* London, 1763.

Malton, Thomas. *A Compleat Treatise on Perspective in Theory and Practice on the true Principles of Dr. Taylor.* London, 1779.

Mitchell, Julien. "My Search for the Elusive Jennie Churchill," *The New York Times,* 26 October 1975.

Morning Post and Daily Advertiser, The. London, 1772.

Muir, Kenneth. *The Comedy of Manners.* London, 1970.

Mullin, Donald C. *The Development of the Playhouse.* Berkeley and Los Angeles, 1970.

Murphy, Arthur. *Gray's Inn Journal.* London, 1753-1754.

————. *The Life of David Garrick, Esq.* 2 vols. London, 1801.

Nicoll, Allardyce. *The Development of the Theatre.* 3d ed. New York, 1946.

————, *A History of English Drama, 1660-1900.* Rev. ed. 6 vols. Cambridge, 1952-1959.

Nolte, Fred G. *The Early Middle Class Drama, 1696-1774.* New York University Ottendorfer Memorial Series of Germanic Monographs, No. 19. Lancaster, 1935.

Noverre, Jean Georges. *Lettres sur la danse et sur les ballets.* Stuttgart et Lyons, 1760.

Odell, George C. D. *Shakespeare from Betterton to Irving.* 2 vols. New York, 1920.

Olson, Elder. *The Theory of Comedy*. Bloomington, 1968.

Pedicord, Harry William. *The Theatrical Public in the Time of Garrick*. New York, 1954.

Phillips, James E. and Bertrand H. Bronson. *Music and Literature in England in the Seventeenth and Eighteenth Centuries*. Los Angeles, 1953.

Pocock, J. G. A. *Politics, Language, and the Time: Essays on Political Thought and History*. New York, 1971.

Public Advertiser, The. London, 1752.

Purdon, Edward. *A Letter to David Garrick on the Opening of the Theatre in 1759*. London, 1759.

Pyne, William Henry. *Wine and Walnuts*. 2 vols. London, 1823.

Redgrave, Samuel. "Loutherbourg" in *A Dictionary of Artists of the British School*. Rev. Ed. London, 1878.

Rosenfeld, Sybil, and Edward Croft-Murray, "A Checklist of Painters working in Great Britain and Ireland in the Eighteenth Century," *Theatre Notebook* (Spring 1965).

St. James's Chronicle, or British Evening Post. London, 1761.

Saussure, Ferdinand de. *A Course in General Linguistics*. New York, 1966.

Schneider, Ben Ross, Jr. *Index to The London Stage, 1660–1800*. Carbondale, 1979.

Sherbo, Arthur. *English Sentimental Drama*. East Lansing, 1957.

Smith, John Harrington. *The Gay Couple in Restoration Comedy*. Cambridge, 1948.

Smith, Winifred. *The Commedia dell' Arte*. New York, 1964.

Southern, Richard. *Changeable Scenery: Its Origin and Development in the English Theatre*. London, 1952.

Spencer, Christopher, ed. *Five Restoration Adaptations of Shakespeare*. Urbana, 1965.

Steele, Richard. *The Tatler*. London, 1709-1711.

Stein, Elizabeth P. *David Garrick Dramatist*. New York, 1938.

Stone, Geo. Winchester, Jr. "Garrick's Long Lost Alteration of *Hamlet*," *PMLA* XLIX (September 1934).

_____. "Garrick's Production of *King Lear*; a Study in the Temper of the 18th-Century Mind," *Studies in Philology*, XLV (January 1948).

Stone, Geo. Winchester, Jr., and George M. Kahrl, *David Garrick, a Critical Biography*. Carbondale, 1979.

Stratman, Carl J. *Bibliography of English Printed Tragedy*. Carbondale, 1966.

Tave, Stuart M. *The Amiable Humorist: A Study in the Comic Theory and Criticism of the Eighteenth and Early Nineteenth Centuries*. Chicago, 1960.

Twining, Thomas. *Poetics of Aristotle*. London, 1789.

Walpole, Horace. *The Letters of Horace Wolpole*. Ed. Mrs. Paget Toynbee. Oxford, 1903–1905.

————. *Correspondence with Sir Horace Mann*, 11 vols. Ed. W. S. Lewis et al. New Haven, 1954–1971.

————. "Thoughts on Comedy," in *The Idea of Comedy*. Ed. W. K. Wimsatt, Jr. Englewood Cliffs, 1969.

Weaver, John. *An Essay Towards the History of Dancing*. London, 1712.

————. *The Loves of Mars and Venus*. London, 1717.

————. *Anatomical and Mechanical Lectures on Dancing*. London, 1721.

Weekly Magazine, The. London, 1760.

Westminster Magazine; or the Pantheon of Taste, The. London, 1783–1785.

Whitehall Evening Post, The. London, 1718–1800.

Wilkinson, Tate. *Memoirs of his own Life*. 4 vols. York, 1790.

Williams, John. (Anthony Pasquin, pseud.). *An Authentic History of the Professors of Painting, Sculpture, and Architecture who have Practised in Ireland. To which are added Memoirs of the Royal Academicians, being an attempt to Improve the Taste of the Realm*. London, 1796.

Wilson, John Harold. *A Preface to Restoration Drama*. Boston, 1965; Cambridge, 1968.

Index

Abel, C. F., 152
Abrams, Harriet, 64, 123
Acis and Galatea (dance), 60
Act of Settlement, 47
Addison, Joseph, 9, 15, 19, 37, 39, 197
   Cato, 3, 7, 39
   Drummer, The, 15
   Spectator, 9, 196
Aesop. See Vanbrugh, Sir John
Afterpieces (discussed), 35–70
Agamemnon. See Thomson, James
Alchemist, The. See Jonson, Benjamin
Alcibiades. See Otway, Thomas
All in the Wrong. See Murphy, Arthur
Amanti Gelosi, Gli. See Cocchi, Gioacchino
L'Amour Costante. See Leo, Leonardo
Angelo, Henry, 96
Anne, Queen, 46
Arden of Feversham. See Lillo, George
Aristotle, 8, 20, 90
Arne, Michael, 118
Arne, Thomas Augustine, 64, 118, 123, 124, 139
   Masque of Alfred, 130
Arne, Mrs. Thomas A., 150, 151
Arnold, Samuel, 124
Art of the Fugue. See Bach, J. S.
As You Like It. See Shakespeare, William
Audience, middle-class, 25
Audience-actor relationship, 74
Audience chamber, 75; relationship with stage, 79

Augustan comedy, 14
Augustan phase of 18th-century drama, 4, 13, 18
Auletta, Piétro, 138
   Orazio, 138
Austrian Succession, War of, 50
Author's Farce, The. See Fielding, Henry
Avant scène, 76
Avison, Charles, 119
Aylward, Thomas, 118
Ayscough, George Edward
   Semiramis, 104, 105

Bach, Johann Christian, 152
Bach, Johann Sebastian
   Art of the Fugue, 28
Baddeley, Sophia, 103
Baker, Thomas, 14
   Fine Lady's Airs, The, 14
Balcons, 76
Ballad opera, 13; discussed, 65
Ballets, 68
Banditti, The. See Durfey, Thomas
Barnum and Bailey, 28
Baroque, 87
Barthelemon, Francois Hypolite, 118, 119, 143, 148, 158
   Orpheus, 143, 144, 150–158
   Pélopida, 150
Bartholemew Fair, 81
Bates, William, 118
Battishill, Jonathan, 118
Baxter, Richard (dancer), 61
Beauchamps, Pierre, 198
Beaux Stratagem, The. See Farquhar, George
Beggar's Opera, The. See Gay, John

239